DATE DUE

12/31/05		7/13/09
3/21/09		

Demco No. 62-0549

**METROPOLITAN COLLEGE
OF NEW YORK LIBRARY**
75 Varick Street 12th Fl.
New York, NY 10013

Jane's

Counter Terrorism

Second Edition

Rohan Gunaratna
Peter Chalk

Copyright 2002 by Jane's Information Group

"Jane's" is a registered trademark

Published by Jane's Information Group
Sentinel House, 163 Brighton Road, Coulsdon,
Surrey, CR5 2YH, UK
Tel: (+44 20) 87 00 37 00; Fax: (+44 20) 87 00 10 06
e-mail: info@janes.co.uk

All rights reserved. No part of this publication may be reproduced, stored in retrieval systems or transmitted, in any form or by any means, electronic, mechanical, photocopying, recording or otherwise, without prior written permission of the Publishers. Licenses, particularly for the use of the data in databases or local area networks, are available on application to the Publishers. Infringement of any of the above rights will be liable to prosecution under US or UK civil or criminal law. While every care has been taken in the compilation of this publication to ensure its accuracy at the time of going to press, the Publishers cannot be held responsible for any errors or omissions or any loss arising therefrom.

Printed and bound in the United Kingdom by Biddles Ltd

Registered with the Library of Congress

Cataloging-in-Publication Data available upon request

ISBN 0-7106-23577

Publisher's Note

Rohan Gunaratna
Dr Rohan Gunaratna is a terrorism specialist at the Centre for Study for Terrorism and Political Violence at the University of St Andrews, Scotland and an Honorary Fellow at the International Policy Institute for Counter Terrorism, Israel. He has also served as Co-Director of the UN University Project on Managing Contemporary Insurgencies, and as a Principal Investigator, Terrorist Trajectories Project, UN Terrorism Prevention Branch. In his role as a consultant on counter terrorism to governments and corporations, he has visited Asia, the Middle East, Sub Saharan Africa and Latin America. He is author of eight books on armed conflict including Inside Al-Qaeda: Global Network of Terror (Columbia University Press, 2002) and Global Terror - Unearthing Support Networks that Allow Terrorism to Survive and Succeed (New York University Press, 2002). He has written articles for Jane's Intelligence Review and is a contributor to Jane's World Insurgency and Terrorism and Jane's Sentinel Security Assessments.

Peter Chalk
Dr Peter Chalk is a Policy Analyst working in the Project Airforce and National Security divisions of the RAND Corporation, Washington DC. During 2001 he worked on projects examining unconventional security threats in Southeast Asia, new strategic challenges for the US Air Force (USAF) in Latin America and evolving trends in national and international terrorism. He was also a major contributor to the First Annual Report of the Gillmore Commission, a Congressionally mandated advisory panel established to assess US domestic response capabilities for terrorism involving weapons of mass destruction. Prior to joining RAND, Dr Chalk was an Assistant Professor of Politics at the University of Queensland, Brisbane, and a Postdoctoral Fellow in the Strategic and Defense Studies Centre of the Australian National University, Canberra.

In addition to his academic posts, Dr Chalk has acted as a research consultant in the UK, Canada and Australia and has experience with the UK Armed Forces. He is author of Non-Military Security and Global Disorder. The Impact of Extremism, Violence and Chaos on National and International Security (Macmillan, 2000) and West

European Terrorism and Counter-Terrorism. The Evolving Dynamic (Macmillan, 1996), in addition to numerous journal articles and other scholarly publications in the security studies field. Dr Chalk has lectured widely on terrorism, piracy and "grey area phenomena" before government, intelligence, police and military audiences in North America, Europe, Sri Lanka and Australia. He is currently a member of the Standing Committee of the Washington-based International Research Group on Political Violence (IRGPV) and serves as Associate Editor of Studies in Conflict and Terrorism, one of the foremost international journals in the area of low intensity conflict. He has written for Jane's Intelligence Review, Jane's Navy International and Jane's Islamic Affairs Analyst.

Charles Clive Newey
Charles Clive Newey is a Civil Engineer. A graduate of Leeds University, his long professional career includes two years designing military works in the Middle East and 14 years working for the UK Ministry of Public works (Later the Property Services Agency) on the design of both civilian and military buildings at the height of the cold war and the IRA terrorist threat. In 1982 he transferred to the Foreign Office where he worked on major projects for the overseas estate, including several years as project manager for the development of the brief and design for the new Moscow embassy. Subsequently he led a large multi-disciplinary team working on major projects and minor works including the development of building techniques to mitigate the increasing threat of terrorist attack. He has written on building security issues for Jane's Intelligence Review.

John Hill
John Hill is a freelance journalist specialising in international security. He is a regular contributor to Jane's Intelligence Review and Jane's Foreign Report.

Trifin J Roule
Trifin J Roule, a Research Fellow at the University of Pittsburgh, is Assistant Editor of the Journal of Money Laundering Control and Project Manager for a multi-year US government study devoted to the study of terrorist finance and money laundering trends in more

than 60 jurisdictions. Mr Roule is also a consultant for a World Bank project that analyzes the use of natural resources to fund terrorist groups and regional conflicts, and a frequent contributor to ABC News. He has written a number of articles for Jane's Intelligence Review, Jane's Islamic Affairs Analyst, and Jane's Terrorism and Security Monitor.

This book is based on current research, knowledge and understanding, and to the best of the author's ability the material is current and valid. While the authors, editors, publishers and Jane's Information Group have made every effort to ensure the accuracy of the information contained herein, they cannot be held responsible for any errors found in this book. The authors, editors, publishers and Jane's Information Group do not bear any responsibility or liability for the information contained herein or for any uses to which it may be put.

CONTENTS

CHAPTER 1: THE TERRORIST THREAT
1.1 Definition What is Terrorism?...4
1.2 Terrorist organization and infrastructure.................................8
1.3 Terrorist leadership...9
1.4 Terrorist aims and objectives...11
    1.4.1 Ideological terrorism...11
    1.4.2 Ethnonationalist terrorism...12
    1.4.3 Politico-religious terrorism..12
    1.4.4 Other categories..13
1.5 Motivation: Why people join or support terrorist groups..........14
1.6 Conclusion...17

CHAPTER 2: TERRORIST TRAINING AND WEAPONRY
2.1 Training..21
2.2 Terrorist weapons..28
    2.2.1 Explosives...28
    2.2.2 Firearms..37
    2.2.3 Dual technologies...40
    2.2.4 CBRN weapons...41

CHAPTER 3: TERRORIST TACTICS AND TARGETS
3.1 Assassination..50
3.2 Armed assault...52
3.3 Ambush...53
3.4 Hijacking...54
3.5 Kidnapping..55
3.6 Suicide terrorism...56
3.7 Aviation terrorism..57
3.8 Maritime terrorism...66

CHAPTER 4: TERRORIST FINANCING AND FORENSIC ACCOUNTANCY
4.1 Terrorist financing...77
    4.1.1 Domestic financing..79

4.1.2 Diaspora and migrant financing...79
4.1.3 Co-ethnic and co-religionist financing......................................82
4.1.4 State sponsorship...82
4.1.5 Low-level and organized crime...83
4.1.6 Financial crime...85
4.1.7 Investments and legitimate businesses..................................87
4.1.8 Non-governmental organizations..87
4.1.9 Individual financiers..87
4.1.10 Community organizations..88
4.1.11 Public and private donor and other benevolent organizations...88
4.2 Forensic accounting and terrorist finance.....................................88
  4.2.1 Sources of information...88
  4.2.2 Information obtained by the examination of terrorist financial networks 89
  4.2.3 International efforts to overcome obstacles to tracking financial activities of terrorist group...92
4.3 Conclusion..94

CHAPTER 5: NATIONAL RESPONSES TO TERRORISM
5.1 Intelligence...99
  5.1.1 Monitoring and control of intelligence activities....................103
5.2 Emergency legislation..105
5.3 Use of special anti-terrorist response teams..............................109
5.4 Control of the media...112
  5.4.1 Security of information versus the public's right to know 115
5.5 Targeting of terrorist leaders and members 115
  5.5.1 Targeted killings and Al-Qaeda...118
5.6 Legitimating socio-economic and development initiatives........118

CHAPTER 6: US HOMELAND SECURITY
6.1 The historical and legal context for US homeland security........125
6.2 National security thinking and homeland security......................126

6.3 Preparing and organizing for new homeland security threats..........127
   6.3.1 Presidential Decision Directive 39 (PDD-39) and the Weapons of Mass Destruction Act (NLD)..........127
   6.3.2 Presidential Decision Directives 62 and 63 (PDD-62, PDD 63)..........127
   6.3.3 Other related initiatives..........128
   6.3.4 Funding..........129
6.4 Reorganising homeland security post September 11..........130
6.5 Main areas of current homeland defence..........133
   6.5.1 Supporting first responders..........134
   6.5.2 Biological terrorism..........135
   6.5.3 Border security..........138
   6.5.4 Homeland security and technology..........140
   6.5.5 Role of the military..........141
6.6 Conclusion..........142

CHAPTER 7: SECURITY MEASURES

7.1 Introduction..........145
7.2 Understanding the threat..........145
   7.2.1 Large stand-off vehicle bomb..........145
   7.2.2 Vehicle bomb close to building..........146
   7.2.3 Proxy vehicle bomb..........147
   7.2.4 Under-site bomb..........147
   7.2.5 Parcel bomb..........148
   7.2.6 Hand grenade..........148
   7.2.7 Evacuation attack..........148
   7.2.8 Rocket-propelled grenade..........149
   7.2.9 Mortars..........149
   7.2.10 Long-range sniper..........150
   7.2.11 Close-range gun attack..........150
   7.2.12 Drive-by attack..........151
   7.2.13 Mob attack..........15
   7.2.14 Military-style occupation..........152

7.2.15 Infiltration by armed personnel	152
7.2.16 Kidnap as leverage	153
7.2.17 Gas attack	153
7.2.18 Poisoning of water supply	153
7.2.19 Bacterial attack	154
7.2.20 Infrastructure	154
7.3 New developments	154
7.4 Information gathering	155
7.5 Threat assessment	155
7.6 Combating the threat	157
7.6.1 Large vehicle stand-off bomb	157
7.6.2 Smaller vehicle bomb close to building	159
7.6.3 Proxy vehicle bomb	159
7.6.4 Under-site bomb	160
7.6.5 Parcel bombs	160
7.6.6 Thrown bombs and hand grenades	162
7.6.7 Evacuation attack	162
7.6.8 Rocket-propelled grenade	162
7.6.9 Mortar attack	163
7.6.10 Long-range sniper	163
7.6.11 Close-range gun attack	164
7.6.12 Drive-by gun attack	164
7.6.13 Mob attack	165
7.6.14 Military-style occupation	166
7.6.15 Kidnapping	166
7.6.16 Gas attack	166
7.6.17 Poisoning water supply	167
7.6.18 Bacterial attack	167
7.7 Moving to an alternative existing building	169
7.8 New building design considerations	169
7.8.1 The site	170
7.8.2 The perimeter	170
7.8.3 The layout of the site	171

7.8.4 The main building..173
7.9 Operations...177
7.10 Attack reaction..178
7.11 Procuring advice...179

CHAPTER 8: BEST PRACTICES FOR RESPONSE TO TERRORIST ATTACKS

8.1 Pre-event planning...183
   8.1.1 Creation of Single Incident Management and Command Systems..183
   8.1.2 The identification of specialized response capabilities.......184
   8.1.3 Information/intelligence sharing............................184
8.2 Components common to all terrorist responses........................184
   8.2.1 The incident management system........................184
   8.2.2 Integrated leadership at the scene.........................185
   8.2.3 Co-ordination with the military.............................185
   8.2.4 Resource requirements......................................186
   8.2.5 Initial actions...187
   8.2.6 Scene control..189
8.3 Components specific to different types of terrorist attack........190
   8.3.1 Conventional attacks..190
   8.3.2 Large-scale incidents..191
   8.3.3 Exotic...194
   8.3.4 Medical response to an exotic attack....................198
8.4 Summary of basic steps in response............................206
Appendix..208

CHAPTER 1: THE TERRORIST THREAT

1.1	Definition: What is terrorism?	4
1.2	Terrorist organization and infrastructure	8
1.3	Terrorist leadership	9
1.4	Terrorist aims and objectives	11
1.5	Motivation: Why people join or support terrorist groups	14
1.6	Conclusion	17

CHAPTER 1: THE TERRORIST THREAT

The face of terrorism is rapidly changing. At the dawn of the 21st century, terrorism has emerged as the single biggest security threat to both governments and societies. Hitherto perceived as a law and order problem, terrorism today is regarded as the priority national security threat. Governments are using every tool of statecraft – intelligence, law enforcement, military, political, diplomatic, economic and financial means both to combat and to reduce the threat of terrorism. Terrorism has replaced the threat of nuclear confrontation, the predominant threat during the Cold War.

Al-Qaeda's co-ordinated multiple suicide airborne attacks aimed at destroying America's outstanding landmark targets: the World Trade Center, the Pentagon, and the White House, on September 11 2001, demonstrated the escalating terrorist threat posed to civilian and military infrastructure. The attack conducted by 19 suicide hijackers killed 3,100 citizens from 78 countries. According to Bruce Hoffman of RAND, Washington Office, only 14 terrorist attacks killed over 100 people in the 20th century. Until September 11, the terrorist attack that killed the largest number of civilians was in Abadan, Iran, when 440 people were killed in 1978. Furthermore, the total number of US fatalities from three decades of international and domestic terrorism was under 3,000. With September 11, the worst of terrorist attacks ever, the threshold for terrorism globally has increased. Terrorism has moved from a tactical to a strategic threat, prompting governments to invest unprecedented resources both in pre-empting terrorist attacks and in the consequence management of mass casualty attacks.

Unlike during the Cold War, the bulk of the major terrorist groups have developed a presence outside their immediate theatres of conflict. Furthermore, like governments, contemporary terrorist groups co-operate and co-ordinate their actions. With the exchange of ideas, technologies, and personnel, the terrorist intentions, capability and opportunities for attack have dramatically increased. Often terrorism is a by-product of protracted armed conflicts. Conflict conditions create the milieu for the spawning and growth of terrorist groups. With the increase in the number and intensity of terrorist and guerrilla conflicts during the last decade, two thirds of the countries of the world are affected by political violence.

As of 2002, there were 23 high-intensity conflicts (where over 1,000 people die per conflict per year); 79 low-intensity conflicts (where between 100 and 1,000 people die per conflict per year) and 38 violent political conflicts (where under 100 people die per conflict per year). According to Dr Albert J Jongman of the Interdisciplinary Research Programme on Causes of Human Rights Violations (PIOOM) in the Netherlands, there are 612 politically motivated groups, mostly with guerrilla and terrorist capabilities, active in 140 conflicts. Of these groups only about 40 organizations have developed an external reach and pose a threat to international security.

The most affected geographic region by terrorist violence is the Asia Pacific region. In the scale of violence, South Asia is followed by Southeast Asia, Oceania and Northeast Asia. Afghanistan, Pakistan, India, Sri Lanka, Indonesia and the Philippines are experiencing high-intensity conflicts. Myanmar, Bangladesh, and Nepal witness low-intensity conflicts. The Asia-Pacific is closely followed by Sub Saharan Africa. In Sub Saharan Africa, the Horn of Africa and Southern Africa follow Central Africa. Angola, Burundi, Chad, Congo, Guinea, Nigeria, Rwanda, Sierra Leone, Sudan are experiencing high-intensity conflicts. Cameroon, Central African Republic, Brazzaville Congo, the Democratic Republic of Congo, Ethiopia, Ivory Coast, Kenya, Liberia, Nigeria, Senegal, Somalia, South Africa, Tanzania and Uganda are experiencing low-intensity conflicts. In Latin America, Colombia continues to witness the most violent conflict. Peru, Mexico, and Guatemala witness low-intensity conflicts. In the Middle East, Algeria and the Israeli-Palestinian conflicts produce the highest fatalities and casualties. Iraq, Iran and Lebanon are witnessing low-intensity conflicts. In the Former Soviet Union, the Caucuses, notably the conflict in Chechnya is followed by low-intensity conflicts in Central Asia. Until September 11, North America and Europe witnessed the lowest fatalities and casualties. Countering the terrorist threat requires an understanding of the nature of terrorism, and the typology and motivation of terrorist organizations.

1.1 Definition: What is Terrorism?
In the spectrum of political violence, terrorism is a unique form of violence. Terrorism is a political campaign backed by threats and acts of violence. It must be systematic, deliberate and seeking to influence a wide audience by generating fear. It primarily targets civilians with the intention of competing for and taking political control of the public. Other forms of political violence include attacks against infrastructure (sabotage), political leaders

Definition: What is terrorism?

(assassination), military (guerrilla warfare), and genocide (ethnic cleansing). While attacks against civilians (soft targets) are the commonest in the initial wave of terrorist operations, subsequently terrorist groups develop the capability to attack security forces (hard targets). Today, about 45 per cent of all attacks staged by terrorist groups are against security forces personnel. The tactical repertoire of contemporary terrorist groups include forms of political violence other than terrorism. For instance, National Liberation Army (ELN) has sabotaged gas and oil pipelines in Colombia, Basque Fatherland and Liberty (ETA) has assassinated moderate politicians in Spain, Free Aceh Movement (GAM) conducts guerrilla warfare against Indonesian security forces, and Liberation Tigers of Tamil Eelam (LTTE) have cleansed Sri Lanka's northern province of Muslims.

Terrorism differs from common crime. While terrorism is driven by political motive, crime is driven by economic motive. With the decline of state sponsorship, terrorist groups increasingly resort to crime to build their capacities and capabilities. For instance, the Revolutionary Armed forces of Colombia (FARC) extorts money from foreign companies in Colombia, Abu Sayyaf Group (ASG) kidnaps foreigners, Islamic Movement of Uzbekistan traffic narcotics, Revolutionary United Force of Sierra Leone (RUF) smuggle diamonds, Armed Islamic Group of Algeria (GIA) steals cars, and Al-Qaeda engages in credit card fraud. Therefore, contemporary terrorist groups traverse along the political violence-criminality nexus. Overall, terrorist groups are armed political parties. Strategically their goal is always political; operationally, to build support and operational infrastructure; tactically, to build military power, accumulate economic wealth and gain political strength.

There are two forms of terrorism. Domestic terrorism, also referred as national terrorism, refers to acts of terrorism committed within the territorial borders of a country involving citizens and interests only of that country. International terrorism refers to acts of terrorism involving citizens or the territory of more than one country. Almost all the major terrorist groups developed an external presence during the post-Cold War period. By building robust external support networks, even domestic terrorist groups have developed an international dimension. Therefore, the distinction made during the Cold War between domestic and international terrorism is of little relevance today especially towards understanding and responding to the threat of terrorism.

The vast majority of incidents of terrorism are domestic but they are largely unreported in the international press especially if they occur in the developing world. Incidents of international terrorism constitute between 8 and 12 per cent of all incidents of terrorism. Most government agencies and private research institutions collect data only of a few domestic or regional terrorist campaigns. RAND, the US State Department and a few other government agencies collect data on international terrorism. The overall terrorist threat is skewed because most terrorism analysts map terrorist trends and patterns by examining only incidents classifiable as international terrorism. The decade preceding September 11 witnessed a steady decline in the incidents of international terrorism largely due to international co-operation. However, the overall incidence of terrorism increased due to an increase in domestic terrorism. The overall increase in terrorist incidents is attributed to the numerical increase and the intensity of intrastate conflicts.

The US state department defines terrorism as premeditated, politically motivated violence perpetrated against non-combatant targets by subnational groups or clandestine agents, usually intended to influence an audience. Non-combatant includes, in addition to civilians, military personnel who at the time of the incident are unarmed and/or not on duty. The US state department considers as acts of terrorism attacks on military installations or on armed military personnel when a state of military hostilities does not exist at the site, such as bombings against US military bases both at home and overseas.

The US justice department defines terrorism as the unlawful use of force and violence against persons or property to intimidate or coerce a government, the civilian population, or any segment thereof, in furtherance of political or social objectives. The Federal Bureau of Investigations (FBI), an agency of the justice department describes terrorism either as domestic or international, depending on the origin, base, and the objectives of the terrorists. Domestic terrorism is the unlawful use, or threatened use, of force or violence by a group or individual based and operating entirely within the United States or its territories without foreign direction committed against persons or property to intimidate or coerce a government, the civilian population, or any segment thereof, in furtherance of political or social objectives. International terrorism involves violent acts or acts dangerous to human life that are a violation of the criminal laws of the United States or any state, or that would be a criminal violation if committed with the jurisdiction of the United States or any state.

Definition: What is terrorism?

These acts appear to be intended to intimidate or coerce a civilian population, influence the policy of a government by intimidation or coercion, or affect the conduct of a government by assassination or kidnapping. International terrorist acts occur outside the United States or transcend national boundaries in terms of the means by which they are accomplished, the persons they appear intended to coerce or intimidate, or the locale in which the perpetrators operate or seek asylum.

The US defense department defines terrorism as the unlawful use of, or threatened use of force or violence against individuals or property to coerce or intimidate governments or societies. It is often used to achieve political, religious or ideological objectives.

In the Terrorism Act 2000, United Kingdom, terrorism means the use or threat of action is designed to influence the government or to intimidate the public or a section of the public within or outside the United Kingdom. Terrorism is also the use or threat of action for the purpose of advancing a political, religious or ideological cause. Terrorism involves serious violence against a person; involves serious damage to property; endangers a person's life, other than of the person committing the action; creates a serious risk to the health or safety of the public or a section of the public, or is designed seriously to interfere with or seriously to disrupt an electronic system.

Instead of defining terrorism, 12 UN conventions criminalize a set of specific threats and actions as terrorist. They are in the areas of internationally protected persons, safety of aviation, safety of maritime navigation, safety of fixed platforms at sea, hostage taking, protection of nuclear material, manufacturing explosives, bombings and financing. The post-September 11 policy working group on the UN and terrorism delineated the broad characteristics of the phenomenon of terrorism as an act meant to inflict dramatic and deadly injury on civilians and to create an atmosphere of fear, generally for a political or ideological (secular or religious) purpose. The world body is under significant pressure to adopt a UN definition of terrorism.

There are over 100 definitions of terrorism. As no one definition has gained universal acceptance, a working definition of terrorism might be as follows. Terrorism is the threat or the act of politically motivated violence directed primarily against civilians. Some supporting the Palestinian, Kashmiri, and Kurdish struggles have argued that they are legitimate campaigns and therefore Palestinian, Kashmiri, and Kurdish actions against civilians are not terrorism. They have also argued that when a campaign is legitimate, the fighters are freedom fighters and not terrorists. Whether a campaign is legitimate or not, deliberate attacks against civilians to achieve a political goal is terrorism. Killing civilians, including women and children, is not an act worthy of a freedom fighter. Irrespective of legitimacy, perpetrator, location and time of the attack, terrorism is a method.

1.2 Terrorist organization and infrastructure

A terrorist organization consists of the terrorist group and its support base. The terrorist group includes the leadership, the middle level cadres and the recruits who are constantly trained and retrained and assigned political and military activities. The lifeblood of a terrorist group is dependent on support it generates from its likeminded ethnic, religious or political sympathizers. Terrorist support base consists of collaborators, supporters and sympathizers who provide political, financial and military support. Not all support is voluntary. Coercion, intimidation, robbery and organized crime are the norm in terrorist methods of generating finances. The strength and the size of the group depend on the support base. The ability of the group to sustain its operations depends on the capacity of the support base to replenish the group's human losses and material wastage.

Terrorist groups have two operational wings – an overt/semi-covert political wing and a clandestine military wing. While the political wing engages mostly in support functions, the military wing engages in operational functions. The political wing operates through front, cover and sympathetic organizations often taking the face of commercial, socio-economic, educational, cultural, religious, welfare, humanitarian and human rights organizations. These terrorist affiliated infrastructures, some of which are legally registered as charities and non-profit organizations both within and outside the conflict zone build political and financial support for the military wing. Terrorist will use these affiliated infrastructures to disseminate propaganda; generate recruits, supporters, and sympathizers; raise and launder funds; secure forged, adapted and genuine identifies; hire, rent or buy safe houses and vehicles; gather intelligence; procure weapons, dual technologies and other supplies; and transport supplies to the theatre of conflict.

The terrorist operational network falling within the purview of the military wing is responsible for mounting final reconnaissance or surveillance of the intended target and executing the operation. To ensure operational security, terrorists assigned to conduct intelligence and military operations are organized by way of compartmentalized cells. Although the bulk of the active terrorist groups are from the developing world, they have established significant support networks in North America, Europe and Australasia. Liberal democracies are conducive for terrorist groups to establish state-of-the-art propaganda, fund raising, procurement and shipping infrastructures. Some of the support networks mutate into operational networks that conduct assassinations, bombings, ambushes and direct attacks.

1.3 Terrorist leadership

Terrorist leadership consists of core and penultimate leaders. They formulate the ideology, develop concepts, delineate strategies, decide on the tactics and direct the organization. Often terrorist campaigns continue for decades because the leadership recruits fresh members and generates support to replace the members killed or captured and the weapons and munitions wasted. Despite the high fatalities and casualties among the terrorists, terrorist groups have survived because the targeting has been at the membership and not the leadership.

Often the membership is expendable but not the leadership. The capture of Abimael Guzman, the founder leader of Sendero Luminoso, Rohan Wijeweera, the founder leader of the Janatha Vimukthi Peramuna and Abdullah Ocalan, the founder leader of the Kurdish Workers Party, seriously weakened their groups. Similarly, after Shoko Asahara was captured, its new leader, Fumihiro Joyu, rejected the violent and apocalyptic teachings of its founder. After the arrest of Fusako Shigenobu, the leader of the Japanese Red Army, in November 2000, she announced her intention to abandon violence and pursue democratic politics. On April 4 2002, shortly after the death of its leader, Jonas Savimbi, the National Union for the Total Independence of Angola (UNITA) signed a ceasefire agreement with the government of Angola. Therefore, it is paramount to target the terrorist leadership, Osama bin Laden in the case of Al-Qaeda, Refai Ahmed Taha Musa in the case of the Islamic Group of Egypt, Prachanda and Bhattrai in the case of the Nepali Maoists, and Manuel Marulanda in the case of FARC. However, there are limitations to destroying or weakening a terrorist group by targeting the leadership. Although the Palestinian Islamic Jihad nearly suffered total collapse after Mossad operatives in Malta assassinated its leader Shiqaqi, the conditions in Palestine led to the re-emergence of the group under the leadership of Ramadan Shallah. It is important to realise the removal of a leader is not a panacea. The new leader of the terrorist group can be much more effective, deadly and unpredictable compared to the known assassinated leader. Although not assassinated by a state, the assassination of Al-Qaeda founding leader, Abdullah Azzam, in Peshawar, Pakistan, by Egyptian terrorists, created the conditions for Osama bin Laden to assume the mantle of Al-Qaeda leadership. Especially if the group has widespread appeal and the support base is large, targeting the leadership is unlikely to be an effective strategy. Therefore, targeting the leadership will be effective when a group is at the formative phase. Nonetheless, targeting the leadership even at the mature phase of a campaign can break the momentum of a terrorist campaign and create opportunities for weakening a group's influence on the wider support base.

The capture of a terrorist leader is preferred to assassination. On capture, most leaders portray a poor image of themselves. With the elite forces of Turkey and Sri Lanka capturing Ocalan, the PKK leader and Wijeweera, the JVP leader, they pleaded not to be tortured. Like the execution of a terrorist leader, the assassination of a terrorist leader inevitably elevates the dead leader to the rank of a martyr. Thereafter, the dead leaders ideals are likely to be the inspiration for a new generation of committed terrorists. However, there is a danger a terrorist group will engage in hostage taking and kidnappings to seek the release of their imprisoned leaders. For instance, the Abu Sayyaf Group kidnapped a number of Americans in the Philippines and Malaysia to seek the release of Ramzi Ahmed Yousef, the World Trade Center bomber of 1993 and Sheikh Omar Abdel Rahman, the leader of the New York landmarks bomb plot of 1995. Similarly, Ahmed Saeed Omar Sheikh of Harakat-ul Mujahidin kidnapped three Britons and one American in New Delhi, in 1994, to seek the release of Maulana Masood Azhar. When the Indian government did not respond positively, the group kidnapped five Western tourists and killed four of them in Kashmir, in 1995. Finally, Harakat-ul Mujahidin secured the release of their leaders in Indian custody by hijacking an Indian airliner with 155 passengers and crew in 1999. While the leaders provide the broad framework for action, the middle level cadres or experts plan, prepare and execute operations. Therefore, in the counter-terrorist agenda, targeting the penultimate leaders or the middle level cadres is equally important. After identifying potential recruits, the experienced middle level cadres indoctrinate and train them to become fully fledged terrorist operatives. Acting as co-ordinating officers or agent-handlers, the middle level cadres provide tactical direction. For instance, the losses of Muhammed Atef, the military commander and Abu Zubaidah, the head of external operations of Al-Qaeda have been major blows to the organization. Similarly, with the Shin Bet assassination of Yahiya Ayyash the Engineer, Hamas suffered the loss of its most experienced bomb maker. However, dependent on the availability of human and material resources, terrorist groups adapt to the changing circumstances and recover. For instance, Ayyash's death made Hamas aware of the risk of provided training in bomb making only to a few. Hamas trained an unprecedented number of Palestinian terrorists in bombmaking and dispersed them throughout the West Bank and the Gaza Strip.

1.4 Terrorist aims and objectives

To advance their aims and objectives, terrorist groups develop ideologies or belief systems. The secular and religious ideologies are designed by terrorist ideologues to politicize, radicalize and mobilize the actual and potential followers of terrorist groups. By conducting a terrorist campaign within an ideological framework a terrorist group seeks to advance its aims and objectives. Although the aims differ according to the ideological orientations of the groups, the objectives range from gaining recognition at local, national and international levels; intimidate and coerce both the target population and the government; and provoke the government to overreact for the purpose of generating greater public support. Three principal ideological strands have generated the ideological fuel required to spawn and sustain terrorist campaigns around the world.

1.4.1 Ideological terrorism

Ideological terrorism is driven by left and right wing ideologies. Marxism, Leninism and Maoism provide the ideological fuel to left wing terrorist groups to advance their aims and objectives. They seek to overthrow existing regimes and establish communist and socialist states. Most of the groups driven by left wing ideologies - Communist Combatant Cells (CCC) of Belgium, Red Army Faction (RAF) of Germany, Red Brigades (RB) of Italy, Action Direct (AD) of France – disintegrated with the end of the Cold War. Although the ideological justification for these groups to continue ended with the death of the Soviet Empire, a few groups driven by left wing ideologies survived in the poorer regions of the world. They include FARC in Colombia, Tupac Amaru Revolutionary Movement (MRTA), Sendero Luminoso (Shining Path), New Peoples Army (NPA) in the Philippines and Peoples War Group

(PWG) in Andhara Pradesh in India. Of these groups, FARC, Nepal Maoists and NPA pose a severe national security threat to Colombia, Nepal and the Philippines. Among the left wing groups still active in Europe are the Revolutionary Organisation 17 November and Revolutionary Nuclei, both of Greece, and the Revolutionary People's Liberation Party (DHKP-C) in Turkey.

Groups driven by right wing ideologies include the Ku Klux Klan, Aryan Nations (Church of Christian Aryan Nations, Church of Jesus Christ Christian), Aryan Liberation Front, Aryan Brotherhood, Arizona Patriots, the American Nazi Party (National Socialist Party, United Racist Front) and the (United Self-Defense Forces of Colombia: AUC). A group driven by a right wing group conducted the bombing of the Alfred P Murrah Federal Building in Oklahoma City on 19 April 1995. Overall, groups driven by right wing ideologies pose a low threat compared to other categories of terrorism. In contrast to the left wing groups, the bulk of the right wing groups are located in North America and in, and racist groups. These groups attack immigrants and refugees, mostly of Asian and Middle Eastern origin.

1.4.2 Ethnonationalist terrorism

The first wave of ethnonationalist campaigns was by national liberation movements directed against the Colonial rulers. They included the Irgun and Lehi opposing the British rule in Palestine in the 1940s and French rule in Algeria in the 1950s. Contemporary groups driven by ethnonationalism can be divided into three sub categories. They are groups fighting for autonomy, unification, or reunification (irredentism). For instance, Al Aqsa Martyrs Brigade, Jammu and Kashmiri Liberation Front (JKLF), and the Liberation Tigers of Tamil Eelam (LTTE or Tamil Tigers) are fighting for independence from Israel, India, and Sri Lanka respectively. The members of these groups are motivated by Palestinian, Kashmiri and Tamil nationalism. Similarly, Continuity IRA and Real IRA are fighting for unification or reunification with the Republic of Ireland. Likewise, the PKK is fighting for linguistic and cultural autonomy for the Kurds in Southeastern Turkey. In comparison to the other categories, ethnonationalist conflicts produce the largest number of fatalities and casualties, internally displaced persons and refugee flows and the biggest human rights violations. Groups that have adopted virulent ethnonationalist ideologies pose a significant threat to their opposing ethnic communities and governments.

1.4.3 Politico-religious terrorism

Groups driven by religiosity include those from the Christian, Jewish, Sikh, Hindu, Buddhist and Islamic faiths. They include Army of God in the US, Kach and Kahane Chai of Israel, Babbar Khalsa International of Punjab, India, Aum Shinrikyo (recently renamed Aleph) of Japan, Islamic Resistance Movement (Hamas), Palestinian Islamic Jihad (PIJ), and Armed Islamic Group of Algeria. Aum, an apocalyptic group, aimed to take over Japan and then the world. In contrast to other Islamist groups campaigning within their territories, Al-Qaeda and Lebanese Hezbollah (to a lesser extent) have a global or a universalistic Islamic agenda. To justify violence, politically motivated religious leaders propagate corrupt versions of religious texts often misinterpreting and misrepresenting the great religions.

Of the religious category of groups, Islamists or groups motivated by radical Islamic ideology are the most violent. Two pivotal events in 1979 – the Islamic Revolution in Iran and the Soviet intervention in Afghanistan – led to the increase in number of groups driven by Islamism. By holding on to US hostages for 444 days, the Islamic Republic of Iran defied the US and the anti-Soviet multinational Afghan mujahidin defeated the largest land force, the Soviet Army. After successfully defeating one superpower, the Islamists turned their energies towards building a capability to defeat the remaining superpower, the United States of America, its Allies and friends in the Muslim world. With martyrdom becoming widespread and popular among Islamist groups throughout the 1980s and 1990s, the scale of violence unleashed by Islamist groups has surpassed secular ethnonationalist and left wing and right wing groups. For instance, Palestinian Liberation Organization, Popular Front for the Liberation of Palestine, and Abu Nidal Organisation killed far fewer people than their Islamist counterparts, Hamas and PIJ.

1.4.4 Other categories

Terrorist campaigns are also driven by ideologies that lack mass appeal and therefore are not very common. They are state-sponsored, single-issue and anarchist terrorism.

As terrorism is a low cost, high-impact form of violence, states wishing to advance their foreign policy goals have supported terrorist groups to attack their inimical states. Due to sanctions imposed by the international community against states that sponsor terrorist groups, this clandestine surrogate form of warfare has declined throughout the 1990s into the 21st century. Although the US government accuses a range of countries for supporting terrorism, there is no evidence that North Korea, Iraq, Sudan, Libya or Cuba are actively sponsoring terrorism today. Throughout the 1990s, Sudan and Libya were active sponsors of terrorism. Although the scale of sponsorship has declined, Iran, Syria and Lebanon continue to support terrorism.

Single-issue terrorist groups include violent animal rights and anti-abortion groups that seek to change a specific policy or practice rather than the political system.

Anarchist terrorists seek to overthrow established governments by a wave of bombings and assassinations. The recent wave of protests against globalization parallel anarchist violence from 1870-1920. However, the trajectory of anti-globalization movements is yet to be seen. State response to anti-globalization movements will determine whether we are likely to witness the emergence of terrorist groups espousing the cause of anti-globalization.

Some groups have overlapping ideologies. Although PKK is ethnonationalist, it has a strong Marxist-Leninist orientation. Similarly, the original ideological disposition of the LTTE was Marxist-Leninist. Likewise, Hamas and PIJ are religious, but they have a strong nationalist dimension. Although the Al Aqsa Martyrs Brigade is ethnonationalist, it has a strong religious dimension. In order to survive, the ideologies of groups tend to shift with the changes in the political environment. Groups driven by leftwing ideologies operating in North America and in Western Europe declined in strength and size at the end of the Cold War. The post-Cold War period witnessed a resurgence of ethnicity and religiosity. As a result, groups driven by ethnicity and religion account for about 70 to 80 per cent of all terrorist groups. Furthermore, the ethnonationalist and religious groups have the greatest staying power. Unlike left wing or right wing conflicts, ethnonationalist and religious conflicts are protracted.

1.5 Motivation: Why people join or support terrorist groups
By the cunning use of propaganda, terrorist groups have a high capacity to indoctrinate and motivate their ethnic and religious brethren to join them as full time and part time members, collaborators, supporters and sympathizers. Protracted socio-economic and political conflicts create the conditions for

the spawning and sustenance of virulent ideologies. By means of propaganda, disseminated by the word of mouth, sermons and lectures, leaflets and booklets; print media, radio, TV and the Internet, terrorist ideologues indoctrinate members, supporters, sympathizers and potential recruits. Those indoctrinated join, collaborate, support or sympathize with terrorist goals, aims, and objectives. Theorists have long argued that conditions of poverty, lack of education and unemployment produced terrorist recruits and supporters. However, Osama bin Laden comes from the richest non-royal Saudi family and his principal strategist, Dr Ayman Al Zawahiri, is from one of the most educated families in Egypt. Although those who live in poverty, unemployed, or underemployed are most vulnerable to ideological indoctrination, it is not depravation or relative depravation but ideological indoctrination that generates recruits and supporters for terrorism. As the socio-economic and political conditions in the global south, Asia, Africa, Middle East, Latin America, and the former USSR, are conducive for the inculcation of terrorist ideologies, the bulk of the terrorist groups are located in the poorer regions of the world. Both territorial and migrant communities harboring actual and perceived grievances and aspirations provide significant political, economic and military support for terrorist groups.

Often the most committed members of terrorist groups are those who are directly affected by political violence often by a state or a state-sponsored group. Those who have suffered the loss of their mothers, fathers, brothers, sisters, wives, husbands, sons, daughters, friends, other loved ones and their schools and homes become the most committed. The victims perceive joining or supporting a terrorist group as a vehicle to seek revenge or as an alternative form of government. By its own political and military actions, it is hard for a terrorist group to grow in strength and size. Often to generate widespread public support, terrorist groups provoke security forces to over-react. A restrained law enforcement response is therefore critical to prevent terrorist groups from expanding its support bases, essential for both recruitment and sustenance.

As the end goal of a terrorist group is always political, terrorist groups are armed political organizations. Therefore, the motivation for a person to join a terrorist group is similar to that of joining a political party. The only difference is that a terrorist group uses violence while a political party uses non-violent means to influence its audience. Many join terrorist groups because they have failed to achieve their political goal by political means. In their minds, the terrorist justifies the use of violence because there is no other path available. However, unlike most political parties that are democratic and where dissent is tolerated, almost all the terrorist groups are totalitarian movements led by dictators. The internal and external political environments of members are controlled with no or limited access to the outside world. Like members of a cult, members of a terrorist group share certain values and beliefs. Singularly and collectively, its members believe that they could accomplish the aims, objectives, and goals of the terrorist group. As a member of a terrorist group, the group dynamics increase and decrease terrorist motivation.

While ideology is the key factor, there are other single or multiple motivations for a person to join or support a terrorist group. For instance, the belief that the political process has failed and the only way to achieve the end goal is to support or use terrorism. The belief that by employing terrorism – as opposed to democratic means - it is feasible to achieve the end goal. The person can be driven to support or join a terrorist group by leftist or rightist indoctrination, ethnic affinity or common religious belief. Terrorist ideologues can also raise the level of consciousness that the community has been wronged or deprived. More than depravation it is relative depravation that makes persons rebel. Furthermore, the belief that by joining or lending support to the terrorist group will correct the situation. Sustained terrorist indoctrination can construct new grievances (insecurity) or exacerbate existing grievances (education, employment opportunities; linguistic, cultural rights; land – settlement and colonization; regional autonomy). Similarly, by heightened propaganda, the aspirations of an affected community – for instance, to statehood, can be elevated. The impressionable young are particularly vulnerable to indoctrination. Some recruits are driven by altruistic reasons – a genuine desire to sacrifice his or her life for the people, the land, or for any other ideal could drive a recruit or a serving member to commit an act of terrorism. With terrorist propaganda, inculcating the belief that sacrifice creates a better future, attracts fresh recruits and increases the commitment of existing recruits. The belief that death is inevitable and that government troops would harm a potential recruit because of differences in ethnicity, religion or ideology can drive a recruit to join a terrorist group and contribute to the cause before dying.

As much as hopelessness, revenge is another powerful motivation. Revenge, a wild form of justice, is often triggered when the security forces harm an individual, his or her loved ones and property. Joining or supporting a terrorist group is perceived as the only avenue of extracting revenge. Although conscription is not widespread and is often highlighted by governments for propaganda purposes, terrorist groups also coerce some recruits to join or support them. In an atmosphere of fear and uncertainty, a potential recruit can be threatened by a terrorist group to join or support a group. Such recruits harbor the belief that joining or supporting a terrorist group would facilitate protection of his or her family from the terrorist threat. Some are attracted to terrorist and guerrilla groups by the membership of a secret organization, magnetized by weapons, shining boots and uniform. They feel a sense of excitement or being different from the rest of society. Some join or support a terrorist group for social recognition or social acceptance – a romantic notion of being a key figure or a special person, even a sort of crusader. As opposed to the ordinary public, by being a terrorist, one can command power and strength. As contemporary terrorist groups engage in organized crime, from trading in diamonds to trafficking in narcotics and human smuggling and credit card fraud, to fund their existence and operations, joining a terrorist group is perceived lucrative by a few. For criminal reasons driven by personal gain and greed for the purpose of accumulating wealth, a person can join a terrorist group. Often in conflict zones, the opportunities for livelihood are limited. Instead of starving, a potential recruit prefers to join a group in order to survive and reduce the burden on the family and at times even to feed the family.

1.6 Conclusion

Research demonstrates that a terrorist group by its own action cannot be successful. Often government over- or under-reaction generates overwhelming support and recruits for terrorism. Inappropriate government actions can drive individuals to become terrorists or support terrorism. Mass arrests by the security forces – including arrests on mistaken identity or on false information provided by a personal enemy – can humiliate and turn a non-terrorist sympathizer into a terrorist sympathizer. Similarly, collateral damage by the security forces where death of a family member can motivate one to join a terrorist group. Therefore, intelligence is paramount to accurately identify and pin-pointedly target the terrorist and the terrorist infrastructure. For every terrorist killed or captured, if the terrorist group can recruit five, the battle is lost. The policy of collective punishment meted out in Israel and in some other theatres of conflict has proved to be counter productive. Often, when a colleague is killed, the security forces tend to enforce collective punishment. To prevent such counter-productive actions, especially over-reaction, there should be accountability and oversight at all levels in the counter-terrorist organization. By investing in counter-propaganda, the motivation to join or support a terrorist group can be eroded. After criminalizing support meant for terrorist groups, governments should erode the legitimacy of the group. Targeting the terrorist rank and file with counter-propaganda and offering irresistible incentives for desertions and surrenders can weaken a group from within. Non-military methods are equally or more important than military methods. The political and economic measures are enduring and can have a lasting impact on a terrorist group as well as a terrorist support base.

CHAPTER 2: TERRORIST TRAINING AND WEAPONRY

2.1	Training	21
2.2	Terrorist weapons	28

CHAPTER 2: TERRORIST TRAINING AND WEAPONRY

Terrorist groups pose a significant threat to domestic, regional and international security because of the access they have to professional training and weaponry. The quality of training and weaponry available to terrorist groups has dramatically changed over the years. During the Cold War years, the USSR and its satellite states, as well as the United States and its allies, provided training to a number of terrorist and guerrilla groups. These superpowers controlled the level of training, weapons and targeting to ensure that the conflicts did not escalate from a Cold War to a Hot War.

In the last three decades, terrorist training infrastructure has moved from the Middle East to Asia. In the 1970s and 1980s, the Syrian-controlled Bekaa valley in Lebanon was the main center for training for over 40 foreign terrorist groups. As a result of the Oslo Accords, the center of gravity in international terrorism shifted from the Middle East to Asia in the 1990s and Afghanistan became the major center for training at least 24 groups until US intervention in October 2001.

2.1 Training
Today, terrorist groups have access to the same level of training available to security forces personnel. Four factors facilitated terrorist access to professional training.

- First, the US and allied sponsorship of anti-Soviet mujahi groups throughout the 1980s included provision of field manual (FM series) reserved for the US military, including the US special forces. For instance, in the New Jersey home of Sayeed Nosair, the FBI recovered secret US military manuals originating from the J F Kennedy Center for Special Warfare in Fort Bragg, North Carolina.

- Second, several former security forces personnel from Egypt and Algeria and the US participated both in the anti-Soviet and the subsequent global jihad campaigns that followed in the 1990s. For instance, an Egyptian Captain Ali Mohommad, who later joined the US Special Forces as a Sergeant, was Al-Qaeda's principal military instructor in Afghanistan, Sudan, Somalia and Bosnia and also trained Osama binLaden's bodyguard contingent.

- Third, privatization of security, proliferation of security companies and former security forces personnel willing to serve as both trainers and mercenaries especially at the end of the Cold War. For instance, when the Sri Lankan government purchased Medium Landing Craft (LCMs) the LTTE clandestinely hired experts from Swan Hunter, the manufacturer of the LCMs, tounderstand the vulnerabilities and limitations of LCMs.

- Fourth, certain intelligence agencies of governments continue to provide training to foreign terrorist groups as a means ofadvancing their foreign policy aims and objectives against inimical states. For instance, the Revolutionary Guards of Iran continues to train Hezbollah. As such, a well connected or a well-endowed terrorist group could always gain access to high-quality training hitherto reserved for professional militaries.

Nonetheless, most terrorist groups operate under constant pressure from their governments. Dependent on the need, resources and opportunities, terrorist groups impart both ideological and physical training to its recruits. Although physical training appears as the most important component of the two and governments respond to disrupt terrorist access to physical training, what is absolutely critical is ideological training. To inculcate commitment of a fresh recruit to the aims and the objectives of the group, ideological indoctrination is considered paramount. Therefore, terrorist groups emphasise ideological training, which is usually imparted by ideologues. After the initial training of a recruit, ideological training does not cease but is continuous as long as he or she retains membership of the group. Often both the motivation and endurance of a terrorist, especially to survive in a hostile zone, depends more on his or her commitment to ideology. More than the physical training, ideological training ensures the staying power of a terrorist. For instance, most of the September 11 suicide hijackers lived in the US for over one year without changing their mind because of the high-level indoctrination they had received over the years. Even after Zacarias Moussaoui was captured three weeks before September 11, it is his belief in Al-Qaeda's aims and objectives that has precluded him from divulging the organization's elaborate plans and preparations as well as the identity and location of Al-Qaeda members and leaders in the United States.

Training

Ideological training differs from group to group. If the organization is driven by ethnonationalist ideology, its members will be indoctrinated about the suffering of their ethnic brethren and the need to sacrifice life so that future generations will be able to live in safety. The opposing ethnic community will be portrayed as subhuman, evil, and destructive. Furthermore, the member will be indoctrinated to the point where he or she will believe that only by waging a sustained terrorist campaign will they be able to recover their homeland. Similarly, the members of an Islamist group will be made to believe that it is a Muslim's duty to wage jihad. Almost all the Islamist terrorist groups waging Jihad in Palestine, Algeria, Kashmir, Bosnia, Chechnya, Afghanistan, Eritrea, Somalia and the Philippines are driven by the Salafi school. Members of this branch are indoctrinated to worship and love Allah above all else. They do not even believe or follow the Imams and the Sheikhs. They only pledge their allegiance to Allah and to his Messenger. Contemporary ideologues draw from the writings of Sayed Abdul A'la Maududi, the founder leader of the Pakistani political party Jamat-I-Islami and Sayed Qutb, the ideologue of the Egyptian Muslim Brotherhood who sanctioned the use of violence for the establishment of Islam. They also appealed for the return of the Koran and Sunnah, with the principles of Islam applied to modern society by the use of rational judgement in religious matters. Maududi and Qutb reaffirmed the function of Islam in politics and civilised societies under the control of secularism and the Western development paradigm of democracy. They were both against the Western political thought especially the concept of sovereignty and called for the establishment of a 'revolutionary vanguard of true believers' to organise Islamic states. By citing the successes of the Iranian revolution of 1979 and the anti-Soviet Afghan jihad (1979-1989) they build confidence to take on their enemies, both Muslim regimes friendly to the West and the West itself.

Physical training takes three forms: basic, advanced and special. Basic training, also known as recruit training, involves physical and weapons training. The training course could last from a week to four months, dependent on the opportunities available for training as well as the sophistication of the terrorist group. For instance, a member of a Palestinian group lacks the opportunities for extended training like a member of a Chechen group. Therefore, a Hamas or a Palestinian Islamic Jihad member living in the occupied territories may train for a few days before embarking on a suicide mission. As the execution phase of a suicide attack against an Israeli target is short, the Palestinian suicide terrorist does not need extensive physical training. In contrast, a member of Al Ansar Mujahidin in Chechnya assigned to infiltrate Moscow and conduct a spate of bombings will receive extended training so that he will be psychologically and physically fully prepared to meet the numerous challenges likely to face him in his long-range, deep penetration mission.

Although the training to be a guerrilla is different from that to be a terrorist, the curricula imparted by terrorist groups to its members is very similar. It is because most terrorist recruits trained to attack civilians must learn how to engage the security forces, if or when confronted by them. For instance, a terrorist tasked to plant a bomb in Srinagar, infiltrating across the line of control in Kashmir, must learn how to move at night and engage Indian border guards if or when confronted. Furthermore, the terrorist training imparted to its members assigned to fight in rural or urban environments is very similar. Most terrorists learn on the job - they survive and progress not according to plan but opportunity. Nonetheless, the sophisticated terrorist groups train its members on how to fight in built-up areas. The training to be a terrorist is much shorter than the training to be a guerrilla, but most terrorists receive both terrorist and guerilla training. As terrorists primarily attack soft targets and guerrillas primarily attack hard targets, the terrorist as well as guerrilla training builds confidence in the recruits.

The curriculum and duration of the training for a recruit is dependent on the environment. If the terrorist has to survive a longer period in the battlefield in a guerrilla role, then he or she is trained for a longer period. This is to prevent demoralization and desertion as well as injury and death. A poorly trained terrorist in a guerrilla role is likely to suffer injury and die, demoralizing other members, facilitating desertion and restraining recruitment. Training and retraining is the key to success of a terrorist group whether operating in a terrorist or a guerrilla context. Therefore, most sophisticated groups continually train to ensure their members are mentally and physically prepared for battle at all times.

The advanced training imparted by a terrorist group is akin to government special forces or commando training. It is an advanced infantry-training course where the terrorist receives harder training to increase his or her confidence as well as endurance. Usually, the best members are provided the limited opportunities available for advance training. Many terrorists that receive advanced training end up as group or sub group leaders or as trainers. In contrast, special training imparts specialized knowledge, from communication to intelligence gathering or use of specialized weapons or weapon systems such as sniper or heavy caliber weapons. As terrorists are cost conscious they are unlikely to waste excessive resources training a terrorist in aspects of warfare beyond his or her mission. Therefore, dependent on their special qualities, orientation and aptitude, terrorists are handpicked for missions and trained to ensure the success of that mission.

The sophisticated terrorist groups of the world impart model training, a fourth category of training that specifically trains the member for his or her mission. For instance, the terrorists assigned for September 11 were trained to fly commercial aircraft. Similarly, the terrorists assigned to bomb the US diplomatic targets in East Africa in August 1998 were trained to drive vehicles. The terrorists assigned to ram an explosives-laden boat onto the USS *The Sullivans* in January and USS *Cole* in October 2000 were trained to pilot boats. Model training imparts the knowledge the terrorist requires to accomplish the mission assigned to him or to her. Model training helps the terrorist to gain stealth, speed, and surprise. The numbers that train in the higher training categories, advanced and special training including model training are kept small. This is to reduce the risk of capture of a trainee thus protecting the secrecy of the intended operation.

Some recruits bring with them special skills having served in the military or the police. Furthermore, military and police service are methods of obtaining professional training for some terrorists. For instance, Ahmad Jabril, the leader of the PFLP-GC is a former Captain in the Syrian army; Namangani, the founder leader of the Islamic Movement of Uzbekistan was a former Soviet paratrooper; and Said Bahaji, an Al-Qaeda member of the German cell, was a former soldier in the Bundeswehr. Similarly, the two Al-Qaeda military commanders Muhammed Atef and Abu Ubadiah al-Banshiri had served in the Egyptian police and the army. Both Algerian and Chechen terrorist groups had several former military officers occupying important positions in their ranks. Some terrorist groups such as Al-Qaeda even request its supporters and sympathizers, including those living in Western Europe, to join security forces for the specific purpose of obtaining training from police and the military. This was invaluable because of the quality of specialized training imparted on how to mount surveillance or reconnaissance, manufacturing explosives and explosive devices and use of firearms. With the loss of Afghanistan, it is likely that terrorist groups that relied heavily on the training infrastructure in Afghanistan will seek to join security forces and obtain professional training.

The curricula of the multi-volume *Encyclopedia of the Afghan Jihad* indicates the cumulative body of knowledge in the possession of contemporary terrorist groups. The first 10 volumes are on tactics; security and intelligence; hand guns; first aid; explosives; grenades and mines; tanks; manufacturing (improvisation of arms and explosives); topography and land surveys; and weapons. The cover of each volume shows a belt-fed machine gun standing on a window ledge next to a copy of the Koran. In each volume, the treatment of the subject is extensive. For instance, a chapter in the volume on tactics titled The effect of desert land on operations is subdivided into the following sections: advance, attack, defense, withdrawal, movement and transport, shortage of water, supplies and maintenance. As terrorists operate in a range of environments, the encyclopedia caters for it – operations in rural, urban, mountainous, and jungle environments are covered. The 7,000 page encyclopedia is simply written by veterans of the Afghan war and does not require high-level education to understand. It has trained a new generation of post-Soviet mujahidin to fight in regional conflicts such as Kashmir, Mindanao, Chechnya and Algeria as well as in terrorist campaigns. Every theatre has its own manual – for instance, when the Arab trainers who fought in Afghanistan went to Bosnia they wrote a manual especially for the Bosnian mujahidin.

Al-Qaeda uses a manual of the Islamic Group of Egypt for its terrorist training. Recovered in Manchester in the UK, the title on the manual is *Declaration of Jihad Against the Country's Tyrants (Military Series)*. The title is imposed on a drawing of the globe through which a sword pierces through the continent of Africa and a section of the Middle East. In its introduction, the manual is dedicated to the "young Moslem men who are pure, believing and fighting for the cause of Allah. It is my contribution towards paving the road that leads to majestic Allah and establishes a caliphate according to the prophecy." The 18 lessons include a General Introduction, Necessary Qualifications and Characteristics for the Organization's Members, Counterfeit Currency and Forged Documents, Organization Military Bases, "Apartments Places" – Hiding, Means of Communication and Transportation, Training, Weapons: Measures Related to Buying and Transporting Them, Member Safety, Security Plan, Definition of Special Operations, Espionage (1) Information-Gathering Using Open Methods, Espionage (2) Information-Gathering Using

Covert Methods, Assassinations Using Poisons and Cold Steel, Torture Methods, Prisons and Detention Centers. The manual describes techniques and tactics that could be used to perpetrate violence, such as the use of improvised explosives devices, use of poisons, and so on. The manual draws heavily from US, British and other field manuals especially those produced for the education of their elite forces. In the dissemination of information, the principle of need to know and operational security is meticulously followed by Al-Qaeda. Other manuals include the widely distributed *The Terrorist Handbook* produced in the West.

The training of Ahmed Saeed Omar Sheikh, the terrorist accused of kidnapping and murdering the American journalist Daniel Pearl, provides insight into the training of a terrorist. Together with 20 other recruits, Omar Sheikh proceeded to a training camp in Afghanistan staffed by Harakat-ul-Mujahidin and visiting Al-Qaeda instructors. The Khalid bin Waleed camp – previously known as Salman Farsi Camp – offered a 40-day 'Istakbalia' course. After morning prayers in the mosque, Omar Sheikh engaged in physical exercise until 0800. After breakfast, he received instruction in the use of small and medium firearms, especially Kalashnikovs, until lunch. After resting for two hours and prayers in the mosque, religious education and physical training followed. For firing practice each recruit, including Omar Sheikh, was provided six rounds. Recruits including Omar Sheikh were also entrusted with night security duties. Of the eight instructors, Omar Sheikh mostly stayed with Ayubi alias Abu Anjwari from Karachi, an educated muhajir. Although Omar Sheikh suffered a bout of diarrhea and returned to his uncles at Lahore he voluntarily went back to the camp after a hiatus of 10 days.

On completion of the recruit training Omar Sheikh was selected for a specialized training course from September to December 1993. According to claims made by Omar Sheikh to his Indian interrogators, he received training from serving members of the Special Services Group of Pakistan (SSG). It is likely that Omar Sheikh received training from former members and not serving members of the SSG, who serve as instructors in training camps, including those in Afghanistan. The specialized terrorist training course followed by Omar Sheikh matches the standard course tailor made for the mujahidin provided by former members of SSG. Omar Sheikh told his interrogators that he received training in surveillance and counter surveillance, art of disguising, interrogation, cell structure, secret meetings, secret writings, cryptology and codes, free wrestling and moving (how to enter a room by kicking the door open, falling on the floor and shooting if somebody suspicious is in the room). On the principles of planning and conducting operations, Omar Sheikh was trained in reconnaissance, checking of equipment, selection of persons for an operation, assignment of tasks, approaching the target, method of attack, use of signals for withdrawing, system of communication and first aid. In addition, Omar Sheikh also received training in urban warfare, use of assault rifles, light machine guns, rocket launchers, night movement, raids and ambushes.

It is apparent there is a generation of terrorists with knowledge comparable to regular soldiers in service of governments. Well-funded groups have hired some of the best available special forces trainers in the world. Therefore, to fight contemporary terrorism, it is essential to provide highly specialized counter-terrorism training to troops assigned for counter terrorism functions. As most terrorists are better trained, better armed and better motivated, regular troops and policemen are likely to be unsuccessful without specialized training. The response of the German police to the massacre of Israeli athletes in the Olympic village, Munich, in 1972, provides an insight to the difficulty of fighting terrorism without creating elite forces. Training and equipping highly specialized counter terrorist forces remain at the heart of sound planning and preparing to fight contemporary terrorism.

2.2 Terrorist weapons

Terrorist weapons include factory-manufactured and improvised explosives, small arms and light weapons as well as dual technologies. A few terrorist groups, however, have an interest in developing, acquiring and using Chemical, Biological, Radiological and Nuclear (CBRN) weapons. Nonetheless, the bulk of the weapon types used by terrorists consists of conventional weapons, especially firearms and improvised explosive devices.

2.2.1 Explosives

Terrorist groups can obtain factory-manufactured explosives by theft, manufacture and terrorist explosives, and terrorist state sponsor. Furthermore, sophisticated terrorist groups purchase both military and commercial explosives using forged and adapted end user certificates. Under the cover of transporting general cargo, terrorist groups transport explosives by land, sea and air. Terrorist groups have gained access to two main types of explosives: fragmentation and incendiary. Terrorists use the following explosives to construct their improvised devices – Semtex, Research Department explosive X (RDX: also known as Cyclonite or Hexogen), Pentaerythriol-tetranitrate (PETN: Pentrite), Composition 4 (C4), Trinitrotoluene (TNT), Ammonium Nitrate (fertilizer), and dynamite. The availability of explosives, associated technologies and expertise enable terrorist groups to build Improvised Explosive Devices (IEDs) to attack land, sea and aerial targets. A basic IED has four components: an explosives charge, an initiator, a power source and an activation switch. The IEDs are activated by physical, water or atmospheric pressure, remote control or radio frequency electronic signal, electronic pulse (detonator box), photo electric cells, motion and heat detectors, radiation trigger, circuit connection, electronic or acid activated time switch and fuse wire.

Almost all the explosives demonstrate fragmentation, blast pressure and incendiary effects. The shrapnel – glass, nails, spikes, ball bearings, barbed wire and other pieces of metal – in the device makes it more lethal. Furthermore, if placed in a metal container the fragmentation is even greater. If the target is an enclosed structure of concrete with windows, the fragmentation will include shattered pieces of concrete and flying glass.

Sometimes Hamas, PIJ and Al Aqsa Martyrs Brigade added warfarin (rat poison), an anti-coagulant, to the bomb device that ensured the injured bled to death. Blast pressure can be positive, the outward wave of air, and negative, the vacuum created that sucks air into the point of explosion. With the explosion, building walls and complete floors collapse, and objects and people are flung at great speed. On occasions those exposed to a blast can appear unaffected but, in reality, most do suffer a range of internal injuries. Even when they are brought to hospital, they may appear well but could be suffering internal hemorrhage that takes time to become apparent. Often their lungs are ripped apart, liver and other internal organs are damaged, and eardrums and eyes injured. The incendiary effects, lasting a fraction of a second, ignite skin, hair and other inflammatory material. Some devices are specially designed to start a fire. The victims suffer from physical and psychological consequences: shock (pale face, abundant sweating and slowed pulse), loss of consciousness, concussion, meningeal hemorrhages and encephalic lesions, as well as panic attacks (trembling, fear, confusion and amnesia).

The scale of destruction to humans and infrastructure depends on the quality of the explosive, the way it is packed and the nature of the target. As low-velocity explosive has a limited shelf life and is susceptible to friction, heat and static electricity, terrorists prefer high-velocity explosives, which are more destructive, stable and mouldable to any shape and size. With activation, explosives are transformed in three ways: combustion resulting in burns, deflagrates with a progressive blast effect, and detonates with shattering, sudden blast and shock effects. The blast, the mechanical effects produced by an aerial shock, can vary dependent on the explosive charge. While a 30 kg charge of explosives has a lethal radius of 5.5 m, a 200 kg charge will have a radius of 25 m. With experience, terrorist explosive experts position explosives and shrapnel to cause maximum damage. The metallic additives give higher pressures of the order of 25 per cent than pure explosives. If the explosive charge is spherical and detonated at its center, it will emit spherical waves whose effects are identical in all directions. If the charge is cylindrical or parallel piped the waves will be concentrated in certain directions. For instance, to increase the kill radius some suicide terrorists of the LTTE have an explosive charge with layers of ball bearings both in the front and back of their body. Furthermore, the pressure and temperature of the ambiance can alter the effect of the shock waves. Some terrorist targets are susceptible to greater damage than others. For instance, to conduct a mass casualty suicide terrorist attack against a military target it is necessary for the soldiers to be inside a building. Together with the US marine barracks (241 killed) and the French paratrooper HQ (58 killed), Hezbollah also planned to attack the Italian component of the Multi National Peacekeeping Force in Lebanon in 1983 but they could not conduct a suicide attack against the Italian target because the Italian troops were in tents. The devices were 60 per cent RDX, 39 per cent TNT and 1 per cent wax designed to coat and desensitize the explosive long enough for the driver to reach the target. Terrorists are continuing to develop new technologies and tactics to improve their efficiency and efficacy. According to J L Marret of the Ecole Speciale Militaire de Saint-Cyr, France, there is a constant race to improve the reliability of bombs as well as a race to improve their power-to-weight ratio.

Terrorists are constantly improving their devices. After a caller accidentally phoned the cell phone of two Continuity IRA members, a father and son, who were constructing an explosive device to be activated by dialing the cell phone number, it blew up mutilating the son's groin and nearly killing the father. To eliminate another accidental explosion, Continuity IRA's next set of devices had two cell phones. This meant the Continuity IRA bomber had to dial both the cell phones to activate the device. Similarly, the security forces too constantly improve their methods for detecting terrorist devices. Because the countermeasures save lives, the technological advances and innovations are often kept secret even between friendly governments. For instance, the UK government rarely shared the devices they developed to counter PIRA's remote-control devices even with their US counterparts for fear that it would leak to PIRA. Often it was a cat and a mouse game where the security forces and the terrorist group attempted to counter each other's techniques, technologies and tactics. In the secret war against explosive devices, this was more evident than in other areas.

There are infinite ways explosives could be used by a terrorist group. *The Encyclopedia of the Afghan Jihad's* volume on explosives illustrates how to use explosives to booby trap several items: a camera, radio transmitter-receiver; packet of cigarettes, a cigarette lighter, a smoking pipe, a bottle of wine, a whistle, electronic equipment, a tape case, a water flask, an electric hand torch, a cake, a chocolate bar, a tooth paste tube, hairbrush, chair bottoms, upholstered mattresses and chairs, letter and parcel bombs, a wallet/purse, a book, raised windows, trapping windows, on a door, beside a frame, inside a domestic heater, storage units. The encyclopedia, drawing from historical and contemporary cases also illustrates how to blast big buildings, symbolic statues and bridges. The volume also discusses the classification of explosives according to their natural characteristics, usage, velocity of detonation and their composition. The mujahidin considers the explosives as the 'safest weapon' as it enables them to get away from the enemy and avoid being arrested.

It is not difficult for a terrorist recruit to master bomb manufacturing skills in a short period of time. Knowledge of how to handle as well as how to manufacture explosives and explosives devices is widely available including on the Internet. *The Terrorist Handbook,* for instance, describes how to buy explosives and propellants, acquire chemicals, lists useful household chemicals and availability and the preparation of chemicals. After outlining the theory of explosives under explosive recipes, it describes impact, low and high order and other explosives such as Molotov cocktails, chemical fire bottles and bottled gas explosives. Under 'using explosives', it describes safety, fuze, impact, electric, electromechanical ignition devices, mercury and tripwire switches and radio controlled detonators; fuse, timer and chemical delays; explosive containers out of paper, metal, glass and plastic; advanced uses for explosives (shape charges, tube explosives, atomized particle explosions, light bulb bombs, book bombs and phone bombs). Some of the recipes are wrong and likely to kill the bomber. By popularizing terrorist devices on the Internet, the threshold for terrorism has increased. Security and intelligence agencies have monitored email communication between terrorist groups such as Hezbollah providing Hamas and Palestinian Islamic Jihad with information on how to manufacture explosives as well as improvise explosives devices.

As IEDs could be designed and built for use in a number of situations, they are the favored weapon of the terrorists. Of the range of IEDs, pipe bombs and Molotov cocktails are the oldest and the most frequently used by terrorists worldwide. The fuel for the Molotov cocktails and gunpowder for the pipe bombs is easily obtainable, low cost and the device is easily manufactured. A pipe bomb consists of low-velocity explosives in a tightly capped piece of iron, steel, aluminum or copper pipe sometimes with nails. With detonation of pipe bombs, the explosion will shatter the pipe and its fragments will travel at high speed and strike the surrounding areas. If the outer casing is grooved, the fragmentation is uniform and can be more lethal to humans. Unlike the pipe bomb, Molotov cocktails, consisting of gasoline, diesel, kerosene, alcohol, lighter fuel or turpentine, usually in a glass container are incendiary. A piece of cloth serving as the fuze is lit and the container is thrown at the target. Molotov cocktails, used for the first time by the Russian resistance against German tanks in the Second World War, break on impact and cause death and injury by burning and setting fire to both vehicles and housing.

Letter and parcel bombs are the commonest examples going back to the end of the 19th century. Listing the contents as medicaments for the Czar for his asthma, Russian terrorists dispatched small packages with explosives. In 1895, anarchists targeted a police officer using gunpowder and a small revolver connected to an alarm clock as a detonator but it was opened at the post office in Berlin. In 1972, the PLO dispatched several hundred parcel and letter bombs to targets in world capitals and other places from locations as distant as India. Although explosives detection systems can detect most letter and parcel bombs, they are in use mostly in the developed world. As there are millions of letters and packages passing through post offices and courier companies annually, only a faction are scanned for explosives. Therefore, the threat of letter and parcel bombs is very real.

Guerrillas, or terrorist groups engaged in guerrilla warfare, employ mines. Although some groups have acquired mines by theft or raiding military facilities, most groups operating in rural and jungle environments manufacture mines. Terrorists manufacture vehicle land mines to destroy vehicles as well as anti-personnel mines to injure enemy soldiers and civilians. Often, when the security forces retreat to their camps at night, terrorists lay mines overnight on the roads frequently used by the security forces. The mines are placed just below the surface often in ways to deceive the routine mine clearing teams, if any. Terrorists detonate mines by command wire (manually), by pressure (either a soldier or a vehicle going over a mine), and by remote control. Mines are invaluable weapons in a terrorist arsenal especially when laying an ambush, where the target is taken by surprise. Also by laying mines, terrorist cut out teams can inflict death and destruction and slow down the military reinforcements approaching the ambushed target. Although there is a worldwide ban against the use of landmines, only states adhere to the convention. Attempts by the International Committee of the Red Cross and non-governmental organizations such as International Alert in London, to influence or seek an agreement with terrorist groups to totally abandon the use of mines, have met with partial success.

By laying minefields around their camps, mines helped security forces to protect their camps from attack. In contrast, terrorist groups, especially those operating in rural areas, use landmines (mostly anti-personnel types) against counter-terrorist especially search and destroy teams. After exploding a primary device, some terrorist groups place a secondary device aimed at targeting reinforcing troops. In most countries, the technology to detect landmines is primitive. Although the technology to detect land mines has improved in the recent past, the use of mine detection equipment slows down military operations. As such, most counter-terrorist forces do not use mine detection equipment. In contrast, mine detection equipment is widely used by serving or retired explosives ordinance disposal personnel in mine clearing operations mounted by governments and humanitarian organizations in post conflict situations or during periods of ceasefire. Terrorist mines are easily produced and cost less than a dollar each. Some of the anti-personnel mines consist of two pieces of wood painted in green or brown to blend into the terrain, a torch battery and a small quantity of explosives. A terrorist trainer states that the principle of an anti-personal mine is not to kill but to drive fear into soldiers by injuring one soldier. By not killing but injuring a soldier, he will scream and struggle, making other soldiers reluctant to continue with the mission. If a soldier is killed it would require only one other to carry him but if he is injured it would require four others to carry him. The psychological impact of an anti-personnel mine attack that leads to the loss of a foot, ankle or a leg of a fellow soldier can demoralize others.

By trial and error, the 19th century anarchists who lost several of their members regulated the quantity of explosives necessary to destroy the target. They also developed portable devices or grenades. Terrorist groups use both hand thrown and rocket propelled grenades frequently. A few terrorist groups even manufacture their own grenades. Terrorists lob grenades into moving or stationary vehicles, infrastructure targets such as schools, homes, and offices; and at public meetings. Usually the impact of a grenade is multiplied if it explodes inside a vehicle or a building rather than in an open space. Therefore, when traveling in conflict zones, it is advised to travel by having the shutters of vehicles fully up and to protect the windows of premises with a wire mesh. Furthermore, when a grenade is lobbed it is advised to go down on the floor or take cover behind a structure to evade the full blast of the grenade. Grenades also act as effective personal weapons. Especially when confronted, terrorists use grenades against police and military units as well as others operating against them. Dependent on the grenade type, the composition of the explosives and the fragmentation of a grenade varies. It could be dynamite or plastic explosives. For instance, the Pakistani ordinance factory produces 84-P2A1, a plastic hand grenade, under Austrian license. The ovoid plastic body contains 5,000 steel balls packed around 95g of plasticized PETN and has a kill radius of 20 m.

Information on how to manufacture explosives or an explosive device is available in the public domain. However, manufacturing and transporting explosives and explosive devices require specialized training and extraordinary skill. Otherwise either the bomb maker or the bomber is likely to die or suffer injury during the manufacturing or the transportation phases. Even experts such as Ramzi Ahmed Yousef, the February 1993 World Trade Center bomber in New York, suffered injuries. Experienced terrorist explosives experts do not wish to produce large quantity of explosives because of the risk of sudden explosion due to the creation of hotspots when the cooling of the explosives mixture is not homogeneous. Although most terrorist recruits are taught the theory of explosives, only a handful of the terrorists are selected to become explosives experts. Before the training begins, almost all the terrorist training manuals emphasize the need to identify a correct type of person to undergo the highly specialized explosives course. The candidate should be calm, quiet and intelligent as opposed to a hothead who is likely to kill himself, other members, collaborators and supporters.

To overcome enhanced security measures at airports and seaports aimed at preventing the transportation of explosives to the target location, contemporary terrorist groups are training their recruits to build bombs by using material commercially available in the vicinity of the target. After training terrorists in manufacturing bombs using commercially available material, they are dispatched to target zones without any bomb making material. The terrorists who have memorized the bomb making instructions and formulae rent apartments and use their rooms, garages and kitchens for the purpose of producing the explosives and the explosive devices. For instance, terrorist explosives experts manufacture bombs by using aluminum powder found in paint, hydrogen peroxide found in hair colourant and in treating medical injuries, sulfur used in agriculture, ammonium nitrate used as fertilizer, concentrated sulfuric acid used to kill bacteria, hydrazine used in making flour and hydrazine recovered as specks from welding. For instance, the bombs Al-Qaeda planned to build to destroy the US embassy and the American cultural center in Paris, soon after September 11, was using commercially available chemicals. When Belgian police raided the apartment of Al-Qaeda member Nizar Trebelsi they found a list of chemicals concealed in a book about the German football club Fortuna Dusseldorf (Trebelsi's former employers). The list included acetone, hydrogen peroxide, sulfur, concentrated sulfuric acid, ammonium, hydrazine and glycerin. Some of the chemicals were recovered from Restaurant Le Nil in Brussels by the police on September 20, 2001.

Military explosives, with higher detonation rates, have a greater shattering effect. They are also stable – insensitive to heat, shock, impact and friction. Nonetheless, a home made explosive device could be as devastating as a military explosive device. According to Professor H C Bissco, by combining a number of commercially available products, it is possible to create an explosive or a pyrotechnic mixture. For example, acetone and hydrogen peroxide and concentrated sulfuric acid gives acetone tri peroxide (TATP), the type found in the shoes worn by Richard Reid planning to bomb American Airlines flight 63 from Paris to Miami on December 22, 2001. TATP is manufactured in terrorist bomb factories in the Israeli-occupied areas of Palestine. It is also the favored explosive of the Palestinian terrorist groups – Hamas, PIJ, Al Aqsa Martyrs Brigade, including that of its suicide bombers. Al-Qaeda trained its explosives experts to manufacture TATP, classed as a primary explosive, extremely sensitive compared with nitride and terazene and, therefore, can be used as a detonator. If the terrorist explosives expert was willing to accept the risk of explosion involved in handling it, the synthesis reaction would require a concentration of hydrogen peroxide of the order of 35 per cent and strong concentrated acid of at least 50 per cent in order to obtain an adequate production yield. Thereafter the temperature has to be controlled permanently in order to avoid an explosion. This requires a minimum of equipment and sufficient experience on the part of the terrorist explosives expert. TATP retains its optimal explosives characteristics for two days from manufacture.

Home made explosive devices can also be constructed by mixing ammonium nitrate, a fertilizer, and aluminum and glycerin. The mixture, similar to ammonium nitrate fuel oil, is a non high explosives mixture which requires a powerful initiation by means of an adequate detonator such as TATP. The ammonium nitrate needs to be sufficiently concentrated and porous to contain at least 6 per cent of hydrocarbonated liquid (glycerin) or hydrazine. Ammonium nitrate, aluminum and hydrazine also give a non high explosive mixture. Instead of aluminum, sulfur, too, can be used as a fuel. Acetone, sulfur, glycerin and even aluminum peroxide are easily obtainable from chemists, pharmacies and DIY stores. In contrast, hydrogen peroxide in that concentration cannot be obtained for medical purposes, disinfecting wounds or for coloring hair. Like Acetone, concentrated sulfuric acid is also a precursor in the manufacture of drugs. Although the fertilizer ammonium nitrate can be easily obtained in the open market, its concentration is below 30 per cent, which is too low to be used as an explosive. However, information is available on methods that can be used to increase concentration. Hydrazine is the hardest substance to obtain except hydrazine sulfate, known as hydrazine salt among chemists. Hydrazine sulfate can be turned into hydrazine nitrate by the action of nitric acid. Ammonium nitrate, aluminum powder and hydrazine sulfate can be obtained easily. The sale literature is on the Internet and there is no need for sophisticated equipment to produce explosives.

Every bomb has the signature of a terrorist school if not a group. Every explosive device, diffused before the explosion or components recovered after the explosion, provides an understanding of the technical competence of the terrorist group. The type of explosives and the method of its manufacture can help to identify the group responsible and even at times the bomb maker. The study of the technical capability of a terrorist group can provide clues as to from where the terrorists are obtaining their supplies and the identity of their trainers. Furthermore, it could help to trace the origin as well as predict the terrorist group's technological trajectory.

Contemporary terrorist groups obtain explosives from security forces, state sponsors or by manufacturers deceptively. The Kosovo Liberation Army obtained 80 per cent of its firearms, including its explosives, from corrupt officers of the Serbian military. The PIRA obtained Semtex from Libya from a 1,000 tonne consignment Tripoli received from Czechoslovakia. The LTTE received 50 tonnes of TNT and 10 tonnes of RDX from Ukraine's Rubezone chemical plant by presenting a forged end user certificate signed by the secretary of defense of Bangladesh. While the French intelligence together with its navy interdicted only one PIRA consignment, the LTTE consignment reached Sri Lankan shores on board MV *Swene*. Access to explosives enabled terrorist groups to step up their terrorist campaigns. Even if stringent measures are introduced, there are several tens of thousands of tones of explosives in the hands of terrorist groups, criminal groups and militaries. The key to reducing the threat of terrorism should be a multi-agency task. They range from denying terrorist groups access to funds, punishing corrupt military officers, sanctions against state sponsors, state verification of all transactions, limiting terrorist access to precursor chemicals and, more importantly, international security, intelligence, law enforcement and judicial cooperation.

2.2.2 Firearms
With the end of the Cold War, the international arms market became saturated with armaments. As the international system is state centric, there are grave legal and operational limitations that constrain governments from combating international arms procurement and shipping. To regulate transactions especially to counter illicit arms procurement and shipping, there

is no centralized controlling body. The widespread availability of firearms, notably small arms and light weapons, has increased the threshold for terrorist attacks. There are nearly 50 million copies and variations of the Kalashnikov (AK/AKM), the most used weapon in the world. Next to explosives, this category of weapons, exemplified by systems such as the AK-47, the Type-56, or the M-16, remains the most widely used by terrorist groups. Easy to procure, conceal, transport, train and use, small arms and light weapons will remain the weapons of choice of terrorists in the foreseeable future. Therefore, limiting their availability by denying easy access to conventional weapons is likely to reduce the threat as well as incidents of terrorism.

The widespread availability of weapons has provided terrorist groups access to small arms, medium-size and heavy infantry weapons. The bolt-action rifle that developed significantly during World War II evolved into the Kalashnikov on the Soviet side and the Armalite on the American side. While the Kalashnikov uses 7.62 mm rounds, the Armalite uses 5.56 mm rounds. Small arms are weapons below the belt-fed category of weapons. They include handguns, rifles, submachine guns, and light machine guns. Medium-size infantry weapons are mostly belt-fed machine guns, smaller sized mortars, RPGs, Light Anti Tank Weapons (LAWs) and small caliber wire-guided missiles. Heavy infantry weapons include heavy caliber machine guns, heavy caliber mortars, large caliber wire-guided missiles, shoulder-held anti-tank missile launchers and some rockets below the category of artillery. The more sophisticated groups have procured and used stand-off-weapons - RPGs, LAWs, Surface-to-Air Missiles (SAMs), and small, medium and large caliber mortars. To use most of these weapons limited training is required. For instance, the RPG is a simple and functional weapon effective against 500 m fixed and 300 m moving vehicle and anti-armor targets. Groups with stand-off capabilities not only attack land but sea and aerial targets. During the last decade, the terrorist propensity to procure and employ stand-off weapons has increased. Stand-off weapons enable terrorists to preserve their strength and conduct mass fatality and casualty attacks both on combatants and civilians.

With easy access to the saturated weapons market, groups have replaced their improvised weapons with commercially manufactured weapons. Improvised or homemade weapons tend to be less reliable than commercially manufactured weapons. In the North Western Frontier

Province, Pakistan, a replica of any small arm and light weapon can be manufactured. There are other regions in the world that are awash with weapons. There are huge Soviet and Western stockpiles in Afghanistan and Pakistan. Many countries in Southeast Asia, Sub-Saharan Africa, and the Balkans (mostly Croatia) are known to sell weapons without proper verification. In these regions, terrorist groups have gained access to sophisticated weapons, dual technologies, and professional trainers. Saturated arms markets in Eastern Europe and the Southern-belt of the former Soviet Union and in other regions where Cold War conflicts have ended, feed the international arms pipelines of several terrorist groups. Although, the industrialized world is producing a bulk of the light weapons today, the emerging trend is for developing countries to increasingly invest in producing light weapons. As developing states have less control over arms production and trade, it is likely that the illicit arms markets will grow exponentially in the future.

Often, large-scale purchase of arms by terrorist groups are accomplished with the connivance and at least tacit of the governments of the manufacturing countries. To checking this untoward trend of proliferation, the role of the unscrupulous private arms dealer should be minimized or supervised. The international community should encourage arms transactions at a government-to-government level. On account of the enormity of the illicit arms trade and the profits that accrue to the manufacturing countries this may not be acceptable to such states. In the alternative, governments of the manufacturing states should nominate their arms dealers. The licenses to trade should be renewed annually after reviewing whether their transactions have complied with international and domestic rules and regulations. There is no international tribunal possessing jurisdiction to try violations of conventions towards regulating illicit arms transactions and transportation. A central data bank is yet to be established to collect, collate and disseminate information on illicit transactions. Those involved in the illegal arms trade are not continuously and adequately monitored. As such, they are changing their modus operandi and adapting more sophisticated methods and machinery in a bid to elude detection. Action to counter illicit arms trade should encompass both the trafficking of arms across national borders as well as the high seas. Although the bulk of weapons for terrorists is transferred by sea, it is not an offence for a terrorist group to traffic arms in the international waters. There is no international maritime police organization on the lines of Interpol both to monitor and to counter this activity by identification, interception and arrest of crew and vessels.

2.2.3 Dual technologies

Dual user technologies or dual technologies are civilian equipment but in the hands of a terrorist group can enhance their performance. Terrorist groups procure dual technologies mostly from Western Europe, North America and Asia. Terrorist groups experiment and adapt modern dual technologies such as GPS, mobile phones and pagers to improve and enhance their terrorist performance. When Osama bin Laden moved from Sudan to Afghanistan, in May 1996, the Al-Qaeda cell in the US purchased a satellite phone for its leader from Deer Park in New York. Similarly, Essam Al-Ridi, Osama's personal pilot, purchased a T-39 military aircraft from Tucson, Arizona, converted it to a civilian aircraft and flew it to Khartoum, Sudan, in 1993. Al-Qaeda also purchased scuba diving equipment, range finders and night vision goggles, as well as communication equipment from the US, UK, Japan, Kuwait, and Saudi Arabia. Terrorist groups with maritime terrorist and support capabilities, such as Hezbollah, Al-Qaeda and the LTTE, have purchased speedboats, communication gear, semi-closed circuit underwater scuba, and antennas from Thailand, Malaysia, Australia, Holland, UK, France and Germany.

Most terrorists are more adept at improvisation than innovation. Terrorist can turn most dual technologies into improvised weapons or a component of an improvised weapon. The world watched with horror the terrorist improvising passenger aircraft as guided missiles to attack US targets on September 11. Likewise, terrorists use commercially available technologies such as Pretty Good Privacy (PGP) encryption software to communicate messages. PGP cannot be decoded by government security agencies. Perhaps the most dangerous aspect of terrorist use of dual technologies is the use of laboratory equipment both to produce medicines for curing the ill as well as biological and chemical agents to kill and injure.

Terrorist procurement of dual technologies is difficult to prevent. By monitoring terrorist support activity and targeting terrorist groups it is possible to deny terrorist groups access to dual technologies. As most governments target criminal activities of terrorist groups and not terrorist groups per se, many foreign terrorist groups procure dual technologies from countries around the world. Procuring a dual technology even by an acknowledged foreign terrorist group is not a criminal offence in most countries.

2.2.4 CBRN weapons

Chemical, Biological, Radiological and Nuclear (CBRN) weapons are not synonymous with mass casualty weapons. Similarly, CBRN attacks are not synonymous with mass casualty attacks. Although classified as Weapons of Mass Destruction (WMD), not all CBRN terrorist attacks have resulted in mass casualties. With the exception of the nerve gas attack by Aum Shinrikyo of Japan that killed 12, none of the other chemical, biological and radiological attacks have resulted in significant casualties. Most terrorists have not used CBRN material due to problems of access. Even terrorist groups with access to chemical, biological and radiological materials are reluctant to use them as weapons due to problems of delivery, lack of control (its effects on one's own population), fear of overwhelming retaliation and, in some cases, loss of public support. The trend is for terrorists to conduct mass casualty attacks using conventional means such as hijacked fully fuel laden passenger aircraft used as guided missiles or coordinated simultaneous bombings of high rise buildings and population centers. Nonetheless, a handful of terrorist groups, such as Aum Shinrikyo and Al-Qaeda have expressed a long-term interest to acquire, develop and use CBRN weapons.

Osama bin Laden paid US$1.5 million to a Sudanese military officer and acquired a Uranium canister in 1993. Although Al-Qaeda tested the canister, irradiated from outside, with a Geiger counter, the group was deceived. In addition to employing an Egyptian physicist, Al-Qaeda persisted in its attempts to purchase CBRN material through Russian and Ukranian organised crime groups. At the time the US intervened in Afghanistan, Al-Qaeda had established links with Pakistani nuclear physicists and established a series of front companies for the purpose of obtaining components for developing a CBRN capability. Furthermore, Al-Qaeda had established a special camp next to the Derunta complex for research into high explosives and CBRN weapons. It is most likely that the Derunta complex was experimenting with the impact of a radiological dispersal device.

From Al-Qaeda camps and safe houses, US troops, CNN and other journalists recovered documents on CBRN material. Furthermore, the computer diskettes of Zacarias Moussaoui, the would-be 20th hijacker, had information about the aerial dispersal of pesticides. On the pretext of launching a crop spraying company he had inquired about crop dusting equipment suggesting that the September 11 operation could have been wider in scope.

If Al-Qaeda survives, it may well prove impossible to prevent such a determined group from building a CBRN capability. Even after Al-Qaeda training infrastructure in Afghanistan was destroyed, the trajectory of Al-Qaeda clearly demonstrates the group has been considering using unconventional weapons. On February 20, 2002, Italian police arrested an Al-Qaeda cell consisting of four Moroccans with nine pounds of cyanide and a map pinpointing the location of water pipes that lead to the US Embassy in Rome. On April 11, 2002, 17 people including 12 Germans were killed when an Al-Qaeda member detonated a Liquid Petroleum Gas truck next to the oldest Jewish synagogue in Djerba, Tunisia. On May 8, 2002, US authorities arrested Jose Perdilla alias Abdullah al Muhajir, a Muslim convert and an Al-Qaeda-trained, former American gang member, planning to detonate a radioactive dispersal device in the US. With terrorist propensity to conduct mass casualty attacks, it is a question of time that Al-Qaeda or another terrorist group will acquire, develop and use a CBRN weapon in the foreseeable future. Unless a state sponsor provides a nuclear weapon to a terrorist group, it is highly unlikely that a terrorist group will be able to gain access to a nuclear weapon. However, it is likely that a terrorist group will acquire, develop or use a chemical, biological or a radiological weapon. As preserving biological agents is difficult, a chemical or radiological weapon is most likely of the CBR categories.

Terrorist groups copied state actors that used chemicals as weapons. In the First World War state actors used choking agents, chlorine and mustard gas, causing nearly 100,000 deaths and 900,000 injuries. In the Second World War, Nazis used Zyklon-B gas against Jews, Gypsies and other groups. Since the beginning of the contemporary wave of terrorism, two groups have used these weapons effectively. After besieging the Sri Lankan military detachment in Kiran, Eastern Sri Lanka, the LTTE employed chlorine recovered from a nearby paper mill in Valachchinai against the Sri Lankan troops in 1990. Although it did not kill any soldiers, it made them ill. The direction of the wind changed and the breeze blew the chlorine in an unanticipated direction. There was neither international outrage nor a close study of the chemical terrorism event until the Aum Shinrikyo successfully used chemical agents five years later. Against Japanese civilians, Aum Shinrikyo used and attempted to use Sarin (a nerve gas), VX, mustard gas and phosgene gas. After Aum Shinrikyo killed 12 and injured 5,500 in the Tokyo subway on March 20, 1995, police raided their premises including Satian 7, their production facility, and recovered chemicals sufficient to kill 4.2 million. Although not weapon grade, Aum Shinrikyo scientists manufactured Anthrax by visiting a sheep farm in Australia and also planned to acquire a thermonuclear device from Russia.

Biological (bacteriological: germ) warfare has the potential to kill more humans than nuclear warfare. Of 395 biological toxins, a threat analysis by David Franz in 1988 revealed that 17 are weaponizable. During the Second World War, biological warfare killed several hundreds of thousands of persons. Plague (black death), a rodent-to-human transmitted disease in India created the first known epidemic in China in 1330, Mongol Tatars catapulted plague infested corpses into the besieged Crimean city of Caffa triggering a pestilence. When a few survivors escaped by boat to Genoa, the rats from the ship spread the plague killing a quarter of the European population by 1349. Laboratory samples still exist in government research facilities in the US and in Russia. Sixteenth century Europeans reduced Mexico's American Indians from 30 to 3 million in 50 years by unwittingly introducing measles and small pox. In 1754, the Indian population in the United States was decimated when traders in Pennsylvania gave them blankets exposed to the small pox (cow pox) virus. Although smallpox, caused by variola virus, was eradicated worldwide in 1977, it is a highly contagious disease that kills 20 per cent of all people contracting it. Some populations such as the American Indians had no resistance against disease causing microbes.

Ethnonationalist terrorists have been cautious of not using emerging pathogens due to the risk of infecting one's own population. With the advances in biotechnology and terrorist access to scientists, terrorist ethnic targeting is a likely future scenario. After September 11, Western governments are manufacturing and stocking the small pox vaccine as young people have never been vaccinated and old people have lost their immunity after 20 years. As commercial firms are involved in vaccine production, a terrorist group could always manufacture these agents under the pretext of manufacturing vaccines. A contemporary use of biological warfare was seen when Oregon's Rajneeshee Sect wanted to sway the outcome of an election in 1984. According to RAND's CBRN expert, Dr John Parachini, the Rajneeshees obtained a strain of salmonella from the American Type Culture Collection in Maryland to poison 10 salad bars in the areas they believed the people would vote against them. Although 751 people fell ill no-one died.

As demonstrated in the post-September 11 anthrax attacks, bacteria-induced diseases can vary in rate of infection and lethality. In addition to bacterial and viral agents terrorist groups have expressed an interest to use toxins, such as ricin and botulism. In the 1980s, both the Bulgarian and South African secret services used biological material to kill domestic political opponents. After obtaining ricin from the KGB, they are believed to have killed a Bulgarian dissident in London. Al-Qaeda's Islamic Group of Egypt training manual, recovered in Manchester, lists ricin as one of its toxins. The French police found a canister of botulism in the safe house of the Red Army Faction in 1980. After receiving news that a Japanese tourist had developed hemorrhagic fever upon returning from a game park in Zaire, Aum Shinrikyo scientists travelled to Zaire with the intention of obtaining infected material either from living persons or corpses. At the turn of the millennium, a US member of the Aryan Nations was arrested for obtaining three vials of yersinia pestis bacterium, which causes bubonic plague. In early 2002, the Russian Federalnaya Pogranichnaya Sluzhba (FSB) is believed to have used a biological agent in an envelope to kill Ibn ul Khattab, the head of Al Ansar Mujahidin in Chechnya.

Both chemical and biological agents can be obtained from government laboratories through the terrorist-organised crime nexus. By developing links with rogue scientists, terrorist groups can also produce them in laboratories. As the equipment is dual technology, terrorist groups can also purchase the equipment required to produce these agents in the open market. Although some biological agents are relatively difficult to produce, the process of production is within the reach of contemporary terrorist groups with access to university-qualified members, collaborators, supporters and sympathisers.

Biological toxins, produced by bacteria, fungi, algae, plants and animals, are more lethal than their chemical counterparts. More than the process of production, terrorist groups face a challenge when it comes to dispersal. As biological agents are non-volatile solids they need to be dispersed by the generation of a fine aerosol cloud suspended with droplets containing bacteriological or viral particles. Similarly, aircraft or aerosol generators can disperse chemical agents: nerve, blister, blood and choking agents. Nerve agents, fast acting organophosphate compounds affecting the central nervous system, are absorbed through skin and respiratory tract, kill immediately. Sarin, soman, tabun and VX are examples. Blister agents, affecting eyes, lungs and skin on contact, are persistent agents that remain in the target area for a considerable period of time. Examples include sulfur mustard, nitrogen mustard and Lewisite. Blood agents, highly volatile and dissipating rapidly in air when in a gaseous state, affect the normal exchange of oxygen and carbon dioxide, damaging rapidly the body's tissues. Cyanide, arsine, and hydrogen cyanide are examples. Choking agents, heavy gases delivered at ground level, tend to fill low areas causing the lungs to fill with fluid and the victim to choke, has corrosive effects on the respiratory system. Chlorine and phosgene are examples. According to a post-September 11 Brookings study, Protecting the American Homeland, dispersing smallpox, anthrax, ebola or another deadly agent in a large city could kill 1 million people and cost US$750 billion to the economy. The study rates the likelihood of a biological attack as extremely low.

Construction of a nuclear device is not within the present reach of a terrorist group. However, the US government has expressed concern over a state sponsor, especially Iraq, providing a nuclear device or radiological material to a terrorist group. Although several hundred portable nuclear suitcases and nuclear batteries have disappeared and the black nuclear market is active, terrorist groups are more likely to either attack a nuclear plant or trigger a radiological dispersal device. While nuclear reactors are defensible, after the recovery of maps of US nuclear facilities from Afghanistan, potassium-iodide pills are being distributed to residents within 10 miles of US nuclear plants that is likely to prevent thyroid cancer in children. Although nuclear plants in the US are well protected by containment facilities this is not always the case elsewhere. Similarly, waste and spent fuel from nuclear power plants across the world could be a likely target. In the past 10 years, International Atomic Energy Agency estimated 175 cases of trafficking in sensitive nuclear material. A radiological dispersal device or a dirty bomb could be constructed using nuclear material such as uranium or plutonium from dismantled warheads or from a nuclear power plant. Such a device is unlikely to kill large numbers but will render a large area uninhabitable and generate mass panic. In addition to killing humans and damaging property, the explosives in the device will spew radiation in all directions contaminating people, buildings, sidewalks and topsoil. According to the Federation of American Scientists, the legacy of radiation would last for years. For instance, cesium 137 would lose only half its radioactivity over the next 30 years.

Only a few groups have engaged in radiological warfare in the past. In addition to a Chechen terrorist group placing a cesium-137 device in a Moscow park in late 1995, an unknown person dispersed radioactive uranium-235 in the New York City water supply in 1981. The radiological dispersal events did not produce any fatalities. Compared to deaths resulting from a biological attack (1 million), a nuclear explosion is likely to produce lower fatalities (100,000) and a radiological explosion is likely to produce the lowest fatalities (10,000). Atmospheric and meteorological (climatic) conditions, both the currents in the upper atmosphere and winds can disperse the fall out in different directions and distances.

CHAPTER 3: TERRORIST TACTICS AND TARGETS

3.1	Assassination	50
3.2	Armed assault	52
3.3	Ambush	53
3.4	Hijacking	54
3.5	Kidnapping	55
3.6	Suicide terrorism	56
3.7	Aviation terrorism	59
3.8	Maritime terrorism	66

CHAPTER 3: TERRORIST TACTICS AND TARGETS

Tactics are methods employed by terrorist groups to conduct operations. Targets are either personnel or infrastructure attacked by terrorist groups. Terrorists select their tactics from a tactical repertoire and targets from a wide range of opportunities. The terrorist ideologies provide the justification and framework for the selection of certain tactics and targets. Nonetheless, the availability of resources and expertise determine whether a group can defeat a certain target. The tactics vary tremendously from hi-tech bombings to the simple machete. To retain the element to surprise, terrorists select from a rich and a wide-ranging tactical repertoire. They range from technical manufacture and use of Improvized Explosive Devices (IEDs) such as victim-operated magnetic switches on mines targeting EOD personnel, to the use of simple pipe bombs and the use of the machete and clubs. Terrorist tactics include bombing, assassination, collective attack, maritime attack, mortar attack, mining attack and ambush. For a tactic to be effective it need not be high tech, complex and expensive. Simple, low-tech, low cost tactics such as arson can be theatrical, effective and even disclaimed.

Hijackings, kidnapping and hostage taking belong to one sub category of tactics. As terrorists are copycats, hijackings, hostage taking and kidnappings become fashionable during certain periods. In addition to these tactics, terrorist groups also use threats to advance their aims and objectives. The threat of a violent action to cause fear or coerce an action or inaction is also an act of terrorism. Terrorist targets are human and infrastructure in land, air and sea. While human targets include political leaders, administrators, military personnel, business leaders and population centers, infrastructure targets include aviation, maritime, symbolic and other nationally critical infrastructure. Symbolic and high prestige targets are the terrorist's favorite. By attacking a symbolic or high prestige target, the terrorist group's power and influence is magnified, prompting the government to engage in massive retaliation thus increasing the terrorist influence.

A breakdown of the type of terrorist targets includes:

- Diplomatic (personnel and infrastructure of embassies, high commissions, consulates and interest sections); foreign or domestic businesses (personnel or infrastructure);

- Domestic or foreign military (including UN, NATO, and other peacekeeping missions); transportation assets (buses, trains,train tracks, aircraft, ships, ports);

- Domestic government (personnel and infrastructure);foreign government (non diplomatic personnel or infrastructure);

- Foreign (non diplomatic, tourists and students and infrastructure);

- Religious (personnel or infrastructure such as mosques, temples, churches, synagogues);

- Ethnic or racial (nationality, linguistic group, colour, geographic region);

- General public (random attacks on population centers);

- Humanitarian workers (local and foreign personnel and infrastructure).

As it is impossible to protect all the likely terrorist targets, governments and corporations adopt target hardening: alarms, sensors, closed circuit television (CCTV), special glass, metal detectors, X-ray technology, barriers, vision barriers, fences, heavy barriers, quality training of personnel - which makes it costly for a terrorist group to attack the protected target. However, the key to thwarting a terrorist attack is intelligence, often advance information of terrorist plans and preparations, developed by infiltrating a terrorist group.

3.1 Assassination

Assassination is the targeting of a specific person for a political purpose, retribution or retaliation. This is not a random killing, but focused on an individual for perceived grievances. Executions by self-imposed sub-state courts, kangaroo courts, or judges fit into this category. Often terrorist assassins are motivated through ideological indoctrination to hate the target for his or her action, inaction, nationality, religion, belief system, political position and so on.

Traditionally, assassination has been evident in the case of heads of state or government for the specific purpose of toppling governments. Serving or former world leaders assassinated by terrorist groups, terrorists or terrorist supporters include Anwar Al Sadat of Egypt, Aldo Moro of Italy, Indira Gandhi of India, Rajiv Gandhi of India, Yitzhak Rabin of Israel and Ranasinghe Premadasa of Sri Lanka. By assassinating strong leaders, especially those who fought terrorism steadfastly, terrorists were successful in bringing to office weak leaders willing to compromise or follow a course of inaction. Therefore, leadership targets are strategic targets, aimed at bringing about strategic change. As it has been difficult to target protected persons, terrorists have assassinated important government functionaries, including party leaders, political officials and diplomats. They include Ahmed Shah Massoud, Northern Alliance leader of Afghanistan, Ri'fat al-Mahjub, the Speaker of the Egyptian Assembly, Shykh Muhammad Husayn al-Dhahabi, former Minister of Awqaf in Egypt, Lalith Athulathmudali, Democratic United National Liberation Front leader of Sri Lanka and Ranjan Wijeratna, Minister of State for Defence of Sri Lanka. Despite the Convention on the Prevention and Punishment of Crimes against Internationally Protected Persons, the threat to Very Important Persons (VIPs) has persisted and is likely to grow. Terrorists have also targeted moderates to eliminate support for a negotiated political settlement and journalists who have criticized terrorist groups. Selectively assassinating important leaders demonstrates the vulnerability of a society to terrorism. The ability to penetrate tight security inculcates a sense of fear in the target population. Loss of quality leaders, especially if they enjoyed mass support, has led to mass demoralization. When commanders of militaries are assassinated, it leads to demoralization of troops, especially frontline troops.

With the profusion of small arms throughout many of the conflict areas, assassination has become a common terrorist tactic. Terrorists also use more specialized weapons to breach VIP security – sniper and high-powered rifles, land mine attacks and vehicle bombings. As terrorists are aware that the assassination of a leader leads to massive retaliation, they sometimes will refrain from claiming responsibility. Some groups conduct suicide terrorism to assassinate because they do not want the terrorist who perpetrated the assassination to be caught alive. Before launching the assassination operation, many terrorist groups tend to criticize the target of assassination. To justify the assassination of the target, he or she is portrayed as an unjust person or a human rights violator. Often if there is public revulsion at the political murder, the terrorist group refrains from claiming responsibility for it on grounds that the group will suffer loss of public support.

3.2 Armed assault

The success of an armed assault depends on two aspects. First, initial, continuous and final terrorist reconnaissance/surveillance of the intended target; and second, training, retraining and model training to gain surprise, speed and stealth for the strike team. Based on the data generated by mounting reconnaissance (moving target) or surveillance (stationary target), terrorist planners will design a model on which the terrorist strike team will train to ensure each member is fully prepared. Often the operational commander will participate in the final reconnaissance or surveillance of the target before he or she leads the strike team into combat. Thorough planning and preparation, which are the longest phases in an operation, is the key to the success of the mission. Examples includes Maoists in Nepal attacking police stations in Rolpa, the LTTE attacking civilian settlements in Eastern Sri Lanka, PIRA firing mortars at Heathrow on three occasions over five days, and Abu Nidal Organization attacking Rome and Vienna airports. A form of armed assault is collective attack. This includes tactical maneuvering on an objective involving coordination and tactics, such as an attack on a strategic settlement or a border outpost. It normally involves attacks against protected civilian settlements or military targets.

Most armed assaults are direct attacks involving the use of bombs, grenades and guns. Of the weapons, the bomb remains the most favored terrorist weapon and accounts for about 67 per cent of all terrorist attacks. As the terrorist is far removed from the event, many groups favor the tactic of bombing. As a long-distance weapon, the elements of surprise and shock can be preserved. Bombs differ from mines, rockets, bombs, mortars, artillery or munitions launched from aircraft or ships. Cars, vans and trucks are delivery vehicles of bombs. Although not in all theatres of conflict, vehicle bombs are closely followed by pipe bombs. Vehicle bombs can be either random victim weapons or personal attack weapons. In random victim attack bombs, the bomb is detonated with a timer or a remote-control device. Dependent on the quantity of explosives and the target environment, it is likely to kill several hundred persons. But if the car bomb is positioned strategically it could kill more people. The plan of Ramzi Ahmed Yousef, who parked the car in the basement of the World Trade Centre in February 1993 was to topple one WTC tower on top of the other and kill 250,000 people. In contrast to indiscriminate killing of civilians, terrorist can well target and kill individuals. In that case, the bomb is placed in the engine cavity, under the seat or the chassis.

In contrast to armed assault, non-armed assault includes physical attacks upon a person or persons by a person or group. Terrorist assault therefore includes beatings and stabbings as well as shootings. However, they do not belong to the category of tactical operations. Examples are drive by shootings, random shooting of tourists, or beating up citizens attempting to vote.

3.3 Ambush

In terms of volume of attacks, terrorist ambushing follows terrorist bombing. In contrast to armed assault, an ambush is also a coordinated surprise attack but lying in wait for the target. If the ambush is well planned, those coming within the kill zone of an ambush are unlikely to survive. In a guerrilla situation, it can involve the use of mines and mortars. While a mine attack involves an explosion directed against personnel-on-foot or a vehicle - carrying troops or civilians - a mortar attack involves the use of indirect fire against the intended target. While an ambush against civilians is categorized as an act of terrorism, an ambush against military personnel is categorized as a guerrilla attack.

Hostage-taking: International law defines hostage-taking as the seizing or detaining and threatening to kill, injure, or continue to detain a person in order to compel a third party to do or abstain from doing any act as explicit or implicit condition for the release of the seized or detained person. This December 1979 convention was in response to Iran taking 96 Americans as hostages. The failure of the US to respond decisively led Jimmy Carter to loose his presidency and led to the US policy of 'no negotiations with terrorists'.

Terrorists take hostages, either from an aircraft or by barricading a building, to negotiate demands or to gain world attention. After taking a hostage or hostages, the terrorist group will make a set of demands, which usually include money and safe passage. The international publicity and attention enables the terrorists to highlight their cause. In a few cases, the families, businesses, insurance companies and even governments yield to the demands increasing the threat of terrorism even further. For instance, the Islamic Movement of Uzbekistan kidnapped American tourists after a Japanese businessman paid to seek the release of Japanese geologists kidnapped in Kyrygyzstan. Similarly, after Libya paid ransom money for the release of one batch of hostages, Abu Sayyaf Group kidnapped even more hostages. Likewise, after India freed Ahmed Saeed Omar Sheikh after Harakat-ul-Mujahidin took hostages of passengers in an Indian airline flight, he was involved in the kidnapping and murder of Daniel Pearl, the first US terrorist casualty since the September 11 attacks. The policy of appeasement rarely works with a terrorist group.

Some terrorist groups, such as Hezbollah, FARC, ELN, AUC and Al Ansar Mujahidin are notorious for hostage taking and hostage holding. Although most hostages are eventually freed, a few groups – whether their demands are met or not – kill their hostages. Hostage-taking for large cash ransoms is the fastest growing form of terrorist activity in Colombia, Chechnya, Mexico, Yemen and the Philippines. Even UN peacekeepers, officials and aid workers have been taken hostage in Bosnia, East Timor and Sierra Leone. Many of these countries lack either the resources to control the security environment or the elite units to respond to a hostage taking.

Before hostage-takers start to kill their captives, highly trained hostage negotiators and rescue commandos, with the skills to help end hostage situations, are essential. Investing in training, equipment and sharing each others national experiences can help to lower the threat of hostage taking worldwide. In hostage situations, governments must work together with the media personnel to ensure there is no real-time coverage of a hostage situation as that would take away the element of surprise, preventing the successfully storming of an aircraft or an embassy. Most hostages freed by a group or rescued by the authorities must be psychologically treated for shock and trauma. A few hostages fail to overcome their ordeals and will suffer deep rooted psychological problems with some eventually committing suicide.

3.4 Hijacking

A hijacking occurs when a vehicle or transportation system is forcibly taken over by a terrorist or a group of terrorists. The vehicle or transportation system can be public or a private conveyance (car jacking) and it can be for the purpose of inciting fear and/or murder. In contrast to other tactics, hijackings give mobility, opportunity to highlight their grievance and unparalleled media attention to the terrorists. The hijacking of aircraft, beginning in the 1960s, has been the single biggest threat throughout history. By the early 1970s, Israel eliminated the threat of hijackings by introducing sky marshals and a range of other initiatives. The countermeasures displaced the threat forcing the Palestinian hijackers to consider other options.

Hijacking is not limited to aerial and land transport but also to maritime transport. Muhammad Tokcan, a Turkish citizen of Chechen origin on January 16, 1996, seized a Turkish Black Sea passenger ferry in the northeastern Turkish Port of Trabzon. When hijacked, the Panama-registered ferry, the *Eurasia*, was about to depart for the Russian port of Sochi. The terrorists took more than 200 hostages including 95 Russian citizens and threatened to blow up the ship if Russian forces did not stop their attacks on the Chechens. The hostages were released unharmed after 4 days. Tokcan was imprisoned after surrendering but, under amnesty, was released by Turkey in 2000.

3.5 Kidnapping

A kidnapping occurs when an individual or a group of persons are abducted by force to be used for ransom or coercion. To increase the ransom payment or coercive power, some terrorist groups refrain from immediately publicizing they have abducted a person. Often, the person targeted is a prominent political or military figure, wealthy person or a businessman, and an opponent. As it is a lucrative industry in some countries, terrorist groups such as FARC subcontract kidnappings to other organizations. A few terrorist groups such as Al-Qaeda conducted specialized course, on kidnapping not only for its members but also members of other groups. In addition to demanding funds, terrorist kidnappings are motivated by publicity, gain political concessions, release terrorist detainees and prisoners, and for revenge and retaliation.

Most sophisticated terrorist groups expend significant resources and time planning a kidnapping operation. They monitor the times and routes taken by their potential target. Therefore, the threat of kidnapping can be reduced by conducting counter surveillance and by frequently varying the routes and times of journeys. Some terrorist groups infiltrate the residence or the office of the target to be better prepared for the kidnap operation. Terrorists who do not wish to be taken by surprise develop intelligence of their target's security: whether they carry a firearm or are protected by bodyguards and, if so, their numerical strength, type of weapons and preparedness. To ensure the success of their operation, the more sophisticated terrorists also develop contingency plans, check their vehicle or backup vehicles and study the security of getaway routes. A few terrorist groups seek targets of opportunity where they kidnap their victims not according to a well rehearsed tactical plan.

Although governments prohibit families and businesses from negotiating the release of kidnapped victims by payment of ransom, experience shows that this is virtually unenforceable. Permitting families and companies to pay ransom for the release of a family member or employees provides the law enforcement authorities the best possibility of capturing the kidnappers. A highly trained professional police force can monitor the contacts between the captors and the negotiators. The success of the police has led to remarkably low incidents of kidnap in the US.

Elite counter terrorist forces in Europe were created as a direct result of the failure of the German police to respond to Black September kidnapping members of the Israeli Olympic team from the Olympic Village, in Munich, September 5, 1972. A total of 11 Israelis were killed. In response, West Germany formed GSG-9 and other European governments created their own counter terrorist forces. Within two years, Mossad launched a worldwide manhunt, assassinating all but two of the kidnappers.

The most publicized kidnapping of an individual by a terrorist group was the kidnapping of Aldo Moro, a former Prime Minister of Italy by the Red Brigades on March 16, 1978. Moro's death resulted in a political crisis prompting the Italian government to strengthen the legal framework for fighting terrorism. Within four years of the kidnap and murder of Moro, Red Brigades kidnapped US General James Dozier, who was subsequently released.

3.6 Suicide terrorism
Suicide terrorism is one of the most difficult forms of terrorist threats to manage. Although a suicide terrorist attack is nearly impossible to thwart once the bomber has been launched into battle, by investing in developing high-grade intelligence, a suicide attack can be detected and disrupted in the planning and preparation stages. In a suicide bomb attack, the bomber intends to die and destroy his or her targets by using an improvised explosive or non-explosive device. In contrast with a non-suicide terrorist who seeks to survive to fight another day, a suicide terrorist is indoctrinated to kill and die with the completion of the mission. As the suicide terrorist concentrates maximum attention and effort to destroy the target and not to protect

themselves, it becomes difficult to stop a suicide attack once the bomber has been launched. Traditional law enforcement is based on the principle of deterrence by punishing the perpetrator. While destroying his or her target, the suicide terrorist defies punishment by actively seeking death. The element of suicide terrorism is what enables a terrorist group to inflict severe damage to targets such as the US Marine Barracks in Beirut, US diplomatic targets in East Africa, the USS *Cole*, the World Trade Center and the Pentagon. By being willing to die, a terrorist retains a high potential to destroy asymmetric targets that cannot be successfully attacked using non-suicide terrorist operations. Furthermore, by integrating suicide terrorism with the CBRN realm, the potential for destruction is unprecedented.

Since the beginning of the contemporary wave of suicide terrorism with Hezbollah in Lebanon in the early 1980s a total of about 320 attacks have been conducted. Although the largest number of groups that conduct suicide attacks are Islamist, secular groups especially the ethnonationalist groups have conducted the largest volume of attacks. Today, there are 14 terrorist groups have developed the capability to conduct suicide operations. They are Al-Qaeda, Jayash-e-Muhammad, Harakat-ul-Mujahidin, Islamic Group of Egypt, Egyptian Islamic Jihad, Al Ansar Mujahidin, GIA, Hamas, PIJ, Al Aqsa Martyrs Brigade, BKI, LTTE, PKK and DHKP-C. As suicide terrorism is cost effective and hard to defeat, the number of terrorist groups developing this tactic is steadfastly growing. In addition to Al Ansar Mujahidin of Chechnya, there is unverified information other Chechen groups as well as Uigurs separatists have conducted suicide attacks. In addition to Hezbollah, there are other Lebanese as well as Syrian groups that conducted suicide attacks in the 1980s. However, these groups are not active in a terrorist context at this time. The suicide terrorist tactic has spread from Islamist terrorist groups to ethnonationalist and even to left wing groups during the past two decades. The latest group to adopt this tactic is the Revolutionary People's Liberation Party (DHKP-C) in Turkey, a left wing terrorist organization. A DHKP-C suicide bomber killed himself, a police officer and injured seven others at the regional police headquarters on 3 January 2001. Another suicide bomber detonated himself at a police booth in the public square, Istanbul, killing two policemen, injuring an Australian tourist (wholater died from his injuries) and over 20 others on September 10, 2001.

A suicide bomber may be launched to reach the target either on foot or in a land, sea or aerial vehicle. The six types of suicide improvised explosive devices (IEDs) operational at present are:

- the human-borne suicide IED also known as the suicide body suit;

- the vehicle- (three wheeler, car, van, lorry) borne suicide IED;

- the motor cycle-borne suicide IED;

- naval craft-borne suicide IED;

- scuba diver-borne suicide IED; and

- airborne (microlight, glider, mini-helicopter, passenger aircraft) suicide IED.

All these categories have been successfully used or attempted in South Asia and in the Middle East. The September 11 attacks were the first suicide attacks in the West. As the tactic of crashing passenger aircraft was cost effective, it is likely to be repeated again. The largest number of suicide IEDs used has been with bombers wearing the suicide bodysuit. A suicide terrorist's vest could contain up to 600 ball bearings to increase the lethality of the explosive device. A female suicide terrorist could evade standard security checks by concealing a device in her lower abdomen.

As terrorists are cost-benefit conscious, there have been only a handful of attempts of terrorist groups to purchase aerial vehicles, train pilots and conduct airborne attacks. Suicide terrorist attack, whether by a light aircraft or a passenger aircraft is most difficult to detect or thwart. Lack of metal makes it difficult for light aircraft to be detected on radar. Even if guards are posted to observe a light air vehicle zeroing on a target, the aerial vehicle does not provide an adequate heat signature to launch a surface to air missile. As terrorist groups faced difficulties of using light aircraft to strike ground targets due to limited range, weather sensitivity and lack of accuracy, Al-Qaeda overcame it by using passenger aircraft to attack ground targets. Although other groups have planned and prepared for suicide airborne attacks, Al-Qaeda is the first terrorist group to use this tactic. Al-Qaeda developed this tactic because by a land suicide attack it was not possible to gain access to the World Trade Center, the Pentagon and the White House, America's most outstanding landmarks.

Terrorist groups continue to develop methods to counter the measures developed by security forces against suicide attacks. For instance, a research unit of an Asian terrorist group hired a police dog handler from France to add repellents to explosives to shield the suicide bomber from detection by sniffer dogs. In addition to conducting intelligence operations and enacting protective security measures to counter the terrorist threat, governments and non-governmental organizations can develop non-military operations to reduce the threat of terrorism. These measures can include reforming the education system, formal and informal education, the use of the media, and other prophylactic measures such as improving the quality of life of the violence affected areas. Furthermore, sustained measures using educators, clerics and other prominent figures to counter the Islamist ideology of misinterpreting, misrepresenting and propagating a corrupt version of the Koran is essential. The Islamic clerics constituting the leadership of terrorist groups intertwine Islam with earthly force stressing on sacrifice with the intention of increasing the appeal of martyrdom operations. To contain the spread of terrorist propaganda videos, many with graphic footage reinforcing the demonic impression of the opponents, disseminating terrorist propaganda must be criminalized. Otherwise, suicide terrorism will persist and even grow as a phenomenon. Terrorists are yet to realize the full potential of suicide terrorism especially in target rich countries of the West.

3.7 Aviation terrorism
The first wave of hijackings began in the early 1960s with Cuban refugees armed with grenades, bombs and guns grew steadfastly from 1967. Gradually, the hijackings that began with one hijacker increased to a group of hijackers. Furthermore, they began to develop a better understanding of the functioning of the aircraft and crew. They also developed better methods to conceal their weapons and used more sophisticated weaponry. Although the hijackings continued until the end of the Cold War, the anti-hijack pact of 1973 between US and Cuba reduced the threat significantly.

The contemporary wave of terrorism began with three members of the PFLP, armed with pistols and grenades, hijacking an El Al Boeing 707 en route from

Rome to Tel Aviv on July 22, 1968. The first flight to be hijacked inbound or outbound to the Middle East, the flight was diverted to Algeria, a country unfriendly towards Israel. The PFLP neither wished to kill 10 crew and 38 passengers nor destroy the aircraft but to humiliate Israel. The hijackers injured the copilot and, on landing in Algiers, the passengers were freed. Due to increased security never again would El Al be a victim of a successful hijacking. Israel also followed a policy of retaliation. For instance, when El Al Flight 253 was taxiing to take off from Athens to Paris, on December 26, 1968, two terrorists armed with grenades and machine guns attacked the flight killing one and injuring another passenger and setting the one engine on fire. In retaliation, helicopter-borne Israeli commandos raided the international airport in Beirut and blew up 12 Lebanese-registered aircraft. Multiple hijackings and mass seizure of hostages took place when PFLP terrorists commandeered four jet airliners from September 6 to 12, 1970. They were Pan Am Flight 93, carrying 153 passengers and two crew members from Amsterdam; Trans World Airlines Flight 741, carrying 141 passengers and 10 crew from Frankfurt; Swissair Flight 100, carrying 143 passengers and 12 crew from Zurich; and British Overseas Airways Corporation Flight 775, carrying 114 persons aboard from Bahrain. One aircraft was blown up in Egypt after emergency evacuation, the other three flights were diverted to the Jordanian desert, evacuated and simultaneously blown up. The terrorists failed to hijack a fifth aircraft, El Al Flight 219, with 158 persons aboard shortly after take off from Amsterdam, when Captain Uri Bar-Lev threw the aircraft to a left bank knocking off the male and female hijackers at the very moment they approached him. While a steward attacked the male hijacker, a young American passenger attacked Leila Khaled, a female hijacker and tied her up with a string and a necktie. Both the steward and the male hijacker suffered gun shot injuries, the hijacker fatally and the grenade Khaled dropped failed to explode due to a faulty spring. Together with male hijackers, Khaled had hijacked Trans World Airlines Flight 840 carrying 113 persons - bound from Rome to Tel Aviv via Athens on August 29 1969 - to Damascus, Syria and, after passenger evacuation, destroyed it.

To evade airline security countermeasures terrorist groups continued to improve their methods of hijacking. For instance, Black September (responsible for the Munich massacre) hijacked Sabena Airlines Flight 517 from Brussels with the aid of two unsuspecting Palestinian women smuggling firearms and explosives in their cosmetic cases and in special girdles. When the aircraft stopped in Vienna, the two male members of Black September boarded and subsequently took control of the aircraft. The terrorists became bolder as they commandeered the plane to Israel. When it arrived at Lod Airport on May 9, 1972, the hijackers threatened to blow up the Boeing 707 demanding the release of more than 300 imprisoned Arab terrorists. Israeli commandos disguised as mechanics burst into the cabin and opened fire, killing the two males and capturing the two female hijackers. At Heathrow in the UK, another terrorist Nizar Hindawi duped his pregnant Irish girlfriend to take a bomb on board but an alert El Al security officer discovered it. Every incident led to new counter measures. Introducing thorough security, ranging from metal detectors, searching passengers and their baggage before boarding and subsequently sky marshals led to a decline of hijackings. The introduction of highly trained, motivated and tough sky marshals with a mandate to negotiate, capture or kill the hijacker or hijackers drove fear into many hijackers. However, with the exception of Israel that had at least one sky marshal on each El Al flight, most countries did not wish to post sky marshals on all flights. Other measures such as magnetometer archways, X-ray machines, passenger profiling, bulletproof partitions between the cockpit and the cabin, and armored luggage and cargo areas have reduced the threat even further. However, not all airlines adhere to strict security procedures and guidelines and they suffer a higher proportion of hijackings. Under the auspices of the International Civil Aviation Organisation (ICAO), a cooperative response against aviation terrorism was developed in Tokyo 1963, The Hague 1970 and Montreal 1971 resulting in a series of UN conventions.

Despite international initiatives the threat has persisted. Although aircraft are prone to hijacking, as an aircraft has a limited supply of fuel and food, the duration of aircraft hijackings are limited. However, national flag carriers in particular remain vulnerable. With constant upgrade of aviation security, the last three decades witnessed Middle Eastern and other terrorist groups using a range of weapons and diverse methods to attack civil aviation. In addition to planting IEDs in cargo, carrying firearms on board and firing surface to air missiles, terrorists used grenades and thereafter with security becoming tight, knives. A grenade is a suicidal weapon, where the hijacker too was likely to die, proved to be a particularly effective weapon inside aircraft. Once a grenade is armed, after the pin of a grenade is pulled, if the terrorist releases the grenade, the timer will start its count down to the explosion. Grenade attacks in cabins inflict personal and structural damage, immediately depressurizing the aircraft, even causing the aircraft to crash. More people have been killed in aircraft bombing using IEDs than in aircraft hijackings and accidents. In many ways, the terrorist groups such as Hezbollah, Babbar Khalsa International (BKI), and LTTE went down the road of sabotage bombing, a far more lethal threat, due to enhanced measures to prevent hijackings, did not wish to risk the capture of its members, or international outrage.

The BKI perpetrated the single worst act of aviation sabotage on June 23, 1985. Their motivation was to avenge the Indian security forces attack on Golden Temple in Amritsar, Punjab to flush out Punjabi terrorists and the massacre of 5,000 innocent Sikhs following the assassination of the Indian Prime Minister Indira Gandhi by her Sikh bodyguards. An Air India Boeing 747, originating from Montreal destined to Bombay, broke in mid air following the explosion. The Boeing 747 dived into the sea about 110 miles (175 km) east of Cork killing 329 passengers, mostly Canadian citizens of Indian origin. The authorities were able to recover only the bodies of 132 victims and 3 to 5 per cent of the structure of wreckage of the aircraft resting on the seabed at 7,000 ft (2,000 m). Simultaneously another bomb placed on board CP Air Flight 003 originating from Vancouver meant to be loaded on to Air India Flight 301 from Tokyo to Bangkok exploded at the Narita airport killing two and injuring four ground workers. Had the detonation not occurred prematurely (perhaps due to a flaw in the timer or timing), the explosion would have killed another aircraft load of passengers. The masterminds of the operation lived in Vancouver until they were arrested and convicted in 2000. Although the BKI poses a lesser threat today, the group continues to operate in the West drawing support from radicalized members of the Sikh community. The bombing of Pan Am Flight 103 over Lockerbie, Scotland in December 1988 demonstrated the role of state sponsors in targeting civil aviation, a threat the Western intelligence community took seriously. In the case of the Lockerbie incident, the bomb, hidden in a cassette player killing 269 people, was a direct retaliation to the US bombing of Tripoli, Libya in 1986, killing the 15 month old adopted daughter of Colonel Gaddafi. The covert operation by the Jamahariya Security Organisation (Libyan intelligence service) prompted the CIA and its British counterpart, MI6, to launch operations to assassinate Gaddafi. A Western intelligence agency provided UK£100,000 to the Libyan Islamic Fighters Group, an Al-Qaeda associate group, to kill the Libyan leader in 1996, demonstrating the degree of threat the Western intelligence community perceived Gaddafi was posing to international security.

Since the mid-1980s, the technology used to detect explosives has vastly improved. However, technologically advanced terrorist groups continue to develop explosives and methods to evade detection. For instance, Ramzi Ahmed Yousef, the 1993 World Trade Center bomber developed an explosive device with nitroglycerine that was virtually undetectable at airport controls. The detonator of the bomb, activated by an altitude meter, causes the mid air explosion of the bomb. Yousef tested the bomb on a Tokyo, Japan bound flight from Cebu in the Philippines on December 11, 1994, with the intention of destroying 11 US airliners over the Pacific in early 1995. The test explosion occurring at 30,000 ft (10,000 m) on board Philippine Airlines Flight 434 killed one, injured ten other Japanese and blew a hole in the fuselage when over Okinawa where the plane landed. Together with the first Al-Qaeda pilot Abdul Hakim Murad, Yousef planned to crash dive aircraft onto the Pentagon and the CIA Headquarters in Langley. Similarly, the GIA hijackers, after hijacking an Air France Airbus from Algiers, planned to crash it on the Eiffel Tower in Paris with 283 passengers on December 26, 1994. In Marseille when the terrorists requested a complete fuelling of the aircraft, GIGN French anti-terrorist commandos stormed the plane, killed all the four terrorists and freed the passengers. The operation injured 13 passengers, three crew and nine commandos.

The continuing threat of airliner bombing and hijacking prompted governments to enhance X-ray and other advanced explosive and metallic detection systems. Similarly, comprehensive positive passenger baggage matching, first done manually and later electronically, ensures that no unauthorized unaccompanied baggage is loaded on to an airliner. With the privatization of security, standards of management, training and morale of airport security tended to decline resulting in security lapses worldwide including in Europe and North America. Although it has become increasingly difficult for hijackers to smuggle a gun on board, it has not been difficult to smuggle improvised explosive devices (IEDs), grenades, knives, and box cutters. Until September 11, largely due to lax security, the rate of detection of these weapons has been low. Considering the detection and confiscation of several hundred sharp instruments at airport controls every day, a repeat of a scaled down version of September 11 is not unlikely. If the threat persists, hand searchers of all luggage and frisking passengers would become a necessity. It is apparent that September 11 has led to an erosion of the public confidence of the aviation industry, especially its grave failure to protect passengers and crew. Despite the continuing threat, the public fear of flying after September 11, and the need to fly is likely to improve aviation security further.

In addition to the terrorists trained in flying schools in Western Europe and in North America, terrorists have also been trained in flying schools from Australia to Pakistan and Sudan during the last decade. As most countries, especially western liberal democracies, targeted the criminal activities of terrorist groups, as such learning to fly was not a criminal offence and therefore throughout the 1990s Britain, France, Australia and other countries turned a blind eye to terrorists and their known local supporters learning to fly.

In addition to the suicidal hijacking threat, there are other forms of terrorist threats that are persisting. A number of terrorist groups, including Al-Qaeda, attempted to infiltrate airports with the intention of planting bombs in airline cargo. For instance, an Al-Qaeda cell in northern Germany penetrated airport security in Amsterdam during the planning stage of September 11 with the intention of planting bombs in American passenger planes. Similarly, terrorist attacks on airline staff continue, such as Hesham Mohamed Hadayet's attack, killing two and injuring four, at the El Al's ticket counter at the Los Angeles international airport on July 4, 2002. Although he is unlikely to have had a direct link with Al-Qaeda, it appears that he was influenced by the Al-Qaeda ideology of Muslim's duty of jihad, killing unbelievers, especially Jews and crusaders. In response to September 11, he removed the sticker 'Read the Koran' in front of his door but replaced it before he launched the attack suggesting that he was an Islamist. The shooting has prompted authorities to screen all passengers at a remote site before entering the airport. It is also likely that tight security prevented Hadayet from boarding an aircraft with a firearm.

Heightened levels of airport security are likely to prompt terrorist groups to shoot down aircraft using missiles. Although the military aviation industry suffered as a result of the proliferation of Surface-to-Air Missiles (SAMs), this threat is gradually extending to the commercial aviation realm. Two-dozen terrorist groups that have gained access to SAMs could target flying targets effectively. Several hundred high-speed jets and helicopters have fallen prey to SAMs during and after the anti-Soviet Afghan period. The most popular of the SAMs are shoulder-fired heat seeking missiles. Examples of these are the Russian SA-7 US and the FIM-92A Stinger, with a maximum range of 5,500 m and an altitude of 5,250 m. The relatively short range of these platforms means most aircraft could be targeted only when flying low, during take off or landing. Although the Congress in 1985 approved the transfer of SAMs to the Afghan mujahidin and to UNITA in Angola, the CIA expressed reservations. In the 1990s, the CIA unsuccessfully attempted to buy back Stinger missiles that survived the anti-Soviet Afghan campaign (1979-1989). During the same period, many terrorist groups purchased SA-14s, an advanced version of the SA-7. For instance, the LTTE office, in Paris, in 1994, purchased SA-14s from Bulgaria and used them against both military and commercial aircraft in the second half of the 1990s. In December 2001, a Sudanese member of Al-Qaeda fired a Stinger missile at a US warplane near the Prince Sultan airbase in Saudi Arabia. By enhancing perimeter security, flying outside the missile's range and by using antimissile flares, military aircraft have minimized the threat but commercial aircraft remain vulnerable to terrorist attack. With the decline in the threat of hijacking, including suicide hijacking, due to increased security, the threat of SAMs to the aviation industry is likely to increase.

The single biggest threat to the aviation industry will remain the terrorist use of explosives. As such, both governments and corporations continue to invest significant resources to improve the rate of detection of explosives. Post-September 11 explosives detection equipment and trace explosive detection equipment has a success rate of over 90 per cent. Trace explosive detection equipment was introduced at airport controls after an Al-Qaeda operative, Richard Reid, tried to destroy a US airliner in December 2001. This lab-style equipment analyses the items on the passenger to find out whether he or she has come into contact with explosives. The items could range from the passenger's money to tickets. As such the threat of an attack launched out of the West is likely to recede but not against the West. Where a terrorist group cannot target a national carrier from a Western country in the West, they are likely to penetrate security in a developing country and successfully target a carrier providing passage to Western nationals. Although national authorities throughout the international aviation system are enjoined to abide by the security standards laid down by ICAO, most developing countries lack the resources to implement a well-designed, well-managed and adequately resourced national aviation security system. An international authority in aviation security, Paul Wilkinson, recently called for a thorough system of international inspection and enforcement of aviation security and safety standards.

3.8 Maritime terrorism

The maritime security environment altered significantly even before September 11 with the October 12, 2000 attack on the USS *Cole*. In this attack two Al-Qaeda suicide bombers rammed an explosives-laden skiff, killing 17 and injuring 42 US naval personnel and inflicting extensive damage to the Arleigh-Burke class destroyer. The international alarm and publicity generated by the USS *Cole* incident triggered two other terrorist groups, one Asian and another Middle Eastern, to mount similar terrorist attacks. Four suicide stealth boats of the LTTE breached the heavily fortified defenses of the Trincomalee naval base on October 23, 2000. The explosives-laden boats destroyed one and damaged a second fast personnel carrier. A Hamas suicide boat attempting to ram an Israeli naval craft exploded prematurely with insignificant damage to the naval craft on November 7 2000. Three attacks within four weeks demonstrated the copycat effect, a phenomenon not uncommon among modern terrorist groups, where they copy tactics and targeting practices from one another. However, the low cost, high-impact attack prompted several terrorist groups to plan and prepare for targeting objects at sea.

Although a relatively new environment for most terrorist groups, the application of land techniques and tactics at sea is not too difficult. The idea of attacking a US warship was born in May 1998, when the USS *Mount Vernon* visited Aden for three days. When Osama bin Ladin was informed by the leadership of the Islamic Army of Aden Abayan, an associate group of Al-Qaeda, he dispatched an operational commander to plan the operation, targeted at the USS The Sullivans. On January 3, 2000, Al-Qaeda's TNT-laden boat was brought from an Al-Qaeda safe house by a trailer and launched into sea but, due to excess weight, the boat sank within minutes of launch. Deprived of high-grade intelligence on Al-Qaeda, the US intelligence community failed to realize it had been targeted. Within 10 months, Al-Qaeda mounted a second operation, this time using C-4, a plastic explosive. Like most sophisticated terrorist groups, Al-Qaeda too had a steep learning curve where it improved its know-how constantly. In keeping with its doctrine of maximizing its successes and minimizing its failures, Al-Qaeda dispatched the USS *Cole* masterminds to Kuala Lumpur to plan an attack on another US ship visiting a Malaysian port in 2000. The Malaysian Special Branch also disrupted a plan by the Kumpulan Militan Malaysia, a terrorist group, to ambush a US ship in 2001. In December 2001, the Singaporean Internal Security Department (ISD) disrupted a plan by Jammah Islamiyyah (JI), of

Singapore, to ambush a US ship in early 2002. Among the recoveries in Singapore was a map with an off shore `kill zone' marked to attack US naval vessels. Around 1997, JI leader, Bin Jaffar, in Singapore, came up with the idea of killing US sailors on leave as they traveled from the Sembawang Wharves to the Yishun transit station in northern Singapore. Bin Jaffar and his associate, Bin Abas, plotted to put a bomb in a parked motorcycle and set it off as sailors got off a shuttle bus and walked to the metro station. A JI surveillance video of the targets was recovered both in the bombed rubble of Al-Qaeda military commander Mohommad Atef, in Afghanistan, and Bin Jaffar's apartment. Since the closure of US bases in the Philippines in the early 1990s, Singapore has become the US military's most important resupply point in Southeast Asia where an average of 100 Navy vessels a year stop, and several thousand sailors take shore leave. Although ISD has disrupted the JI organization in Singapore, and Malaysia and the Philippines have followed suit, the failure of Indonesia to disrupt the JI organization, especially its failure to arrest the JI leadership, continues to threaten security both in Southeast Asia and Australasia.

Al-Qaeda's successful attack on USS *Cole* and attempted attacks on the USS The Sullivans and other US warships off Malaysia, Singapore and Gibraltar demonstrates the continuing threat posed by this one group. In addition to Al-Qaeda, Hezbollah too has mounted surveillance on US warships at least in Southeast Asia.

Prior to September 11, 2001, the international community, including the US, had no effective system to monitor the movement of terrorists operating across borders. In preparation for the USS Cole bombing, its masterminds, Khalid Almihdhar and Nawaf Alhazmi, visited Kuala Lumpur in January 2000 and met with Al-Qaeda's Asian leadership, Hambali and Sufaat, planning a similar operation in the Malacca Straits. Despite their visit to Malaysia coming to the attention of the CIA, Almihdhar and Alhazmi entered the US under their own names and participated in the September 11 attacks. The lessons of September 11 are being incorporated into the US counter-terrorist doctrine but, slowly, the FBI, the lead US agency for fighting terrorism is laying the foundation for an international terrorist tracking system. The preparedness of the international community to fight the post-Cold War wave of terrorism, called the `new terrorism', has been poor. The post-Cold War terrorist is highly mobile, well educated and willing to die for his or her beliefs. In many ways, international and national security, intelligence and law enforcement agencies are developing the framework for fighting the new terrorism only after September 11.

An exploration of the maritime dimensions of the new terrorism reveals the terrorist know-how and technology to attack ships has proliferated. In addition to the recovery of a manual referring to sea mines in Afghanistan, a 1,086 paged Harakat-ul Mujahidin terrorist training manual in Arabic titled *Mujahideen ki Lalkaar (War Cry of the Mujahideen)* was found in Rishkhor, near Kabul, by Sandeep Unnithan and Mohammad Waqas. Under the section, techniques for disabling ships, the manual read: "A warship can be immobilised by placing 1.2 kg of plastic explosive on the propeller shaft. A mere 1.3 kg can destroy the engine ... 4 kg on the base can sink it ..." Although Afghanistan is landlocked and over 500 km from the sea, the Harakat family of terrorist groups operates from Australia to the Balkans and from the UK to Canada. Unlike the terrorist groups of the Cold War, all the major groups active today have established external networks and, as such, they influence the conduct of each other directly and indirectly. Like governments, most contemporary groups learn from one another, either by direct transfer or indirect emulation of technology, techniques, and tactics. The threshold for maritime attacks has escalated with the increased interaction between Caucasian, African, Middle Eastern, and Asian terrorist groups in Afghanistan and elsewhere.

In addition to targeting ships and other objects at sea, a terrorist group could use a ship both to transport supplies and personnel and as a weapon. After September 11, the International Maritime Organisation (IMO) warned that terrorists "could use hijacked oil tankers or liquefied natural gas carriers". It is impossible to check each container that arrives in major ports. The carnage from detonating a conventional or a non-conventional device on board a ship inside the New York harbor, the third largest in the US and located in the center of the city, is likely to kill and injure a number far exceeding the death toll of September 11.

Despite the looming threat, less than five per cent of all terrorist groups have developed maritime support and attack capabilities. However, as demonstrated, any determined terrorist group can develop a maritime capability, including a terrorist capability, in a short period of time. Replicating land capabilities in the maritime environment is not difficult, although maritime infrastructure of terrorist groups is vulnerable to detection.

Therefore, only a few terrorist groups with maritime capabilities have attacked commercial and military shipping in a sustained manner. Most terrorist groups have emulated pirates and staged surface attacks both to send a political message and to accumulate general cargo. On board fast boats terrorists have fired at ships mostly with RPGs, LAWs and heavy machine guns.The attacks have been infrequent because most commercial and military ships navigate the deep oceans and most terrorist groups can operate only within the coastal or territorial waters.

When ships divert from the shipping lanes and navigate to ports of call, the marine police, coastguard or the navies of host countries protect them. Therefore, the risk of terrorist attack on commercial and military shipping is low except when they navigate along narrow sea-lanes that are not secured or well policed. Examples include the Islamic group of Egypt conducting terrorist attacks against cruise liners sailing on the Nile river in the 1990s. Polisario have staged similar attacks off Morocco. Al-Qaeda and its associate groups planned to stage suicide attacks and destroy US and British warships in the straits of Malacca in 2000/2001 and Gibraltar in 2002. Terrorists have also fired at ships from low- and high-trajectory weapons based on land. For instance, the Portuguese terrorist group, FP-25, claimed responsibility for an unsuccessful mortar attack on six NATO warships in the Port of Lisbon on January 28, 1985. There have been similar attacks off Greece. Therefore, commercial and maritime shipping is vulnerable to terrorist attack by sea (surface when moving and underwater when stationary) and by air.

Anchored or berthed ships, especially when in port, are vulnerable to underwater attack by terrorist groups. Maritime terrorist attacks involving the use of underwater explosives is few but lethal. Only a few groups with access to military explosives, essential to construct an underwater explosive device, can stage an underwater attack. Furthermore, only a few groups have members also trained as divers. Al-Qaeda manuals recovered in Afghanistan and intelligence of an attack in the making in the US indicated that the group had access to trained divers willing to die. It is mostly groups with past and present access to state sponsorship that conduct underwater maritime terrorist attacks. They place underwater explosive devices on the hulls of vessels, especially under the engine room. Damage to any part of a ship can be repaired without much difficulty except to the ship's engine. In the past, a number of state level intelligence agencies, together with their naval counterparts, provided underwater demolition training to a number of terrorist and insurgent groups. Underwater maritime terrorist attacks inflict significant damage to boats and small ships but not big ships. Terrorist groups have not yet perfected the art of transporting large underwater explosive devices and attaching them to the hulls of ships. The LTTE has used underwater scooters, purchased from Denmark, to attack Sri Lankan and foreign ships off northeastern Sri Lanka. As most ships do not have hooks in the hull to attach an explosive device, terrorist divers tie the device to the ship's propeller. To inflict greater damage, suicide divers position the device under the ship's engine and detonate the device. Therefore, using the commonly used underwater explosive device, a terrorist group cannot inflict a mass casualty attack on crew and passengers. In underwater warfare, only terrorist groups with access to military explosives pose a sustained high threat to maritime security. However, a terrorist group can strategically place a sea mine on a shipping lane or ram a target with a boat laden with explosives. Therefore, the threat to commercial and military shipping is high from terrorist mine warfare and maritime surface warfare.

Using front shipping companies, flags of convenience and by changing their names frequently, terrorists use ships to smuggle members, weapons and supplies as well as to smuggle humans, narcotics and other contraband. A few Middle Eastern groups, including the Palestinian Authority (PA), enjoying state sponsorship and others such as Al-Qaeda, LTTE, KLA, ASG and MILF have contracted or acquired ships that can navigate over long distances. For instance, *Karine A*, a Tongan flagged ship with 50 tonnes of rockets, mortars and explosives was seized by Israeli commandos in international waters in the Red Sea in January 2002. Registered to an Iraqi national, the ship was used by the Palestinian Authority to smuggle weapons from Iran. By rigging the ship as a bomb, some terrorist groups have expressed an interest to use the ship as a weapon. Others have expressed an interest to ship containers laden with explosives to target either ships or ports. After Norwegian intelligence uncovered, in December 2001, that Al-Qaeda owned or controlled 23 ships, a number of ships have been searched by US special forces and other military forces. Prior to September 11, Western intelligence agencies only monitored (as opposed to interdiction) terrorist ships as they posed limited or no threat to Western interests.

As passengers and crew, terrorists clandestinely or deceptively gain access to ships and plant explosive devices. A homemade bomb was found on a crowded Sydney ferry and safely defused in 1997. No injuries were reported and no claims of responsibility were made. In 1988, Abu Nidal Organisation exploded a bomb aboard the City of Poros tourist ship, killing 9 and injuring approximately 100 in Greece. Similarly, terrorists have gained access to ships under the cover of darkness and attacked ships. Seven Italian soldiers were killed while they slept aboard their ship at the port of Jilel in Algeria in 1994. Over the years, in response to terrorist attacks, maritime security has improved. Until the cruise ship *Achille Lauro* was hijacked by the Palestine Liberation Front (PLF), headed by Muhammad Abu Abbas, in 1985, maritime security was not a serious problem. Fifteen years later Al-Qaeda conducted a devastating maritime suicide attack against the USS *Cole*. Since then, both commercial and military maritime industries have invested significantly in security. Nonetheless, terrorist groups, too, have expressed a greater interest to exploit the maritime environment. The terrorist success, industry's fear and public alarm generated after the USS *Cole* attack drove several terrorist groups to consider developing maritime capabilities. The threat to the maritime industry continues to escalate with terrorists planning to develop mini submarines throughout the 1990s, use explosives laden ships as weapons to attack port cities in the aftermath of September 11, attack warships in the Indian Ocean by crashing commercial airliners on to them in early 2002, and plant explosives in cargo containers. With stepped up security, the trend is for maritime terrorist attacks to be few but more lethal.

Terrorist groups operating in the maritime environment continue to learn from one another. Like exchanging land and aerial technologies, terrorist groups continue to exchange maritime technologies, techniques and tactics. The initial knowledge base of terrorist groups of maritime technologies improved with state actors providing specialized training and resources. For instance, the CIA-trained Cuban exile groups in the US staged the largest number of terrorist attacks against Cuban and Soviet maritime targets throughout the 1960s. In return, several Latin American and Middle Eastern groups received similar training from the Soviet bloc countries. Several other countries, such as India, copied the provision of underwater demolition techniques to foreign terrorist groups operating against their inimical states. In addition to state sponsorship, maritime conflicts between states increased the threshold for maritime terrorism. The Arab-Israeli conflict and the Iran-Iraq war led to the proliferation of maritime terrorist technologies. During the post-Cold War period, state to state conflicts in the maritime environment declined. There are a few exceptions, such as a North Korean ship sinking a South Korean ship, killing four and injuring 18 on June 28 2002. Although a few terrorist groups innovate their own technologies, techniques and tactics, most terrorist groups are copycats and receive or emulate know-how and resources from state actors.

Post-September 11 measures include governments hiring additional immigration and investigative personnel, development of machine-readable, tamper resistant visas and other travel and entry documents using biometric identifiers, advanced notification of all cargo, vessels, crew, passenger and other personnel arrival and departure information and civil penalties to those who fail to conform. In addition to arrangements with foreign governments to search and seal US-bound cargo in their ports, it became mandatory for all vessels to inform government 96 hours before entry to a port. Especially after the successful suicide bombing of the oldest Jewish synagogue in Djerba, Tunisia, using a liquid petroleum gas vehicle on April 11, 2002, there is fear Al-Qaeda will use a ship with dangerous cargo to attack a port. The threat posed by liquified natural gas and petroleum tankers is likely to persist until ports create special areas to service such vessels. In the light of the new threat, the US has amended the definition of "Certain dangerous cargo" to include any explosive materials, oxidizing materials, blasting agents, spontaneously combustible products in bulk packaging, highway route, controlled-quantity radioactive material, controlled shipments of fissile material and bulk cargoes such as butylenes oxide, chlorine and elemental phosphorous.

While countering the conventional threat, the US will also need to invest more in thermal, infra-red, chemical, biological and radiological detection systems. In addition to declaring all US ports as security zones, the US coast guard will develop passenger-profiling systems to screen all commercial vessels with the intention of identifying high interest vessels for closer examination. With several tens of thousands of ships entering US ports, with as many as 4,000 containers in one ship in some cases, the US government will have no option but to invest in better quality intelligence. Together with Lloyds Maritime Intelligence Group, London, Maritime Intelligence Group, Washington DC, has developed the best vessel profiling system to date. Furthermore, the US coast guard established protection zones for a distance of 500 yards around all US naval vessels in navigable waters of the US. The US government stipulated that non-military vessels are not allowed to enter within 100 yards of a US naval vessel, whether underway or moored, unless authorized by an official patrol, US Coast Guard or a US naval vessel. Open ports such as New

York and New Jersey came under restrictions with revised traffic management plans and vessels were barred from within 150 yards of Liberty and Ellis Islands. Furthermore, vessels and persons were prohibited from approaching within 175 yards of the United Nations building on the East River and vessels are to remain at least 25 yards away from bridge piers and abutments, overhead power cables, and tunnel ventilation points. While clarifying and amending various other restrictions in the wake of September 11, the US also eliminated the requirement that deep draft vessels enter the port via Ambrose or Sandy Hook Channels as well as the security zones around piers 90, 92 and 94 on the Hudson River. The security of cruise ships also came under greater scrutiny. The threat is likely to be displaced from the US, Atlantic and Pacific waters to other zones where protection of US naval vessels is shared by host navies, coast guard and maritime police authorities. Port security will include cargo security where containerized cargo will be identified, tracked, screened and physically secured by standard seals and locks; personnel security; and foreign port assessments including screening containerized cargo, access restrictions, vessel security, certification of compliance with security measures and security management. Future security of US, allied and coalition partner maritime assets will depend on the ability and the willingness of Western governments to work with the rest of the world to enhance maritime security worldwide.

CHAPTER 4: TERRORIST FINANCING AND FORENSIC ACCOUNTANCY

4.1	Terrorist financing	77
4.2	Forensic accounting and terrorist finance	88
4.3	Conclusion	94

CHAPTER 4: TERRORIST FINANCING AND FORENSIC ACCOUNTANCY

4.1 Terrorist financing

Terrorist financing, the lifeblood of terrorist groups, has evolved dramatically during the past 30 years. Only the creative and the innovative terrorist groups survived the Cold War-Post-Cold War transition. The dramatic decline in state sponsorship led several groups to abandon violence as a means to political power. Post-Cold War terrorist groups are dependent on organized crime for survival and sustaining operations. The trend is for sophisticated groups with an international reach to move from 'dirty-clean' money routes to `clean-clean' money routes. Penetration of legitimate businesses, from manufacturing to trade and investment, is evident. Today, all the major terrorist groups enjoy a trans-boundary presence. With traditional state sponsors distancing themselves, several Middle Eastern, Asian, African, and Latin American terrorist groups generate support for terrorism in North America, Europe and Australasia. The political and economic conditions in these liberal democracies are conducive for foreign terrorist groups to establish support infrastructure far from their theatres of conflict. These liberal democracies, where the freedom of association, organisation and demonstration are protected by constitution, are particularly vulnerable to terrorist infiltration and operation. Many host countries tacitly provide as much or even more support as traditional state sponsors to sustain contemporary terrorism. As terrorist groups have become highly mobile during the last decade, they move rapidly in search of new opportunities. Liberal democracies and some emerging democracies tacitly host more terrorist support structures than any other political and geographic region. Only by sharing the burden of response between host and target terrorist states can terrorism in the 21st century be effectively countered and suppressed. As they are not within the jurisdiction and, in some cases, the operational reach of target states, a shared response between host and target states is pivotal. To combat externally supported terrorism, the target governments are dependent on host governments for intelligence, security and judicial co-operation.

The traditional law enforcement response of attacking only the criminal activities of terrorist organizations has neither mitigated nor deterred terrorism. This is largely due to the failure of the community of nations to attack the non-criminal infrastructures generating the finance for terrorist groups. As such, states addressed the criminal aspects of terrorism, such as murder and arson and not the political aspects of terrorism, such as propaganda and fundraising. The international environment permitted most terrorist groups to generate support in one theatre in order to fight in another theatre. The community of nations recognized the need for an international response to terrorism even during the Cold War. A well formulated, multipronged, multidimensional and a multinational response became feasible only after the end of the East-West confrontation. After recognizing this threat, the international community responded by formulating a UN convention on the suppression of the financing of terrorism, which calls on national governments to dismantle front, cover and sympathetic organizations, especially of foreign terrorist groups operating on their soil. Despite a UN convention, impediments in developing a global strategy to suppress the financing of terrorism still remain. In the past, host governments were confronted with legal, political and operational impediments in disrupting terrorist front, cover and sympathetic organizations engaged in fundraising. Most countries lacked comprehensive legislation to regulate their financial and banking institutions. Legislation in some countries forbade their operational agencies from mounting surveillance on any one particular community vulnerable to contributing funds to a terrorist group. Similarly, some terrorist-infiltrated ethnic and religious communities exerted constituency pressure on politicians to legitimize their cause in return for the ethnic and religious vote. Likewise, liberal democracies such as Canada, UK, France, Switzerland, Germany, all of Scandinavia, Australia and New Zealand permitted foreign terrorist groups to raise funds openly and even issue receipts to their contributors. The reality is most host-governments permitted foreign terrorist groups to operate on their soil unless the terrorists directly threatened either host domestic or foreign interests.

Aside from preserving the core and penultimate leadership and ideologically indoctrinating the support base, building the financial, supply and logistical infrastructure is paramount for the success of any group. Sustained support, whether domestic, international or both, enabled the terrorist leadership to replenish the losses and wastage in rank and file. By creating innocuous front, cover and sympathetic organizations, terrorists drew support from domestic and foreign governments, intergovernmental and non-governmental organizations and individuals. As registered charities in liberal democracies and in some emerging democracies, terrorist groups generate support, evade tax, launder and transfer funds for procurement. The broad latitude of democratic space facilitates several Asian, African, Middle Eastern and Latin American terrorist groups to exploit open societies and liberal immigration laws. In response, the terrorists establish bases, gateways or 'springboards' to either stage or transit terrorist operations. Dependent on the host laws and strictures, most terrorist groups moved from diaspora-migrant 'taxation' to investment in enterprise (trade and businesses). Any host government turning a blind eye to terrorist infrastructure disseminating propaganda and raising funds risks the group's graduation to terrorist training and procurement. The incremental escalation of support is intimately linked to the incremental escalation in violence. Disrupting financial infrastructure, constraining access to sophisticated weaponry, expertise and other resources, could appreciably affect the sustainability of a terrorist campaign.

The study of opportunities available and strategies adopted by terrorist groups to accumulate economic wealth reveals that the post-Cold War political climate facilitates terrorist groups to accrue significant international and domestic political, economic and military support. As international terrorist infrastructures are unconstrained by national jurisdiction, they are a greater threat to national and international security. International terrorist infrastructures disseminate propaganda, lobby foreign governments and potential supporters, raise funds, invest funds in trade or businesses, procure weapons and hire expertise, recruit and train personnel and ship personnel, weapon and other supplies to the theatres of conflict.

4.1.1 Domestic financing
All terrorist groups enjoy varying degrees of domestic or territorial financial support. However, only some groups generated most funds domestically. Domestic support, both individual and corporate, can be voluntary (contribution) or involuntary (coercive). To ensure a continuous flow of finance, terrorist groups institute either a mandatory or an ad hoc tax. Many of these forms of financing are better described as organized crime, discussed later.

4.1.2 Diaspora and migrant financing
The conflicts of the 1990s generated unprecedented displacement and refugee flows. This, in turn, facilitates the formation of diaspora and ethnic networks which provide the rudimentary international infrastructure for insurgent/terrorist groups to operate overseas with relative ease. With external support, most insurgent/terrorist groups of the 1990s are

transforming from 'rag-tag' to sophisticated groups. Groups with vibrant external support networks are mostly ethnonationalist groups Irish, Kurdish, Sri Lankan Tamils, Kashmiris, Basques, Croats, Albanians, and Armenians for example. Of insurgent/terrorist campaigns hardest to defeat are those empowered by ethnonationalist sentiments and emotions. They have the longest staying power, their struggles can be dampened more politically and less militarily. However, to make such groups more amenable to negotiation, they have to be militarily weakened and politically marginalized. For instance, had US–UK security cooperation not disrupted the PIRA transatlantic pipeline, the Northern Irish peace process may not have got off the ground. Similarly, had Indo-Bangladesh cooperation not ended Indian support to the Chakmas in the Chittagong Hill Tracts, the Shanthi Bahini rebels would still be fighting the Bangladeshi troops. Towards disrupting insurgent/terrorist support networks, multipronged political, military, economic and diplomatic countermeasures are necessary.

After September 11, terrorist infrastructures tapping their overseas-based communities have become more clandestine. Nonetheless, terrorists continue to raise from their Diaspora and migrants, both individual and corporate, voluntarily (contribution) and involuntarily (coercive). Coercion can be implicit (threat of force) and explicit (use of force). In collateral coercion, force or the threat of force is used against family members in the homeland to make reluctant members of the diaspora-migrant communities to pay. To prevent coming to the attention of the host law enforcement, terrorists or their activists operating overseas prefer to use implicit coercion than explicit coercion.

At a domestic level, countermeasures must be aimed at the country of origin of the insurgent/terrorist organization itself. Central to the success of the anti-insurgent/terrorist campaign is to meet the aspirations and the grievances of the ethnonationalists before the insurgent/terrorist group gathers momentum. As the diaspora represents the thinking of the domestic population, it is imperative for all governments to focus first on altering the internal dynamics that have spawned rebellion. Many governments have lacked the skills and expertise to develop the non-military dimensions of counter insurgency (the political, socio-economic and intentional). At a political level, many governments have failed to develop and implement sustained political and economic strategies to provide an alternative leadership to their minorities from getting sucked into the gun culture.

Therefore, to dampen popular support for insurgency/terrorism, it is imperative to implement political reform, by way of autonomy and enhanced security for the marginalized and the deprived.

If the insurgency terrorist campaign persists, then the insurgent/terrorist groups develop their international infrastructures, some even independent or semi independent of their diasporas. Procurement operations are sustained by finance generated both by diaspora collections and insurgent/terrorist investments. Therefore, the key to restraining procurement is by generating an effective counter propaganda network. Most states have made some headway by launching coordinated counter propaganda initiatives against insurgent/terrorist infiltrated diaspora organizations. Most governments operate overseas through pro-state diaspora organizations and through their foreign missions. Effectively disseminating the 'right' propaganda can strategically weaken the fund-raising capability of an organization. The non-governmental community - commercial, social and religious organizations – have played major roles in curbing the activity of insurgent/terrorist fronts. Many have pressurized host governments to withdraw their support to or even to ban an organization. Permitting propaganda and fund-raising is a political issue. In the US until October 1997 and in the UK until September 1998, it was not an offence for insurgent/terrorist groups to raise funds for perpetrating violence. In continental Europe and in Canada, several groups continue to publicly raise funds to procure weapons.

The key to regulating procurement and shipping, per se, is international and regional inter-agency and security cooperation. Some states have been successful in developing frontline intelligence on the international procurement and shipping operations of their insurgent/terrorist groups. There should also be a political commitment to embark on high-risk operations both overseas and on a domestic level. Many states have failed to thwart the external threat due to lack of a comprehensive understanding of the international networks of their insurgent/terrorist groups. This is a paramount requirement before developing a counter strategy. At a domestic level, there should be institutions created to ensure that there is cooperation and coordination and not confrontation or competition between government intelligence and investigative agencies.

4.1.3 Co-ethnic and co-religionist financing

Contributions from members of an akin ethnicity are co-ethnic support. Co-religionist support consists of contributions from the members of the same faith but always driven by religious affinity. Islamist groups in particular benefited from donations from wealthy Arabs in the Gulf and the Middle Eastern and North African countries. Although there is no conclusive proof, it may be surmised that the habit of providing such donations originated when the Afghans were fighting the Soviets from 1979 to 1989.

4.1.4 State sponsorship

State sponsors, also known as patron states, provide active contributions to terrorist groups to attack inimical states. Usually, foreign policy considerations drive states to sponsor terrorist groups in inimical countries. For instance, the government of India sponsors a number of Pakistani groups and Pakistan sponsors a number of Indian groups. The late 1990s witnessed a decline in state sponsorship. With the international community punishing sponsors, many state sponsors have distanced themselves from funding groups engaging in terrorism as opposed to guerrilla warfare. Finance is the key component of any terrorist support infrastructure. With the international community targeting terrorist state sponsors, the terrorist capacity to independently generate terrorist finance appears to be the key to terrorist survival.

During the height of the Cold War, a large percentage of terrorist groups funded their existence and activities by receiving the active sponsorship of superpowers or their satellite states. Soviet Union and its satellite states provided finance and weapons to MPLA in Angola, SWAPO in Namibia, FRELIMO in Mozambique, ANC in South Africa, PLO in the Middle East, POLISARIO in Western Sahara and the PKK in Turkey. The United States provided finance and weapons to groups in Angola (UNITA), Cambodia (Khmer Rouge) and Nicaragua (FDN: Contras) as well as to Cuban exile groups and the Afghan mujahidin. For instance, between 1980-1989, the CIA provided through the Pakistani Inter-Services-Intelligence (ISI) US$2 billion in weapons and 80 per cent of the CIA's covert budget to Afghan groups. The bulk of the weapons and finance went to Hezb-e-Islami, led by Gulbuddin Hekmatyar, who was vehemently opposed to the US and supported Al-Qaeda, led by Osama Bin Laden. Similar to other agencies that acted as conduits for weapon and financial transfers to guerrilla and terrorist groups, the ISI retained a bulk of the weapons and finance for use in subsequent campaigns including to support the Taliban and Kashmiri mujahidin.

The CIA also supported Sudanese Peoples Liberation Army (SPLA) against Dr Hasan Al-Turabi's National Islamic Front that worked closely with Al-Qaeda. The CIA also supported the Northern Iraqi opposition forces beginning late October 1994. NATO members supported KLA until a UN Security Council passed a binding resolution, in March 1998, forbidding such activity. Turkey supported Chechen groups and while Pakistan supported several Kashmiri and other Indian groups, India supported several Pakistani groups.

4.1.5 Low-level and organized crime

Organized crime differs from low-level, individual and casual crime in the degree of scale and coordination. While organized crime is conducted by an organization, low-level crime is by disconnected individuals. Organized crime can be broadly divided into fraud (percentage from prisoner welfare, social security; illegal logging, cultivating or refining narcotics, video, CD and cassette piracy; taxi scams such as running unregistered taxis; not paying taxes), smuggling (cigarettes, alcohol, narcotics, humans), racketeering (extorting percentages from prostitution, human smugglers, narcotic trafficking, forgers of identity and travel documents, drinking clubs, taxi services), kidnapping for ransom and armed robbery. In addition to developing links with organized crime groups, terrorist groups directly engage in organized crime. For instance, in exchange for weapons, FARC provided cocaine to Russian organized crime groups.

With the end of the East-West confrontation, porosity of borders enhanced terrorist mobility. The geographic range of terrorist organizations, especially operations into Western countries, have increased. Contemporary groups can operate over long distances with relative ease. Most terrorist groups today engage in the narcotics trade, human trafficking, illicit weapon transfers, video, audio and CD piracy, kidnapping, extortion and credit card fraud. As such, they have a lesser need to depend on state sponsors. The international environment also favored many of these groups to establish front, cover and sympathetic organizations in Western European and North American countries. These terrorist affiliates appearing as human rights, humanitarian, cultural and social organizations engage in organized crime. Often migrants from conflict zones facilitate terrorist groups to establish such organizations and conduct such operations. As a result, there is extensive organized crime infrastructure in Canada, Australia, New Zealand, France, Germany, Switzerland, Belgium, Austria and in the Scandinavian countries, mostly in Sweden and Norway. Today the funds raised by terrorist groups operating in these host countries is comparable to and, in some cases more than, the contributions they received from their state sponsors. Weapons, explosives and dual technologies purchased from funds raised through organized crime in Western liberal democracies have gone to kill several thousand civilians and security forces personnel in the global South.

The proceeds from organized crime constituted a small percentage of terrorist financing during the Cold War. Only the innovative terrorist groups, able to develop alternative sources of income, survived the transition from the Cold War to the post-Cold War period. The decline, and finally, the distancing of states from sponsorship, is forcing terrorist groups to become increasingly dependent on organized crime to finance their existence and activities. While most terrorist groups became dependent on the proceeds of organized crime, the more sophisticated terrorist groups generated their finances by investing in legitimate businesses. As the groups engaged in organized crime needed to convert the 'dirty money' into 'clean money' they risked 'dirtying their hands'. In contrast, the groups that engaged in legitimate businesses did not need to launder the 'clean money'.

Traditionally, terrorists used criminal funds or proceeds from organized crime to fund their existence and activities with the sweeping changes in the international environment enabled terrorist groups, the terrorist modus operandi for generating funds is undergoing a major change. With the transition from accruing vast profits through legitimate businesses, should investments and the profits of legitimate businesses owned by terrorists be considered criminal funds? As the motivation of the terrorist group is to use the clean money for illegitimate purposes, it is necessary to think of ways and means of criminalizing the generation of clean money for nefarious activities. With the sweeping changes in the post-Cold War international strategic environment, almost all the major terrorist groups engage in organized crime or transact with organized crime groups. The access to criminal groups has strengthened many terrorist groups. In addition to attempts to procure CBRN material, Al-Qaeda used the criminal groups operating in Europe to purchase weapons. For instance, when the Special Intervention Unit (Escadron Special d'Intervention) raided the apartment of an Al-Qaeda suicide bomber, Nizar

Ben Abdelaziz Trabelsii, on September 13, 2001, they found among his clothes an Israeli-manufactured Uzi submachine gun.

With governments allocating significant resources to combat money laundering, it will become increasingly difficult for groups to rely on the proceeds of organized crime. To evade police tracing, the clever groups are likely to develop and maintain clean money sources. Irrespective of who does it, it is not a criminal offence in most countries to generate funds through businesses and raise funds through charities. Dirty money can be traced back to drugs cartels, alien smuggling networks and so on. The dirty money trail is obvious and relatively easy to trace. Clean money sources are not as easy to trace – they have a legitimate front end and no illegal hook to start with. The future is likely to be more ad-hoc groups using 'dirty – clean money routes' and sophisticated groups using 'clean – clean money routes'. This development in the terrorist environment should be viewed in the light of the latest UN convention on the suppression of the financing of terrorism. It is likely terrorists are a step ahead of the convention, elements of which are now being integrated into domestic legislation by a number of UN member states. The organized crime-terrorist nexus will ensure terrorist survival. With the decline in state and public support – sanctuary, recruitment, finance, and weapons – investment in crime will be essential to maintain a viable terrorist organization. Future terrorist existence and activities are dependent on a sustained and consistent flow of support from organized crime. That means any successful counter terrorist agenda should include measures to combat organized crime too. As such, attrition of the criminal support infrastructure of a group is critical to disrupt, degrade and destroy a terrorist group.

4.1.6 Financial crime

Financial crime, a form of organized crime, is one of the most lucrative methods of generating funds for terrorist groups. Therefore, several groups, especially groups operating outside their territorial borders, engage in financial crime using credit cards and checks. Using a supply of blank credit cards, a card embossing machine, a skimmer (mobile card data reader), a computer, a data reader/writer and cables to connect devices, terrorist support cells operating throughout Europe counterfeited and cloned credit cards raising millions of dollars annually. At points of vulnerability (restaurants, gas stations, garages and stores) a person with access to genuine credit cards would swipe it using the skimmer. Thereafter, the terrorist cell would download it to a computer, save it and transmit it by email to a second cell usually in a second country. This data would be uploaded onto the magnetic strip of any plastic card, or it may be edited and a new name inserted in place of the genuine name. This allowed a number of counterfeit cards to be prepared for a single identity that may have supporting identity documents in that name. It also allows for the use of accounting details of a male to be entered on the magnetic strip of a card which appears to belong to a female or for change in name if the user would not appear to be of that ethnic origin. These plastic cards may be used more than once and data erased and replaced if the card is returned. If the information is entered into a blank card, this would then need embossing if it were to be used where it may be checked. By embossing holograms on credit cards, fraud can be made more difficult through allowing easy visual checks. However, terrorist groups have overcome many of these countermeasures by obtaining genuine cards and replacing the magnetic information with details from skimmed cards.

Support members of terrorist groups using genuine (mostly stolen), forged and adapted identifications established accounts in reputed financial institutions and built strong credit histories by frequently depositing small sums. By putting in cash and taking it out, it builds up a turn over. After churning, building credit histories and generating confidence in the banks, they took huge loans and overdrafts and disappeared, at times making over hundred thousand dollars. Often one terrorist supporter would open a dozen accounts to build a legend around the false identities of the account holders making his time and resources profitable. When one account is being defrauded, the same terrorist supporter will have another dozen accounts in operation under multiple fictitious identities. In world capitals like London, Paris and Amsterdam, some terrorist groups built financial networks to issue checks and amass several tens of thousands of dollars. The depth of activity includes a dozen members stockpiling check books and issuing them all in one go, backed by check guarantee cards. Terrorist modus operandi includes different types of bank fraud including getting a loan, repaying first time and then getting a bigger loan or issuing checks. Most banks did not aggressively investigate these frauds as insurance covered the losses. After September 11 banks have become more alert. However, banks want to open as many accounts as possible and therefore are reluctant to run detailed credit checks on new customers. One of the biggest failures of governments, especially Western governments, of regulating financial crime, is their failure to target the terrorist organization as opposed to criminal activity. By targeting criminal activity and the individuals engaging in it, the activities of the group become increasingly clandestine. Thus financial fraud is more an embarrassment rather than a loss for a bank. Bank frauds are rarely reported and are least likely to be detected. Among the groups that engage in financial fraud are Al-Qaeda, GIA, GSPC, LTTE, PKK, and BKI.

4.1.7 Investments and legitimate businesses

Although money laundering is investment to loose the dirty track and generate clean money, many contemporary groups invest money to generate high profit both in safe and high-risk ventures, including in trade and enterprise and investments. For instance, the LTTE invested in Palmax, a food canning business in Thailand. With the formulation of the UN convention on the suppression of the financing of terrorism in January 2000, more terrorist groups are investing in legitimate businesses to become less reliant on individual contributions that can be easily monitored by government authorities.

Terrorist groups will also indulge in the sale of terrorist literature, audio-visual and other products. To generate funds, terrorist groups produced newspapers, magazines, books, videos, audios, CDs, T-shirts, clocks, watches, radios and other products that promoted their aims and objectives. These are marketed at sympathetic stores or terrorist-organized public and private events.

4.1.8 Non-governmental organizations

Several respectable NGOs active in the political, religious, cultural, judicial, human rights and humanitarian fields, located in the global north, contribute vast sums of funds to poorer and needy organizations in the global south. Usually, the terrorists or their political activists cultivate vulnerable individuals with either compatible ideologies or interests in the NGO sector to channel funds to front, cover and sympathetic organizations of terrorist groups.

4.1.9 Individual financiers

The Afghanistan-based Saudi terrorist, Osama Bin Laden, is the best known of individual terrorist financiers. Several less known individual financiers living in the Gulf support terrorist-controlled welfare, social and religious organizations.

4.1.10 Community organizations
By infiltrating or establishing community organizations, terrorist groups protect their identity and gain respectability. Organizations, as well as individuals sympathetic to terrorists, have little or no hesitation of interacting with community organizations that promote community interests, provide services and incentives and care for the needs of a community. Some community organizations controlled by terrorist groups initiate grant applications under the guise of promoting community interests.

4.1.11 Public and private donor and other benevolent organizations
By operating through registered human rights, humanitarian and other organizations committed to humanity, terrorist groups deceived their donors and benevolent organizations to making considerable public and private contributions. To accumulate and transfer wealth and to evade paying tax, several terrorist groups have sought charity status.

4.2 Forensic accounting and terrorist finance
The use of forensic accounting in major corporate and corruption investigations has steadily increased since the late 1980s. Over the past two decades, forensic accountants, familiar with legislation and banking regulations, have assisted in a series of high-profile corporate scandals. These have included the BCCI and Bank of New York crises. They have also aided the recovery of immense sums of money stolen by former Philippines President Ferdinand Marcos and former Nigerian head-of-state General Sani Abacha. After the attacks on the United States on September 11, 2001, forensic accounting, which integrates accounting, auditing and investigative skills, has been given a more prominent role in the arsenal of weapons used to combat terrorism. As a result, the efforts of forensic accountants routinely assist intelligence agencies by locating terrorist cells, identifying areas at risk for attacks, and exposing the multitude of sources that fund terrorist groups across the globe.

4.2.1 Sources of information
Several sources can be used by forensic accountants in the collection of information related to terrorist financing networks. These include credit card records, bank account transaction records, telephone usage, and computerized data including e-mail.

Forensic accountants frequently initiate investigations into members of terrorist groups through an examination of a credit card account used by a known terrorist. This allows investigators to locate specific bank accounts used by the terrorist group, identify purchases made through the account, and track the movement of individual terrorists. Credit card accounts often contain valuable information, including current and former addresses, and employment information. The name used on the credit card is also often linked to a checking account, which permits investigators to trace the origin and method of funding of the terrorist group, such as cash deposits or wire transfers. Large collections of paper and electronic financial documents are also routinely provided to forensic accountants for review. For instance, since the early 1990s, Israeli forces have assiduously collected financial data during raids on groups that attack Israeli soldiers and citizens. Forensic accountants routinely inspect this information for key pieces of evidence such as names of banking and non-banking institutions and deposit information.

Additional information, collected from telephone records, computers, and pagers, identifies salient financial transactions, and close associates. Ongoing investigations into terrorist groups frequently employ 'sniffers', installed on nearby telephone lines and computer servers, which permit investigators to scrutinize e-mail messages for references to financial activities. The efforts of forensic accountants are also assisted by a wide array of computer software and hardware that data-mine computers and retrieve deleted or damaged computer files and e-mail messages. Computer programs that employ algorithms are also utilized by financial institutions to locate abnormal financial activities, such as an increase in deposits in a long-dormant account. The information gathered from computers and communication equipment, such as the name of a suspected terrorist, is often subjected to link analysis, which establishes associations between suspected terrorists and institutions utilized by terrorist groups, including front companies, charities, and state sponsors. All these efforts by forensic accountants are supplemented with information gathered by police, security and intelligence agencies, including arrest and income tax records, and driving and passport information.

4.2.2 Information obtained by the examination of terrorist financial networks

Since the early 1990s, the efforts of forensic accountants have led to numerous successful financial investigations of terrorist groups. Examples of these include the Abu Sayyaf Group, Al-Qaeda, Basque Fatherland and Liberty Group (ETA), Islamic Resistance Movement (Hamas), Kurdistan Workers Party (PKK) Liberation Tigers of Tamil Eelam (LTTE), and the Real IRA. They have also uncovered a myriad of activities commonly used to raise funds for terrorist groups across the globe; for instance, extortion is a common means of raising funds for a number of groups located in Asia and the Middle East. The Abu Sayyaf Group (ASG) routinely demands monthly 'revolutionary taxes' from local residents, businessmen, and white-collar workers. In addition, intelligence agencies suspect businessmen paid Al-Qaeda operatives extortion money to prevent attacks on their business interests throughout the Middle East. The payments were made to assuage Bin Laden, who repeatedly threatened to initiate attacks against targets in politically moderate Middle Eastern states, such as Jordan and Saudi Arabia. In Sri Lanka, residents in LTTE-controlled territories routinely pay fees to LTTE operatives, and families who fled war-ravaged areas must pay a fee before being permitted to return to their homes. Tamil refugees living abroad in a number of European countries, including the UK and Germany, are also reportedly forced to pay a modest fee to European-based LTTE sympathizers who collect money to support terrorist activities. The hundreds of thousands of Kurdish refugees living throughout Europe are also expected to support the efforts of the PKK, or suffer reprisals from PKK representatives who are involved in a number of criminal activities, including arms smuggling and drug and human trafficking.

The PKK is not the only terrorist group linked by financial documents to narcotics trafficking. The LTTE reportedly has close ties to drug trafficking networks in Myanmar and members of Hezbollah are linked to drug trafficking in Lebanon. The Al-Qaeda network also received millions of US dollars per annum through the production and distribution of opium, which was smuggled through neighboring Central Asian states, or transported to distribution networks in East Africa. Forensic accountants have also associated a number of terrorist groups to other criminal activities, including smuggling. For instance, the Real IRA is active in smuggling assorted goods into the United Kingdom. For example, in November 2001, British customs officers seized an illegal shipment of cigarettes from the Baltic States that was valued at nearly US$60 million. The Real IRA is also linked to a number of counterfeit operations that produce pirated copies of compact discs and videocassettes, which raises millions of dollars each year for the Real IRA. When these illicit profits are coupled with the millions of dollars raised by Irish communities in the United States, the Real IRA can easily afford to recruit new members, construct bomb-making facilities, procure light weaponry and maintain close contact with other terrorist groups, especially in the Americas.

The funds raised through extortion schemes are supplemented with private donations to various terrorist groups. The Real IRA and ETA routinely rely on proceeds collected in beer halls to fund their activities. For example, 'people's taverns' throughout the Basque country collect donations from supporters of ETA and launder the proceeds to purchase weapons and bomb-making equipment. The scarlet-and-green Basque flag displayed next to collection boxes easily identifies the dozens of taverns located across the region that support ETA activities. A review of financial data also uncovered immense sums of money willingly donated by émigré communities to several terrorist groups. For instance, the LTTE receives significant financial support from Tamil communities in Switzerland, Canada, Australia, the United Kingdom, the United States and Scandinavia, which raise close to US$3 million a month for LTTE activities. Moreover, Middle Eastern terrorist groups, such as Hamas and Hezbollah, receive financial support from Palestinian émigrés in Western Europe and the United States. The funds raised by Palestinian émigrés in Western states, however, are dwarfed by the number of donations received from émigrés in the Middle East who offer financial support to terrorist groups, which routinely attack Israeli citizens and armed forces personnel.

The increase in funding from wealthy patrons is an on-going concern for investigators who track terrorist finance. For example, a team of investigators, which included forensic accountants, actively tracked a wealthy donor who supported the LTTE during 2002. The mysterious figure, known as 'KP' was linked to business interests throughout Asia. 'KP' allegedly supplemented his donations with illicit profits from drug and arms trafficking. Another alleged supporter of the LTTE, a physician living in the United States, supposedly pledged millions of US dollars to fund LTTE activities during the 1990s.

The majority of the funds raised by terrorist groups are laundered through front companies to obscure the origin and the destination of funds. Investigations of the financial activities of the ETA uncovered nearly 170 shell companies currently laundering the proceeds of extortion, and 'people's tavern' collections through off-shore zones. Before the September 11 2001 attacks on the United States, the largest investigation into front companies used by terrorist groups was undertaken to discover the source of funding of the Al-Qaeda terrorist group. Forensic accountants working on the trial uncovered a series of businesses in Khartoum involved in areas spanning road and bridge construction, trucking, currency exchange, a leather tannery, and exporting farm products like sesame seeds and peanuts. These companies are believed to have facilitated the movement of funds to Al-Qaeda operatives prior to the East Africa US embassy bombings in 1998. The LTTE launders illicit profits through a shipping network consisting of approximately 12 freighters, which are staffed by personnel loyal to the LTTE. The profits from the multitude of legal and illegal financial activities of terrorist groups are also routinely laundered through long-established money-laundering centers, such as Egypt, the Philippines and the United Arab Emirates (UAE). These states have strong links to financial centers in Europe, Asia and North America and poor records for oversight of domestic financial institutions.

4.2.3 International efforts to overcome obstacles to tracking financial activities of terrorist groups

Tracking funds of terrorist groups is an arduous task. The efforts of investigators are slowed by a number of factors, including the immense sums of money which are transferred daily through alternative remittance systems, such as hawala banking. Forensic accountants have expressed concern for years about the use of the unregulated hawala system that leaves little trace of money transferred around the world. For example, in the mid-1990s, an investigation uncovered a number of money transfer businesses in Toronto that were transferring cash to the LTTE in Sri Lanka. A number of high-ranking Al-Qaeda leaders who planned the September 11 attacks allegedly also used hawalas to transfer funds to cells outside the Middle East. In response to numerous requests from Western and Asian regulatory agencies, the UAE has approved legislation to criminalize hawalas, so as to avoid the appearance that the UAE was allowing terrorist financial networks to use domestic financial institutions to transfer cash abroad. The new legislation states that individuals who are convicted of an irregular money transfer to finance terrorism could receive a seven year prison sentence and a US$272,000 fine. More importantly, in October 2001, the UAE closed two hawalas: Al Barakaat, and a money changer suspected of transferring funds to one of the alleged hijackers who piloted a plane into the World Trade Center on September 11 2001.

The inability of states to regulate charities and domestic financial institutions also inhibits investigations by forensic accountants into terrorist finance. To avoid further censure by Western regulators, the UAE announced a review of the financial activities of charities based in the country. The UAE has a strong internal intelligence capacity that may be lawfully brought to bear to gather information on terrorist finance. This capacity could be effectively used in monitoring the uses of funds by Islamic charities that are suspected of funding Al-Qaeda, Hamas and Hezbollah. Kuwait also responded to criticisms by establishing a ministerial committee to regulate the activities of charities. Efforts to limit the funneling of terrorist finance through charities are bolstered by US efforts to freeze the assets of charities linked to terrorist groups. This is a powerful tool, because the US government has never been forced by a court order to pay damages to groups whose assets were frozen. Efforts to limit the laundering of terrorist finance through domestic institutions were bolstered by the passage of the Anti-Money Laundering Act of 2001 in the Philippines. The Abu Sayyaf Group and the Moro Islamic Liberation Front allegedly received significant funding from Al-Qaeda. The passage of anti-money-laundering legislation will establish the legal framework for a regime, which will permit the tracking of funds allegedly sent to terrorist groups located in the Philippines. The United States has clearly stated that countries whose secrecy laws impede investigations into terrorist finance risk sanctions being instituted.

Recent investigations uncovered another source of funding that troubles investigators. The commodities and futures markets, customarily a secure means of conducting financial transactions with relative anonymity, may have assisted buyers who knew about the September 11 attacks in advance. For instance, forensic accountants uncovered an unusual pattern of purchases in shares of AMR Corporation, which fell 40 per cent since the attacks. Forensic accountants also question a number of purchases of five year US bonds, which rose substantially after the attacks on the United States. The intensive media coverage of these two events resulted in more than US$2 million in profits going uncollected. To prevent future attempts to manipulate market shares and bond prices, major exchange houses installed new computer systems to permit rapid retrieval of buyer information. Furthermore, these firms also currently employ specialists who promptly investigate suspicious market. transactions.

The biggest potential roadblock in tracing the trail of money is the use of cash by members of terrorist groups. Most major financial institutions are required to file a Currency Transaction Report with the federal government whenever a transaction or series of transactions involves more than US$10,000 in cash. Terrorists, however, can easily circumvent this law by ensuring that deposits are below the reporting threshold. Financial institutions are also inadequately prepared to deal with individual terrorists who open or access accounts with false identification, or permit another individual authority to access the account. Efforts are underway to block potentially illicit financial transactions. The United States is currently devising a means to integrate information obtained by intelligence agencies, and financial information from the public sector. This system would permit the immediate freezing of suspect bank accounts, which allows forensic accountants to review the account for links to terrorist activities. The United States expects all major financial centers to establish similar systems to flag transactions conducted by suspected terrorists in the short term.

Another setback frequently encountered by forensic accountants is the refusal of states, such as Iran and Syria, to permit investigators to examine accounts in state-owned financial institutions. Investigators believe that they are refused access to information, because several states routinely fund the activities of a number of terrorist groups. For instance, the majority of Hamas funding is provided by a number of states, including Iran, Iraq, and Syria. Other problems arise when states that are allies of the United States, such as Tajikistan and Venezuela, mask their efforts to fund terrorist groups, because they do not want to be linked to regional terrorist activities. Moreover, some entities, such as the Isle of Man, refuse to acknowledge the possibility that terrorist funding passed through their financial institutions, because they do not want to curtail secrecy provisions that protect their customers' privacy. States, however, are more susceptible to censor from Western financial centers and governmental leaders. Moreover, the taint of assisting terrorist groups will inflict unwanted reputational risk and could limit future efforts by states to fund terrorist activities.

4.3 Conclusion
An immense amount of progress has been accomplished by forensic

Conclusion

accountants in the battle to limit terrorist financial networks. The investigations into various terrorist groups since September 11 2001 have resulted in the freezing of assets and the identification of hundreds of individuals and groups willing to fund such groups. For instance, more than US$100 million in financial assets linked to Al-Qaeda and the Taliban have been frozen, and investigators have identified 189 individuals and organizations suspected of financing or engaging in terrorist activities. But there are still a number of worrisome problems, and terrorists groups will develop new schemes to avoid recent changes to the financial environment. A high degree of success against terrorist groups will only be achieved through a sophisticated combination of aid programs, diplomatic pressure and measures aimed at curtailing terrorist finance. The first step was the passage of United Nations Security Council Resolution 1373, which requires all countries to criminalize terrorist fundraising and block terrorist assets, and provides for an international coalition to combat terrorist financing. The unified approach to combating terrorist financial networks is essential. Investigators learned that the United States declaration of 28 groups in August 1997, followed by a similar British declaration in early 2001, resulted in a number of groups moving operations to Canada and continental Europe (mostly to France and Switzerland). The efforts of forensic accountants identified the major sponsors of terrorist groups. The handful of states that permit terrorist funding to pass through domestic financial institutions are routinely criticized by Western regulatory bodies, and should expect sanctions for failing to adhere to international norms.

President George Bush referred to the September 11, 2001 attacks on the United States as "the first war of the 21st century". Unlike previous conflicts, combatants in the war against terrorism include forensic accountants who track terrorist finances. In the short term, the efforts of forensic accountants will be impaired by the nascent state of terrorist finance legislation throughout the world. The efforts, however, will be assisted by states that recognize the danger terrorism poses to their national security. Western states can assist a number of countries with technical assistance aimed at establishing a legal infrastructure that can seize terrorist finance. Forensic investigations have uncovered the most often used sources of terrorist finance, such as extortion, state sponsors, front companies and donations from radical mosques and expatriate communities. The numerous methods employed to fund terrorist groups illustrate the sophisticated logistic capabilities that link the individual cells or members of terrorist groups across the globe. The individual terrorist may exist on the margins of society, but the global financial system links the individual terrorist to like-minded fanatics across the globe.

CHAPTER 5: NATIONAL RESPONSES TO TERRORISM

5.1	Intelligence	99
5.2	Emergency legislation	105
5.3	Use of special anti-terrorist response teams	109
5.4	Control of the media	112
5.5	Targeting of terrorist leaders and members	115
5.6	Legitimating socio-economic and development initiatives	118

CHAPTER 5: NATIONAL RESPONSES TO TERRORISM

Governments confronted with endemic terrorist threats to their rule have employed a wide range of policies and instruments in an attempt to mitigate internally focused threats and generally safeguard public security. Drawing on examples from several states around the world, these modalities can be variously grouped under the following categories:

- Intelligence
- Emergency legislation
- The use of militarized anti-terrorist response teams
- Control over the media
- Legitimating socio-economic and development initiatives
- Targeting of terrorist leaders and members

This chapter provides an overview of these tools of national policy and assesses their general utility in terms of terrorist mitigation. It also offers some broad principles to guide democratic governments in responding to terrorism in a manner that is consistent with their own defining principles.

5.1 Intelligence
It is widely recognized that current, accurate secret intelligence is indispensable for the prevention and pre-emption of terrorist actions as well as for the successful termination of terrorist incidents when they are actually in progress. It is out of the gathering of such information that databases are created and subsequently used to identify perpetrators, pinpoint safehouses and disrupt supply routes and potential sources of recruits. Moreover, intelligence information performs a vital role in establishing patterns of demands and methods of operation, both of which greatly assist in the process of crisis decision making. Finally, intelligence helps to enhance general governmental understanding of the terrorist phenomenon by providing information and insights on the aims, political objectives, leadership

and motivations of individual members of terrorist organizations.

The importance of the intelligence function is further underscored by the fact that most states confronted with significant terrorist threats retain agencies that are specifically tasked in this area.

Representative examples include:

- The Direction de la Surveillance du Territoire (DST) and
- Renseignements Generaux (RG) in France
- The Centro Nacional de Inteligencia (CNI, formerly the Centro
- Superior de Informacion de la Defensa/CESID) in Spain
- The Security Service (formerly known as MI5) in the United Kingdom
- The Canadian Security Intelligence Service (CSIS) in Canada
- The Intelligence Bureau (IB) in India
- The National Intelligence Bureau (NIB) in Sri Lanka
- The Federal'naya Shuzhba Bezopasnosti (FSB) in Russia
- The Federal Bureau of Investigation (FBI) in the United States
- ha-Mossad le-Modi'in ule-Tafkidim Meyuhadim and Sherut ha-Bitachon ha-Klali in Israel

The successful implementation of the intelligence tool relies on three elements: acquisition, analysis and dissemination. Given the nature of terrorist conflicts, the initial emphasis has to be on the cultivation and use of human-sourced intelligence (HUMINT). Raw data then needs to be analyzed, channeled and coordinated through a centralized intelligence structure to all relevant agencies engaged in tactical operations on the ground. If any one of these elements is missing, the overall intelligence function will be ineffective.

France provides a good example of a state where intelligence has been used highly effectively to augment overall counter-terrorism efforts - the main thrust of which is directed against imported Islamic extremism. Information, which is channeled through the DST, is collected in three main ways. First, the police and security services actively monitor immigrants entering the country, especially those with an Islamic or North African background. All non-citizens are required to carry an identity card, are frequently subjected to random stops and searches and may be arrested in the event of a failure to produce proper documentation. French nationals running hotels and guest houses are also obliged to inform authorities of the arrival and departure of any immigrants that they provide lodging to, either to the local prefecture or the government representative's office.

In addition to these measures, a centralized database has been established that contains the names, addresses and work places of irregular migrants, that is, those lacking proper documentation. The identity of these persons is largely derived from an earlier immigration decree that was designed to regularize the status of any migrant expressing (in the form of a written application) a readiness to 'integrate' into French society. These measures are intended to provide an internal monitoring mechanism that can be brought to bear against Islamic extremist sympathizers, activists with no prior criminal record and militants that manage to pass undetected through external immigration controls.

Second, the intelligence services use informers that have been established or placed within the French Muslim community. In many instances, insiders have been convicted terrorists felons who have gained amnesty in exchange for cooperating with police and intelligence authorities. Gaining HUMINT in this way is something that is specifically sanctioned by the Vigipirate Renforcé program, which forms the basic structure of French counter-terrorist legislation.

Finally, emphasis is given to information provided by the general community. To facilitate this effort, state authorities invest considerable time in information campaigns (publicized through the media) to explain the purpose of terrorism counter-measures and why they are being directed against certain groups and causes.

In the event of a terrorist instance occurring in France, the police immediately initiate a so-called pre-emptive roundup of all known militant activists, sympathizers or foreigners that the authorities have a reason to suspect, based on information provided by the intelligence services. The aim of these so-called 'moping up' operations is to dry up the 'pool' of passive support that foreign-based extremists necessarily have to rely on in order to function in France. Perhaps the clearest example of the policy at work followed the series of blasts on the Paris metro in the summer of 1995 when mass arrests of Algerians suspected of belonging to the Islamic Salvation Front (FIS) and the Armed Islamic Group (GIA) took place (in one raid, 170 individuals were detained).

Counter-terrorist intelligence information also feeds directly into domestic threat assessments and associated programs for physical protection and target hardening. The institution of these measures is designed to be deliberately flexible, allowing specific plans to be upgraded or downgraded according to the situation at hand. Potential vulnerabilities are measured on the basis of the technical, organizational and financial requirements needed to exploit them relative to the known capabilities and tactical preferences of groups operating in France. The aim is not to prevent attacks from occurring under any circumstances (which can never be achieved in an open society that allows democratic freedoms). Rather it is to protect those contingencies that are gauged to be at greatest risk and ensuring that if an act of terrorism does occur, it will not be repeated (as far as possible).

Several aspects of French counter-terrorist intelligence policy are worthy of note. First, the emphasis on an insider, HUMINT oriented, intelligence has been highly successful in disrupting terrorist cells and providing crucial information on their intentions, capabilities and resources. In several instances this has allowed for the effective pre-emption of planned attacks and bombings. Equally, it has contributed to well-developed physical protection programs that are based on rationalized (as opposed to worse case) threat assessment and risk depictions. This has allowed for greater flexibility in target hardening while helping to mitigate the wasteful and inefficient allocation of scarce fiscal resources.

Second, specifically involving the community in information-gathering efforts has enabled the police and intelligence services to achieve a useful 'force multiplier' effect that has greatly enhanced the potential scope of their national surveillance efforts. Because consistent media and information campaigns have accompanied these efforts, they have also helped to give the intelligence services more public face and at least provided a means by which to explain the nature, rationale and purpose of their activities.

Third, the existence of a domestic intelligence agency with a specific anti-terrorist mandate - the (DST) - has facilitated the rapid and effective exchange of information on foreign militants operating in France as well as facilitated the genesis of risk assessments based on a well developed understanding of extremist behavior. In addition, it has allowed authorities to collect information and initiate prompt, pre-emptive investigations against potential, latent threats to the state.

Fourth, close monitoring of immigrant populations has helped to limit the pool of passive support and assistance that foreign-based extremists depend on for operational and logistical purposes. Just as critically, it has enhanced the ability of law enforcement to keep track of immigrants who enter the country on temporary work, visitor and student visas and ensuring, as far as possible, they leave when they are meant to.

5.1.1 Monitoring and control of intelligence activities

It is generally accepted that terrorist operations have a vital role to play in anti-terrorist activity. Nonetheless, concern exists that excessive surveillance can make the general population more reticent to express opinions as well as impact on their overall willingness to participate in particular socio-political organizations. Such effects are deemed highly deleterious as critical debate and civic participation are both considered essential to the effective functioning of any vibrant pluralistic democracy.

Just as important, an uncontrolled intelligence apparatus can quickly come to poison the entire political system by being used to undermine and otherwise suppress legitimate opponents and critics of the government. A pertinent case in point concerns the former Italian Servisio Informazione Democratica (SID). During the 1970s, the agency adopted a policy that can best be described as a 'strategy of tension', which involved the exploitation of the threat of Red Brigade-instigated terrorism to induce greater public demand for more concerted measures against groups with leftist or Communist leanings. The tactic was carried out by means of protecting the activities of proxy right-wing terrorist organizations and, in some instances, directly participating in their attacks. According to one study undertaken by a member of Parliament in Rome, direct secret service involvement can be traced to some of the most serious terrorist attacks ever perpetrated on Italian soil.

These potential effects and dangers highlight the pressing need for adequate control to be exercised over the state's intelligence apparatus. The best way to achieve this type of oversight is to ensure that all covert surveillance operations have a clear and precise mandate, are based on a solid legal basis and are only used to monitor those who the state has a legitimate reason to believe are involved in the perpetration of serious crimes. It is equally vital that intelligence operatives are made fully accountable for their actions to the democratically elected government and, through it, to the legislature and the electorate.

In Italy, for instance, the intelligence services are now amalgamated into a single coordinating agency that is directly monitored by the Prime Minister's office and is answerable to Parliament for both its activities and the use of budgeted funds. A similar approach also forms the basis of the 1989 Security Service Act and 1993 Intelligence Services Act in the United Kingdom, which together provide a framework of controls made up of the Home Secretary, independent members of the judiciary, senior civil servants and members of Parliament serving on an Oversight Committee. Official legislative 'watchdog' commissions of this sort exist in most democratic states throughout Western Europe and North America.

Several governments have also moved to inject greater openness in their intelligence agencies as a way of augmenting accountability and oversight. In most western democracies, for instance, it is common for intelligence files to be published after a given time period - normally 20 to 30 years. The data contained in these files is not generally subjected to review but released based entirely on the date of its original creation. Certain states have also required that their intelligence agencies publish details of their budgets (though not necessarily the specific operational allocations for these monies), while others have greatly relaxed the rules governing contact between serving intelligence officers and members of the academic community.

5.2 Emergency legislation

Emergency legislation is designed to aid governments in capturing and prosecuting terrorists and, thereby, eliminating the threat they pose to society. Most countries reject this particular policy tool on the grounds that significant departures from customary methods of policing, judicial processing, and sentencing would not be publicly accepted as either necessary or legitimate. Several states afflicted by serious campaigns of terrorism, however, have been able to sanction statutory acts that have both enhanced the search, arrest and investigative powers of the police and allowed for the implementation of a variety of extra-judicial, non-court oriented executive processes.

The UK, Germany, France, Spain and the United States all provide good examples of states that have enacted special legislation to deal with terrorist threats in their respective jurisdictions. In the UK no less than three separate Acts sanctioning extra-judicial measures were introduced between 1973 and 2000: the Northern Ireland (Emergency Provisions) Act (NIEPA, 1973); the Prevention of Terrorism Act (PTA, 1975) and the Terrorism Act (2000). In various forms, these initiatives have allowed for pre-emptive arrests prior to the commission of a crime; prolonged detentions for terrorist suspects; broader police powers of search and seizure (which can be carried out without warrants); trial by judge alone; exclusion of subscribed groups from access to the media; and the outright banning of designated terrorist organizations.

Following the September 11 attacks against the United States, the UK moved to further augment the anti-terrorist legislative powers at its disposal by passing the Anti-Terrorism, Crime and Security Act (2001). This latest instrument, among other things, empowers the government to detain people who have committed no crime, bars judicial review of deportation cases, allows authorities to hold terrorism suspects indefinitely without trial and prevents their access to the evidence being used against them.

In Germany, two major anti-terrorist statutes have been passed that have substantially altered the laws of procedure with respect to trial and imprisonment for those accused or indicted with terrorism. In 1974, legislation was instituted that prohibits joint defense in a terrorist trial. This was supplemented by a 1978 law that both gives police the right to undertake multiple residential searches under one warrant and significantly limits lawyers the right of access to their clients if they are believed to be sympathetic to an extremist cause; the 1978 legislation also empowers the state to prevent defense attorneys from ever taking on terrorist cases if they have known sympathies to particular militant groups.

As with the UK, additional measures were passed following the attacks of September 11, including provision for the banning of religious organizations suspected of inciting violence or having terrorist affiliations. This legal change overturned the 'religious privilege' that had been a fundamental component of the post-Nazi German constitution and which had been designed to curb potential state excesses against minority groups.

The basic structure of French counter-terrorist legislation is formed by the Vigipirate Renforcé program, which was first enacted in September 1986. This initiative provided a series of legislative rules regarding the jurisdiction of the courts and the procedures to be applied for those offences that are related to individual or collective attacks 'aimed at disturbing the public order by means of intimidation or terror'. The basic parameters of the program were substantially enhanced following the outbreak of the Second Algerian civil war in the early 1990s and now sanction arrests of high-risk individuals who have yet to commit a crime (and who can be detained for up to 96 hours without formal charges being laid); collective trials for terrorist suspects or their associates; and executive-mandated searches of any premises (without the consent of the owner) that might be instrumental in securing a conviction in relation to a terrorist crime.

In Spain, anti-terrorist legislation was passed in 1980 that allowed terrorist suspects to be held in preventative detention for up to 72 hours, empowered the police to search their homes without a warrant and gave law enforcement officials the right to intercept their mail and telephone conversations. Organic Law No. 8 supplemented the statute in 1984, which additionally empowered judges to ban political organizations, close down media organs that were openly supportive of terrorist groups and extend the duration of detention without trial for a period of up to two and half years.

Finally, in the United States, broad-ranging anti-terrorist laws were passed in the wake of the September 11 attacks in New York and Washington. In addition to an Executive Order mandating the use of closed military tribunals for foreign terrorists (which will not presume the accused are innocent nor

Emergency legislation 107

allow defendants to choose their own legal counsel), several extra-judicial initiatives have been instituted under the auspices of the Uniting and Strengthening America by Providing Appropriate Tools Required to Intercept and Obstruct Terrorism (PATRIOT) Act. Taken together, these various measures:

- Give sweeping new powers of detention and surveillance to the Executive branch of government and law enforcement agencies, and depriving the Courts of meaningful judicial oversight to ensure that the law enforcement powers are not being abused;

- Provide the Secretary of State the authority to designate any up, foreign or domestic, as a terrorist organization, an authority that is not subject to review;

- Create a broad new crime of 'domestic terrorism' which is defined in Section 802 as "activities that (A) involves acts dangerous to human life that are a violation of the criminal laws of the US or of any state; (B) appear to be intended (i) to intimidate or coerce a civilian population; (ii) to influence the policy of government by intimidation or coercion; or (iii) to affect the conduct of a government by mass destruction, assassination or kidnapping";

- Permit investigations based on lawful First Amendment activity if that activity can be tied somehow to intelligence purposes;

- Erode the line between intelligence collecting and gathering evidence for a criminal proceeding and expand the ability of the government to spy through wiretaps, computer surveillance, access to medical, financial, business and educational records and secret searches of homes and offices;

- Permit the government to detain non-citizens indefinitely even if they have never been convicted of a crime.

The use of emergency legislation has undoubtedly provided the UK, Germany, France, Spain and the United States with greater flexibility in prosecuting and punishing terrorists and their sympathizers than would have been possible within the context of the normal criminal justice system.

In practical terms, it has allowed governments to substantially close the operating space available to terrorists, hindered civilian aid to their cause and allowed for important pre-emptive arrests. Moreover, because extra-judicial measures have been enacted in direct response to what are generally accepted as significant threats to internal law and order they have, for the most part, been accepted as a necessary evil that has been imposed on society by the greater evil inherent in terrorism.

To ultimately succeed, however, emergency legislation must take into account, and balance the need to protect institutions in the common name with the equally pressing dictum to avoid draconian measures that unduly infringe on individual rights and freedoms. It is therefore vital that judicial initiatives and modifications not only provide the necessary legal tools for effectively prosecuting and punishing terrorists, but also embrace sufficient safeguards to ensure against arbitrary application and abuse. Above all, emergency legislation must be sensitive to public concerns for preserving civil liberties. Extreme and radical extra-judicial measures, even if enacted as times of exceptional violence and through accepted constitutional frameworks, will not be tolerated if they are deemed to go beyond what is demanded by the specific exigencies of the situation at hand.

The blunt use of emergency legislation is also likely to prove a double-edged sword in practical terms. The arbitrary suspension of due process will almost always impact on the general population at large, which will both feed public frustration and resentment as well as increase the active and passive support base for terrorists. Under such circumstances, intelligence gathering will become far more problematic and what might otherwise have been sound command and coordination structures may even be compromised. Moreover, bad public relations will not provide the security forces with any margin for error in the actual prosecution of the anti-terrorist campaign and will, eventually, require the government to spend precious resources courting a civic population that it has already alienated.

The potential pit-falls associated with the inappropriate use of emergency legislation are well illustrated by the British introduction of internment without trial in Northern Ireland between 1971 and 1975. Even though the measure was initiated at a time of rapidly rising Loyalist and Republican paramilitary violence - 1972 remaining one of the worst years with respect to killing in the province since 'the Troubles' began in 1969 - this particular legal suspension of regular liberal democratic procedure was widely castigated as a blatant example of the direct politicization of the criminal justice system where the rule of law was essentially used to the explicit advantage of one community (the Protestants) over another (the Catholics). More importantly, the policy proved completely counter-productive, galvanizing support for the Provisional Irish Republican Army (PIRA) in addition to further fracturing what was already a highly polarized society.

These lessons should not be lost on governments in North America and Western Europe as they move to enhance the emergency powers at their disposal in the wake of September 11's terror strikes. Certain infringements of civil rights are undoubtedly called for to deal with the contemporary manifestation of terrorism as represented by the transnational Al-Qaeda global network (especially if future attacks come to involve weapons of mass destruction). However, it is equally essential that such measures are mandated through open scrutiny and regular review and discussion. Because terrorism is constantly evolving and changing, it is logical that the legal means to fight it are similarly dynamic and forward-looking. Formal appraisals at defined intervals allow a reconsideration of legislation enacted at time of emergency and provide an opportunity for legal modifications to ensure extra-judicial initiatives remain both relevant and effective.

5.3 Use of special anti-terrorist response teams

Most countries confronted with serious terrorist threats have developed special incident response teams, either within their respective police structures or the military. Prominent examples include the Grenzshutzgruppe 9 (GSG-9) in Germany; the Groupe d'Intervention de la Gendarmerie (GIGN) in France; the Grupo Intervento Speciale (GIS) in Italy; the Grupo Especial de Operaciones (GEO) in Spain; Delta Force and the Federal Bureau of Investigation's Hostage Rescue Team (HRT) in the United States; and Tactical Action Groups (TAGs) in the Australian and British Special Air Service (SAS).

These units are extremely well versed in rapid assault techniques, have extensive knowledge of the use of deadly force, are isolated from the wider community in which they act and operate according to a strict hierarchical chain of command. In the case of police commando teams (often referred to as a 'third force') the principle according to which they act is also extended from one of minimum force (the guiding cardinal of police forces in the modern liberal democratic state) to one of sufficient force.

The ability to call on special anti-terrorist response teams provides governments with a number of specific advantages. The most obvious benefit of such organizations is that they are specifically trained to deal with difficult situations, such as siege breaking and hostage-rescue, employing skills that are not normally found within conventional force structures. These units also do not suffer from conflicting missions, which can be the case for both the military (whose primarily role is external defense) and the police (whose primary role is internal law enforcement). Moreover, they can be deployed at very short notice and reduce the possibility of having to call on armed combat troops for problematic internal security situations.

Certainly, there have been occasions when rapid response teams have formed a useful adjunct to the state's counter-terrorist tool kit. The SAS hostage rescue at the Iranian Embassy, in 1980, is perhaps the most dramatic case in point, although other units have enjoyed equal success such as GIGN's storming of a GIA-hijacked Airbus at Marseilles in 1995. Dedicated anti-terrorist squads have also been used to provide additional security at high-profile public and political events such as the 2000 Sydney Olympics and 2002 Salt Lake Winter Games (covered, respectively, by the Australian SAS and US Delta Force).

The overall utility of specialist anti-terrorist teams is questionable, however. At the very least, these units are extremely expensive to maintain, particularly if they are to be kept at a high state of operational readiness. While this, in itself, is not a major reason for concern - security assets are, by their very nature, costly both in terms of trained manpower and resources - the fact that they are rarely used does raise the issue of their overall cost effectiveness. In Italy, for instance, the changing nature of terrorism and virtual elimination of the Red Brigade's (RB) threat during the 1990s has made the GIS more or less obsolete, with most of the organization's current activities taken up in internal and external training missions.

The most pressing problem associated with tactical response units, however, concerns the appropriate level of force together with the locus and degree of accountability when excessive violence is employed. Obviously, specific actions will depend on the circumstances at hand. In certain cases, they may require the actual elimination of the terrorist (for example, in hostage situations when abductors start to shoot their captives). In others, merely the threat to use deadly force may be sufficient to persuade the terrorist(s) to surrender. Disabling and distraction devices such as stun grenades and CS gas can also play an important role, as they did in the SAS storming of the Iranian Embassy.

This being said, if tactical response units either fail in their missions or appear overly violent for the political sensibilities of their democratic sponsors, they are liable to trigger a groundswell of public opposition to the general detriment of the counter-terrorism effort. Two salutary cases stand out. The first concerns the Italian Nucleo Operativo Centrale di Sicurezza (NOCS), the forerunner to the GIS. Despite gaining an excellent reputation in hostage rescue operations throughout the 1970s and 1980s - most particularly, the dramatic rescue of General James Dozier from the RB in 1982 - the unit's image was irrevocably tarnished by the conviction of five of its members for torturing Red Brigade activists in order to extract confessions. The revelation resulted in the disbandment of NOCS (which was replaced by the GIS in the mid-1980s) and severely curtailed the latitude accorded to Rome's overall counter-terrorist campaign.

The second relates to the deliberate shooting of a Red Army Faction (RAF) terrorist, Wolfgang Grams, during a botched GSG-9 ambush in 1993. This scandal not only devastated the near-legendary image of the unit (almost resulting in its indefinite closure), it also cost the Chief Federal Prosecutor, Alexander von Stahl, and the Interior Minister, Rudolf Seiters, their jobs. In addition, it provided ample fodder for the RAF to legitimize its own position to the direct detriment of Bonn's own domestic and international standing.

Notwithstanding these potential dangers and limitations, many governments that have established tactical response squads tend to view them as playing a crucial role in hardening the 'sharp' end of the government's counter-terrorist options. Moreover, the mere existence of these units is often justified as a useful deterrent to terrorist operations such as aircraft hijackings (assuming the perpetrators are not suicide operatives) and embassy assaults.

The existence of anti-terrorist commando teams will only be tolerated if it is apparent that they have been created to meet a clear and on-going danger.

In addition, it must be clear that any force these units subsequently employ will only be used in a controlled and precise manner and only after all other possibilities have been exhausted. Finally, it may well be prudent to balance the relative deterrent value specialist squads have in counter-terrorism campaigns with more day-to-day security force responsibilities, which would give them a more fiscally justifiable dual-use capacity.

5.4 Control of the media

It is generally recognized that a fundamental link exists between terrorism and the media. On the one hand, an intrinsic element of the modern terrorist phenomenon resides in its function as a form of political communication. By being able to rely on the immediate and extensive coverage of television, radio and newspapers (which in the modern age of mass communication competition cannot afford to ignore 'live action spectaculars') extremists have found it possible to effectively fulfill the propaganda objectives that are so critical to this mode of psychological warfare - namely to instill fear.

Just as importantly, the media has provided terrorists with a ready-made publicity platform from which to air their grievances, legitimize their causes, mobilize potential recruits, disrupt government counter-responses and underscore their political relevance. As Ted Koppel, ABC's former Nightline host, once said: "Without the [media] terrorism becomes rather like the philosopher's tree falling in the forest: no one hears it fall and therefore it has no reason for being".

For as long as the mass media exists, terrorists will hunger for "the oxygen of publicity" (as Margaret Thatcher put it). Equally, as long as terrorists continue to commit acts of violence the mass media will scramble to cover them in order to satisfy the desire of their audiences for the dramatic and, thereby, boost viewing and readership figures. It is in this context that several governments have moved to impose restrictions on the broadcasting of terrorist demands and the reporting of incidents.

During the height of the troubles in Northern Ireland, for instance, the UK's Prevention of Terrorism Act expressly prohibited members and supporters of proscribed groups from being directly heard on the broadcasting media (although their words could be reported there as well as written in the press). In Germany, Article 129a, Section 3 of the Penal Law prohibits the advertising of terrorist manifestos and propaganda. At the more draconian end of the spectrum, Spanish Organic Law No. 8 makes it a criminal offence to support or praise "the activities typical of a terrorist organization or the deeds or commemorative dates of their members by publishing or broadcasting, via the mass media, articles expressing opinion, news reports, graphical illustrations, communiqués"; at one stage Spanish judges were even empowered to close down radio stations as an exceptional precautionary measure.

Direct government control over the media, however, has been vigorously criticized on the grounds that it prevents the press from acting as a forum for independent critical debate and, thereby, directly threatens the essential oversight function performed by the 'fourth-estate'. Even in instances of widespread terrorist activity, the tendency has been to interpret any form of government control as the thin edge of the censorship wedge. Equally, it has been pointed out that a vibrant, independent media can play a useful role in helping to frustrate the aims of terrorists, by denuding extremists of any political veneer (and exposing them as plain murderers), providing a forum of informed discussion on the implications and causes of terrorism, issuing warnings of possible attacks and heightening general public vigilance and awareness to unusual behavior and suspicious packages/vehicles.

Undoubtedly a more preferable solution is for the media to accept self-imposed restrictions on their reporting and information production activities. Regulation of this sort could include such elements as:

- Limitations on direct interviews with terrorists and their supporters;

- Avoidance of reports that could unduly panic the public or otherwise complicate consequence management at the site of a terrorist incident;

- In-house vetting of news stories to ensure that they are accurate, consistent and balanced.

Many major media organizations have adopted guidelines for their staff with the aim of helping to prevent the more obvious pitfalls in terrorism reporting. The Radio Telefis Eireann (RTE) Authority in the Republic of Ireland, for instance, requires that all interviews with designated groups be pre-recorded and only included in broadcasts if first cleared by divisional heads or, if necessary, the RTE Director General. Equally pertinent are guidelines that have been drawn up by CBS News, which emphasize thoughtful, conscientious and restrained terrorism coverage and specify:

- No live reporting of terrorist/kidnapper situations;

- Care in avoiding interference with the authorities' communications channels (for example, tying up telephone lines);

- Use of expert advisers whenever possible to help avoid questions or reports that "might tend to exacerbate the situation";

- Strict observance of 'all police instructions' (although there is provision for the media to report to their superiors any instructions that seem to be intended to massage or suppress the news);

- Balanced and limited news length to ensure that 'the (terrorist) story does not unduly crowd out other important broadcasts of the hour or day'.

Certain governments have also established dedicated organizational structures to provide the media with accurate, complete, timely and understandable information in the event of a terrorist incident. The main rationale behind such initiatives is to ensure, as far as possible, that news organs have the best available information at their disposal and will act as an asset, rather than a hindrance during a crisis situation (particularly in terms of informing the public in a non-sensationalistic and balanced manner). The Joint Information Center (JIC) in the United States provides a good example of this type of initiative. Three main functions are performed by the Center:

- Information production, which involves the development of all printed material for the media, including bulletins, news releases, fact sheets and background material;

- Information dissemination, much of which is conducted either through press conferences or via written and verbal submissions to reporter questions;

- Information analysis, which is essentially concerned with ensuring that all information disseminated to the media is correct and consistent.

5.4.1 Security of information versus the public's right to know

No doubt there are those that would reject self-imposed restrictions and government-fed information as subverting the independence of the media and eroding the principle of the public's right to know. However, the argument that the freedom of the press is an absolute and incontestable value that must always be upheld is problematic. In order to carry out its function in a responsible manner, the media have to retain the option of remaining silent, of 'keeping off the record', of delaying the reporting of certain facts and of respecting the need for centrally mandated information. It is essential that journalists differentiate between the wars of ideas fought within the legitimated institutions of the community and those struggles that take place outside such structures and which rely on violence and intimidation rather than reason and intellect.

5.5 Targeting of terrorist leaders and members

In addition to using the primarily defensive measures discussed above, a few countries have aggressively targeted the leadership of terrorist organizations that pose a threat to the security and stability of the state. This particular policy option represents one of the most extreme counter-terrorism tools available to the state and is generally (though not always) one that is reserved for the most extreme of circumstances.

The methods used to kill targeted terrorists have been varied and ingenious and are often designed to deliver an unmistakable symbolic or political message. Considerable use has been made of clandestine methods such as poisonings, shootings or bombings, which give the state an opportunity to deny involvement in the action and thus avoid any negative public opinion that might subsequently result. In certain cases, however, more open and obvious means have been adopted. This has been particularly evident in the Middle East, where Israel has frequently resorted to the use of AH-64 Apache helicopters and rockets to eliminate Palestinian leaders in the West Bank and Gaza Strip areas.

Assassinations and directed killings - which are seldom, if ever, articulated in the public political arena - are typically designed to serve several primary functions, including:

- The elimination of specific individuals known to be planning or preparing imminent attacks against the state or its interests;

- The disruption of internal organizational command structures in an attempt to bring about leadership changes that are more favorable to government positions;

- The instilling of fear in targeted groups by constantly penetrating their ranks and killing their leaders (which is viewed as a viable and potent form of terrorism deterrence).

The use of assassination as a direct tool of state policy is perhaps most closely associated with Israel. Indeed, many commentators have argued that government-sanctioned murders have been a hallmark of the country's collective counter-terror efforts since at least the 1960s.

As noted above, many of the methods used by the Israeli military and security services have been overt, particularly in the wake of the Palestinian uprising that began in September 2000, where explicit attempts have been made to kill leading figures of Hamas, Islamic Jihad, the al-Aqsa Martyrs Brigade and even members of Force 17 - Arafat's personal bodyguard (see table).

Although these means have opened the Israeli government to significant national and international scrutiny, they have been consistently justified on the grounds that Israel is at war with terrorism and, therefore, the state is perfectly justified in applying the principles applicable to warfare in confronting Palestinian extremism; more specifically, that those who are targeted are no different from combatants killed on the battlefield.

Several other states, however, have aggressively targeted terrorist leaders and members. In Peru, institutionalized killing formed a principal component of President Fujimori's all-out war against Sendero Luminiso (SL, Shining Path) between 1990 and 1993. The bulk of the policy was instituted through the Counter-Terrorism Agency of the Police Force (DINCOTE), which was

Targeting of terrorist leaders and members

Israeli assassinations of key Palestinian militants, 2000-01	
Name	Method of assassination
Massoud Ayad	Rocket attack
Thabet Thabet	Shooting
Samih Maliabi	Booby-trapped bomb
Hani Abu Bakra	Shooting
Abbas al-Ewiwi	Shooting
Yusuf Abu Swayeh	Shooting
Anwar Hamran	Shooting
Mahmoud al-Mugrabi	Shooting
Ibrahim Bani Odeh	Bomb
Jamal Abdel-Razak	Shooting
Hussein Abayat	Rocket attack

Source: "West Rebukes Israel's Assassins," The Guardian, February 15 2001.

essentially given carte blanche to destroy SL following Fujimori's suspension of Lima's Constitution in 1992. Although some terrorists were arrested and tried according to what most societies would consider normal judicial procedures, many simply 'disappeared'. Between 1989 and 1992, it is estimated that the number of SL members killed after capture (without a trial) doubled and that by 1993, most of the organization's primary and secondary leadership had been removed.

A more explicit policy of state-sanctioned assassination was adopted in Spain during the 1980s when the Interior Ministry established death squads known as Grupos Antiterroristas de Liberacion (GAL) to conduct a full-blown 'dirty war' against Euskadi Ta Eskatuna (ETA, Basque Fatherland, Land and Liberty). The GAL network was funded by so-called fondos reservados - secret government resources reserved for 'special purposes' - and mandated to carry the terrorist war back to ETA. Between 1983 and 1987 these units carried out numerous bombings, kidnappings and killings in the Basque regions of northern Spain and southwestern France, taking responsibility for over two dozen murders during the period. French and Portuguese mercenaries carried out many of these assaults, most of who had been directly recruited into the GAL squads by undercover Spanish police intelligence agents.

It is not clear whether assassination and directed targeting as a tool for counter-terrorism yields a net benefit. On the one hand, killings have been instrumental in weakening group structures - as occurred with SL in Peru - and satiating the desire for revenge from angry and frustrated segments of the general population, which has, arguably, been the case in Israel. On the other hand, however, there are a number of significant dangers associated with the policy. Military-styled methods such as the use of helicopter gunships or tanks immediately open the government up to negative public exposure as they have done in Israel. More clandestine tactics can be equally problematic, particularly if the agents carrying out the action are either caught, kill the wrong subject or otherwise alert the public to the government's use of the tactic. The GAL dirty war in Spain, for instance, not only served to legitimize ETA's armed struggle in the eyes of many Basques, it was also instrumental in alienating support for the Socialist government of Felipe Gonzalez and ensuring its ultimate demise in 1996. In Peru, the virtually freehand accorded to DINCOTE had a highly deleterious impact on democratic legitimacy within the country and, in the long term, has failed to entirely eliminate the threat posed by SL.

5.5.1 Targeted killings and Al-Qaeda
In the wake of the September 11 attacks in New York and Washington, there has been growing pressure within the US government to aggressively target the senior leadership of Al-Qaeda. In the case of specific group members generally recognized in American society, such as Osama Bin Laden, the potential for significant negative backlash is probably minimal. Nonetheless, the policy is not without its risks and obstacles. Increased group militancy and greater recruiting potential on the part of the organizations represented by the target may still outweigh the potential positive affects derived. Moreover, it is not apparent that the removal of lesser known figures would be accepted as a legitimate option, particularly if their direct involvement in the September 11 (or other US-directed) attacks was not immediately apparent. Finally, the use of directed killings and assassinations, continues to be hampered by several executive orders specifically prohibiting the action.

5.6 Legitimating socio-economic and development initiatives
States have emphasized socio-economic and development policies in their overall counter-terrorist tool kit. These 'soft' or so-called 'carrot' initiatives

have been designed to address the underlying grievances of conflict-ridden regions that may directly or indirectly fuel unrest or be exploited for anti-government purposes. Functionally, socio-economic and development policies have been directed toward two main, inter-related goals: first, to deprive terrorists of their claim to legitimacy by demonstrating that the government is responsive to the needs of the community; second, to diminish the active and passive support base on which terrorists rely for political, logistical, recruitment and operational purposes.

Poverty does not, in itself, cause terrorism. Many deprived regions do not suffer from this type of violence and many terrorists (for example those that carried out the September 11 attacks) come from well-to-do backgrounds. Nonetheless, as several states have come to appreciate, it does play an important role in exacerbating latent feelings of frustration and aggression and generally providing a contextual environmental that can be readily co-opted and exploited by radicals and demagogues. Certainly this has been the case in a number of regions severely affected by endemic terrorism and civil conflict, including Colombia, the southern Philippines, Northern Ireland, the Spanish Basque country, the Israeli Occupied Territories, Indonesia, Uzbekistan and the Indian sub-continent.

Colombia, Mindanao (the southern Philippines) and Northern Ireland provide three good examples of regions where concerted attempts have been made to mitigate entrenched campaigns of terrorism through socio-economic and development initiatives. In Colombia, an integral component of Bogota's 'Plan Colombia' has involved the provision of aid to support alternative agricultural development projects and boost social programs in the health and education sectors. The policies have been designed both to encourage legal alternatives for farmers and laborers engaged in coca production and to empower local communities by reducing their perceived dependence on the Revolutionary Armed Forces of Colombia (FARC). Roughly US$98 million was set aside for these initiatives between 2000 and 2001, the bulk of which came from the United States and European donors.

The UK has devoted considerable public expenditure to try and boost socio-economic development in Northern Ireland. London has invested in large-scale education, health, housing, infrastructure and urban regeneration programs; jointly funded European Union-administered peace funds that have been used for local development projects; and moved to promote private investment by offering tax incentives to national and multinational communities to move to the Province. The stated aim of these policies has been to move Northern Ireland from a 'contested' to a 'shared' society where sectarian divisions and violence are framed and ultimately subsumed within a wider vision of Catholic and Protestant peace.

Finally there has been some use of socio-economic development in an attempt to address perceived grievances among Filipino Muslims in Mindanao. Most of these efforts have been channeled through a so-called Southern Philippine Council for Peace and Development (SPCPD), which was instituted in 1996 to promote, monitor and coordinate communitarian health, education and infrastructure projects throughout the southern Philippines. At the time of its creation, some US$510 million was pledged to support the Council's efforts in these areas - US$10 million from Manila and US$500 million from international donor bodies (primarily the Organization of Islamic Conferences/OIC).

The experience of these states suggest that legitimating development measures can have a positive bearing on terrorism and associated civil conflict. In particular, they can:

- Contribute towards the expansion of a new middle class that has often taken the initiative in inhibiting local support for terrorist activities and acting as a conduit for conflict resolution;

- Provide tangible economic alternatives to those who actively join or otherwise assist terrorist organizations out of financial desperation;

- Be made conditional on the absence of violence, creating a useful 'stick' for governments and the international community to use against terrorists and community support bases (although over-use of this coercive mechanism obviously risks negating any long-term positive effects that social and economic policies might otherwise have had).

The overall utility of the socio-economic tool, however, depends on its implementation. If measures are enacted in the absence of well-formulated needs assessments and if effective administrators, auditing and fiscal oversight mechanisms are lacking, the impact of policies is liable to be marginal and may actually serve to exacerbate conflict by widening or even institutionalizing existing poverty gaps on the ground. Accordingly, the most successful use of development initiatives has tended to occur when funding disbursement mechanisms are:

- Transparent;

- Developed in close consultation with local leaders and community representatives;

- Geared to meet the specific economic environments and needs of particular conflict zones;

- Channeled through regional administrators that are adequately trained (and equipped) in the use of development aid.

Finally, although legitimating initiatives may serve to dampen the contextual environment surrounding terrorism, they seldom serve to eliminate violence on their own. It is therefore vital development drives are worked into multi-pronged approaches that also embrace wider political, community and security dimensions. Placing too much emphasis on one proxy to the detriment of others will almost certainly result in sub-optimal outcomes.

CHAPTER 6: US HOMELAND SECURITY

6.1	The historical and legal context for US homeland security	125
6.2	National security thinking and homeland security	126
6.3	Preparing and organizing for new homeland security threats	127
6.4	Reorganising homeland security post September 11	130
6.5	Main areas of current homeland defence	132
6.6	Conclusion	142

CHAPTER 6: US HOMELAND SECURITY

Although homeland security has become a topic that has shot to the forefront of Washington's war on terrorism, it is a concept as old as the United States itself - the basic principles and legal justification for which can be found in the Constitution. These historical antecedents took on particular resonance after the September 11 terrorist attacks, leading the Bush administration to outline a strategy and create an organization aimed at upholding two fundamental (constitutionally-explicated) guarantees first 'to insure domestic tranquility' and second 'to provide for the common defense'. The end result has been the creation of a dedicated Office of Homeland Security (OHS), which has combined with an increased role for US law enforcement agencies and the military. This chapter discusses the evolution of homeland security in the United States and examines current planning and programmatics for handling large-scale domestic terrorist contingencies.

6.1 The historical and legal context for US homeland security
Homeland security was a serious issue in the framing of the US Constitution. The anarchy that broke out in Massachusetts during Shay's Rebellion, combined with the powerlessness of the American government to halt the eruptions, had a profound effect on those who attended the Constitutional Convention of 1789. It was during the Summer of this year that these delegates moved to create a stronger central administration capable of 'establishing justice and ensuring domestic tranquility' - an objective that has since been given concrete expression and legal foundation in Articles I and IV of the US Constitution. These clauses state "Congress shall have power...to provide for calling forth the Militia to execute the Laws of the Union, suppress Insurrection, and repel Invasions" (Article IV) and that the "United States shall guarantee to every State in this Union a Republican Form of Government and shall protect each of them...against domestic Violence" (Article I).

Homeland security has changed significantly since the days when these ideas were first formulated. The invading foreign armies, farmers' rebellions and attacking Indian tribes envisioned by the Founding Fathers have been replaced by contingencies that now embrace Intercontinental Ballistic Missile (ICBM) threats from rogue states, mass destruction terrorist strikes originating from within and outside the US and cyber attacks directed against and designed to cripple the country's critical infrastructure system. These new threats and challenges have resulted in a proliferation of laws and bureaucratic organizations that are designed to prevent large-scale attacks from occurring within the continental United States (CONUS) as well as to facilitate rationalized and coordinated responses in the event that such assaults actually transpire.

6.2 National security thinking and homeland security

In the strategic context, homeland security began to influence national thinking in the mid-1990s. Fresh from a victory in the Persian Gulf and challenged by no other military power in the world, US policy analysts became concerned with possible asymmetric threats to the country's interests at home and abroad.

In 1998, Washington released an updated version of the US National Security Strategy (NSS), which reflected these concerns by highlighting the changing and new types of threats the US would face into the new millennium. In particular, it portrayed the increasing likelihood that potential enemies would attempt to attack CONUS in unconventional ways, focusing especially on the specter of nuclear, biological, chemical and cyber terrorism. To address these challenges, the Clinton administration moved to institute an integrated, multi-faceted strategy that combined federal interagency cooperation with a homeland defense program that linked national response assets with capabilities at the state and local levels.

The September 11 attacks on the World Trade Center and Pentagon further highlighted the need for a new rationalized program to avail domestic defense. With his issuance of Executive Order 13228 (EO 13228), President Bush mandated a new Director of Homeland Security to "develop and coordinate the implementation of a comprehensive national strategy to secure the United States from terrorist threats or attacks".

Washington's current plan for homeland security calls for a national program that will be developed over a number of years and which will incorporate all levels of government as well as the private civilian sector. In addition, it seeks to address a wide range of internal defense issues, some of which will require a reorganization of federal agencies, legal reform and greater cost-sharing between separate levels of national and local administration. Just as crucially, the strategy is expected to provide an effective framework for directing federal spending on homeland security and ensuring funds are used in the most cost-effective manner possible.

6.3 Preparing and organizing for new homeland security threats

The specific event that first galvanized the federal government to start thinking about homeland security was the Tokyo subway sarin gas attack carried out by members of Japan's Aum Shinrikyo cult on March 20, 1995. For US policymakers, the assault was taken as evidence that extremists were now able and willing to use Weapons of Mass Destruction (WMD) and that modalities for addressing such contingencies were deficient across the board.

6.3.1 Presidential Decision Directive 39 (PDD-39) and the Weapons of Mass Destruction Act (NLD)

In the immediate weeks following the sarin attack, the Clinton administration issued President Decision Directive 39 (PDD-39). This executive initiative focused on improving overall national response capabilities and enhancing the government's ability to handle and manage the consequences of a WMD terrorist attack on American soil. One year later, Washington passed the Weapons of Mass Destruction Act, more commonly known as Nunn-Lugar-Domenici (NLD) after the three senators who originally sponsored the legislation. The initiative established a national domestic preparedness program, administered by the Pentagon, to educate local officials in 120 cities on how best to respond to an exotic attack involving Chemical, Biological, Radiological and Nuclear (CBRN) agents. The act also proposed training exercises where federal, state and local officials could learn to work more effectively together.

6.3.2 Presidential Decision Directives 62 and 63 (PDD-62, PDD-63)

In 1998, the Clinton administration looked to build on the budding framework for preparing and coordinating against WMD terrorism by announcing two additional Presidential Directives designed to strengthen the nation's defenses against unconventional contingencies: PDD-62 and PDD-63. The first initiative aims to create a new and more systematic approach to fighting generic terrorist threats in the 21st Century, while the second focuses specifically on protecting US critical infrastructures from both physical and cyber attack.

Apart from reinforcing the mission of government agencies charged with combating terrorism, the two PDDs also sought to give clear direction and organization to the many government agencies (federal, state and local) that were now attempting to define their new roles for combating terrorism. As part of this effort, PDD-62 established an Office of the National Co-ordinator for Security, Infrastructure Protection and Counter-Terrorism who was charged with overseeing the relevant policies and programs in the areas of counter-terrorism, protection of critical infrastructure, preparedness and consequence management for WMD.

PDD-63 (which built on the recommendations of the President's Commission on Critical Infrastructure Protection) further called for a national effort to assure the security of the USA's "increasingly vulnerable and interconnected infrastructures", including physical and cyber-based systems in telecommunications, banking, finance, transportation and essential government services. More specifically, the Directive sought to protect those systems that were seen as essential in allowing federal and state governments to perform vital security missions as well as deliver general public health, safety and order. A National Coordinator was instituted and tasked with providing advice regarding budgets for counter-terrorism programs and taking the lead in the development of guidelines that might be necessary for crisis management.

6.3.3 Other related initiatives
In addition to NLD and PDDs 39, 62 and 63, the Clinton administration established several other organizations (overseen by the National Coordinator) to enhance public-private sector cooperation in the area of critical infrastructure protection. These included:

- A National Infrastructure Protection Center (NIPC), which combined representatives from the Federal Bureau of Investigation (FBI), Department of Defense (DoD), US SecretService, Department of Energy (DoE), Department of Transportation (DoT), the intelligence community and the private sector to facilitate information exchange and sharing;

- A National Infrastructure Assurance Council (NIAC), which was meant to bring together private sector leaders and state and local officials to provide policy guidance in the formulation on a national strategy on critical infrastructure protection;

- A Critical Infrastructure Assurance Office (CIAO), which supported the work of the NIAC and which was responsible for handling public awareness as well as various legislative affairs.

6.3.4 Funding
The amount of dollars actually spent on relevant programs and activities is difficult to quantify due to the inclusion of certain expenditures that cannot be separated from larger costs as well as the fact that there is no single/uniform definition of terrorism

Spending on homeland security-related programs more than doubled between 1996 and 2002, from US$9.4 billion to over US$19.5 billion. Most of this money has been devoted to boosting law enforcement capabilities and assuring the physical security of government facilities and employees. Resources allocated for responding to and preparing for terrorist attacks have generally accounted for around 15 per cent of the total counter-terrorism budget, the bulk of which has gone towards training first responders, WMD detection equipment and state and local planning and assistance.

While overall funding levels have been substantial, there has been little oversight on how this money has been spent. The National Coordinator established under PDD-63, for instance, was given neither budgetary nor legal authority over any of the agencies involved in counter-terrorism plans. As a result, most of the efforts made in addressing domestic threats to CONUS took the form of additional funds being allocated to pre-existing organizations (many of which tended to be more interested in protecting their share of the counter-terrorism 'pie' than developing a truly rationalized, coordinated national strategy). In all, over 40 agencies overseen by various congressional committees have received a role in the nation's counter-terrorism plan. The General Accounting Office (GAO) has frequently lambasted the lack of federal accountability and fiscal oversight that is exercised over these bureaucratic bodies, highlighting the wasteful spending that has occurred from resulting (and unnecessary) duplication of effort. The creation of 90 different programs for the single purpose of training local officials in WMD response is a case in point.

The lack of a legislatively mandated federal entity to oversee the task of providing security for the homeland - administratively and financially - was and continues to be one of the most nettlesome obstacles to coordinating domestic defense efforts effectively. Although several Congressionally mandated commissions have frequently pointed to this problem, criticizing the general lack of structure and process in the US strategy, they effected little change in the Executive level prior to the events of September 11.

6.4 Reorganising homeland security post September 11

The events of September 11 and the subsequent anthrax attacks in New York gave added focus to the debate on homeland security in the US. Issues from intelligence and border security to coordination of first responders were all critically revisited with an eye to improving on the organizational deficiencies that surfaced on September 11. On October 8, 2001, President Bush accordingly issued EO 13228 "Establishing the Office of Homeland Security", which created a new framework for coordinating domestic counter-terrorism responses within the United States.

The OHS is run within the White House and was modeled on the National Security Council (NSC). Headed by the Assistant to the President for Homeland Security, it has a staff of 120 and is supported by a supplementary Homeland Security Council (which acts as the main mechanism for ensuring effective development of relevant domestic defense policies among executive departments and agencies). The importance accorded to the new organization was reflected both by the fact that it was been placed within the Executive Office of the President and that the Director, Tom Ridge, a close personal friend of Bush, was assigned cabinet-level status.

The mandate of the OHS was specifically crafted to undertake tasks associated with the coordination of security for the homeland rather than actual management, leaving unchanged the existing authorities of operating departments and agencies. The specific functional parameters of the OHS can be broken down into six main areas:

- Identifying priorities for collection and analysis of information that relates to terrorist threats;

- Preparing for and mitigating the consequences of terrorist threats or attacks in CONUS;

- Preventing terrorist attacks in CONUS;

- Protecting US critical infrastructure from the consequences of terrorist attacks;

- Responding to and promoting recovery from terrorist threats or attacks in CONUS;

- Reviewing and assessing the legal authorities available to executive departments and agencies to implement the goals of counter-terrorism programs in the US.

Although the OHS is given a clear role to coordinate the various efforts in the Executive branch, the Director, in reality, shares his responsibilities and powers with many other officials and agencies - acting as a principal contact person to the President rather than a counter-terrorism 'czar' per se. In formulating a national strategy, for example, the Office is to work with executive departments in addition to state and local governments and the private sector. Equally in the area of intelligence and border security (land, water and airspace), the OHS is required to coordinate with the National Security Advisor, while during the response and recovery phase of a terrorist incident it is stipulated that the Office deal with the National Economic Council (NEC).

The area of critical infrastructure protection raises particular questions pertaining to organization and leadership at the national level. The OHS has been given a broad mandate in this area and is tasked with protecting a wide-ranging list of assets, including energy production, telecommunications, information networks, food and water supply and transportation systems. However, the issuance of a separate executive order- EO 13231 - specifically addressing critical infrastructure issues as well as creating a new Critical Infrastructure Board (CIPB) begs the question whether the OHS can truly act as an effective coordinating body.

In EO 13231, "Critical Infrastructure Protection in the Information Age", the CIPB is tasked with the responsibility for coordinating programs that are intended to protect information systems for critical infrastructure. It is to work in conjunction with the private sector and state and local governments and will consist of representatives of all the White House departments involved with counter-terrorism activities. The CIPB is to be chaired by a Special Advisor to the President for Cyberspace Security, who is to report to the Assistant to the President for National Security and the Director of the OHS who are responsible for defining the Board's role in protecting the physical assets that support crucial information systems. The executive order does not state, however, where actual responsibility for protecting the physical infrastructure lies.

It should also be noted that the director of the OHS has no definitive budgetary authority, with his overall fiscal mandate (currently) limited to four main areas:

- Identifying programs that contribute to the administration's strategy for homeland security;

- Reviewing and providing advice on such programs to relevant heads of departments and agencies;

- Providing advice to the Director of the Office of Management and Budget (OMB) on the levels of funding in departments and agencies for homeland security-related activities;

- Certifying to the OMB that the funding levels specified in the annualbudget submission by OHS Director are indeed necessary and appropriate for the homeland security activities of the Executive branch.

In sum, while its name implies a comprehensive approach to homeland security, the OHS and its Director have been given a much narrower focus. The Office suffers from an acute problem of ambiguity in terms of national leadership and operational responsibilities and lacks the fiscal authority to allow for the effective coordination and implementation of projected domestic defense activities. These various issues will bear in on the ability of the OHS to initiate a truly effective and integrated homeland security policy and raise the question as to whether the wasteful allocation of resources and duplication of effort that was so apparent between 1995 and 2001 will, in fact, be mitigated.

6.5 Main areas of current homeland defence

While President Bush has only communicated the broad policy changes it would like to see implemented, examining his administration's 2003 budget request provides some insights into where improvements and modifications to current practices are likely to come. Four main areas have been emphasized, which reflect both Bush's attempts to shore up certain deficiencies in critical areas associated with defending the homeland and perceived response priorities that would need to be enacted in the event that these safeguards fail (particularly in light of post-11 September assessments):

- Supporting first responders;

- Defending against bioterrorism;

- Securing US borders;

- Employing 21st century technology to protect the homeland.

The table below shows actual and planned spending in each of these priority areas for the years 2002 and 2003.

	First emergency response	Biological terror defense	Border security	Technology for homeland defence	Other homeland security initiatives
2002 Enacted	0.291	1.4	8.8	0.155	3.2
2002 Supplemental	0.651	3.7	1.2	0.075	2.4
2003 Proposed	3.5	5.9	10.6	0.722	5.4

Note: All figures in US$ billions.

6.5.1 Supporting first responders

First responders - local police, firefighters and emergency medical personnel - represent those professionals and volunteers that can make the difference between a contained crisis and a large-scale disaster. However, the capabilities of these services vary greatly on a national basis and in most cases training has not focused on terrorist attacks per se (largely due to limited resources). The result has been inadequate first response preparation at many local levels.

President Bush has identified improving the capabilities of first responders and rationalizing/streamlining their relationship with the federal government as one of his top priorities. Specifically, the administration aims to allocate funds both to avail multi-county simulated exercises and to underwrite the logistic requirements that would be needed in actual response situations. In addition, Washington intends to set up dedicated facilities acrossthe country that can be used as training centers for first responders. One site has already been established for this purpose at Fort McClellan in Alabama. The center will be used to provide instruction on how to handle live chemical agents such as sarin gas. The 2003 budget request calls for US$3.5 billion for these purposes which, even taking into account past supplemental funding, represents a 3.5 per cent increase over 2002 levels.The biggest single budget item under the first responders portion of the homeland security budget is directed at supporting the interoperability of emergency personnel through the establishment of a central communications network. The urgency of undertaking such an initiative was underscored by the lessons of September 11. The inability for firemen to communicate simultaneously with the police, Emergency Medical Technicians (EMT) and other rescue workers was a glaring deficiency, which directly hampered initial rescue and recovery operations at the World Trade Center disaster site.

Significant funds have also been allocated towards adequately equipping and training state and local emergency personnel. As with communications, impetus for this funding reflects the lessons of September 11, particularly:

- The insufficient interoperability of first responder Personal Protective Equipment (PPE);

- Protective technologies that were ill-suited for extended wear during demanding physical labour;
- The lack of familiarity of numerous emergency management personnel with PPE practices such as the proper selection, fitting and maintenance of respirators.

Of all the priorities for homeland security, improving the capabilities of first responders and coordinating these personnel with those of the federal government present perhaps the biggest challenge for the Bush administration. Each state and perhaps local entity will need to provide a comprehensive assessment of the threats it faces and the main consequence management areas where there are significant shortfalls. In order to provide this information, two things are needed. First, strategic guidance will be required from the federal level (as well as the state level in the case of local agencies) to define what aspects of response are critical in managing a particular terrorist threat. Second, in order to ensure funding reaches the most important or deficient areas, states and localities will have to be able to conduct and prepare thorough threat and needs assessments. If either of these prerequisites are lacking, there is a high likelihood of well intentioned resources being misallocated to non-essential programs and non-first line priorities.

6.5.2 Biological terrorism

The question of how to defend against, prepare for and respond to the threat of terrorist attacks involving biological weapons has been a major concern of US government officials since the 1990s. This preoccupation reflects revelations about the scope of the Iraqi biowarfare program post-1990/91, indications that several sub-state groups retain an active interest in acquiring viral and bacterial agents (including Al-Qaeda) and the experience of the anthrax attacks that swept across the eastern sections of the United States last fall.

The Bush administration's plans for addressing biological terrorism involve large fiscal increases that are focused on:

- strengthening infrastructure of state and local systems;

- improving specialized federal capabilities to respond to bioterrorist incidents;

- developing specific new vaccines, medicines and diagnostic tests through research and development.

Overall, the White House has proposed allocating US$5.9 billion to improving the capabilities in each of these three areas. This represents an increase of US$4.5 billion over 2002 spending levels and signals a concerted effort on the part of Washington for creating a national system for dealing with biological contingencies.

State and local health care systems remain the first line of defense against biological attacks as they are most likely to be the first to notice increases in sick individuals presenting with similar symptoms - a potential indicator for a deliberate act of bioterrorism. Containing the spread of disease, having the capacity to handle surges of sick people and protecting those who have yet to be infected are critical elements of an effective medical emergency response system as is coordination among government and health agencies. The Bush administration has identified several deficiencies in these areas that are serving to mitigate overall preparedness against a large-scale bio attack:

- The health care system does not have the requisite surge capabilities to handle large numbers of victims quickly, nor does it possess sufficient facilities to isolate contagious patients;

- The information system linking hospital emergency rooms and public health officials is outdated and insufficient;

- There are few regional contingency plans or agreements betweenhealth care institutions to assist in meeting the demands placed onthese institutions during a bioterrorism attack;

- Infrequent training of health care providers has left many unprepared for handling bioterrorism victims.

To address these problems, several significant funding commitments have been made:

- Upwards of US$500 million is being devoted to enhance hospital healthcare surge capacities and improve overall consequence management of contagious bioattacks;

- US$810 million in supplemental funding is being provided to upgrade public health care preparedness training, strengthen laboratory diagnostic capabilities and help with the development of mutual aid compacts;

- US$329 million has been allocated to modernize the existing communications network that links local acute care providers with state and local public healthcare officials.

Many top federal officials and experts have realized that responding to a large-scale bioterrorism attack can not be handled by a single non-federal jurisdiction. Relevant capacities simply do not exist at the state or local level and an overwhelmed healthcare system could easily cause mass panic and allow diseases to spread more rapidly. To prevent or mitigate such scenarios, the Bush administration plans to allocate US$1.8 billion for federal bio response efforts. Among the top priorities is improving the National Pharmaceutical Stockpile (NPS). The FY02 supplement allocated US$562 million for the procurement of antibiotics to treat diseases such as anthrax, tularemia and plague with the overall aim to have enough drugs on hand for at least 20 million people. An additional US$512 million was spent on smallpox vaccine (the 'nightmare' agent in bioterrorism contingencies) with a further US$100 million investment planned in 2003. A major enterprise partnership scheme between the National Institute of Health (NIH), the federal government, industry and academia is also to be instituted to examine the different types of pathogens that could be used as bioterrorism agents and which medical products should therefore be emphasized in stockpiling initiatives.

Apart from the NPS, considerable emphasis has been placed on maintaining and improving 'push packs' that can be used in the event of either of a biological or chemical attack. These pre-assembled packages contain life-saving antidotes, pharmaceuticals and other supplies that can be distributed within 12 hours of a request. The packs are maintained in secure locations around the United States and are considered a vital component of any multi-phased response to a bio attack.

One final area of concern has to do with the global reach of biological weapons. The current plan for homeland security pushes for more extensive cooperation with scientists in other countries to provide information, research awareness and early warning of potential health threats abroad. In addition, plans are being developed to strengthen the Epidemiological Intelligence Service (EIS) of the Centers for Disease Control (CDC) in Atlanta, which was established in 1951 as an early warning system against biological warfare, but which has been extended into a surveillance types of epidemics.

There are several agencies on the federal level for dealing with the consequences of biological terrorism, including the CDC, the DoD, the FBI, the Department of Health and Human Services (DHHS) and the Environmental Protection Agency (EPA). The Bush administration intends to streamline and integrate this patchwork of jurisdictional responsibility into a more rationalized structure that will provide federal agencies with greater clarity in determining appropriate SOPs and chains of command once a bioterrorist attack has occurred. The OHS is intended to facilitate this effort, although, as noted above, its ambiguous nature casts considerable doubt over whether it will, in fact, be able to achieve this objective.

It should also be noted that although spending levels are high, the challenge of sufficiently preparing for a large-scale bio contingency could easily go beyond any amount of money put towards this task. Moreover, the evolution of the medical system itself seems to conflict directly with many of the plans envisioned for combating bioterrorism. The rising cost of healthcare, for instance, has made profitability a major focal point of hospital administration. Devising a system that is both cost effective while at the same time able to maintain an adequate excess capacity to handle surge situations will require innovative planning as well as substantial federal backing and support.

6.5.3 Border security

Defending the frontiers of the United States has been a vexing issue that has faced almost every President since the inception of the nation. In modern times, concerns have revolved primarily around illegal immigration and drug smuggling. While these problems continue to present substantial challenges, new threats such as transnational crime, terrorism and the proliferation of WMD have required a change in the organization and methods of protecting America's air, sea and land borders. The main dilemma confronting

Washington is how to defend its main ports of entry without adversely affecting the country's open society that is based on a global flow of goods and services.

Traditionally, border security has been a multi-agency task handled primarily on the federal level through the Immigration and Naturalization Service (INS), the Customs Agency, the Coast Guard and the DoD. Following the attacks of September 11, however, there has been growing pressure for a major overhaul of border security. The most recent plan, which has the explicit support of the Bush administration, calls for the creation of an integrated Agency for Immigration Affairs (AIA), to be headed by the Associate Attorney General for Immigration Affairs and embracing two dedicated Bureaus of Immigration Services and Adjudications and Immigration Enforcement (both of which would have equal power and receive the same amount of funding). Although full approval of the plan is still pending, it is envisioned the AIA will, henceforth, assume coordinated control over border security activities. These agencies collectively check over 500 million people who cross US borders every year (330,000 of who are non-citizens), inspecting an additional 11.2 million trucks, 2.2 million rail cars and 7,500 foreign-flagged ships

Overall, the Bush administration plans to allocate roughly US$11 billion to streamlining and improving accountability in the area of frontier surveillance, an increase of roughly 25 per cent over current spending levels. If approved, almost half of this money will be invested in improving border control and inspections through such innovations as:

- Integrated databases and communications systems;

- Electronic entry-exit visa systems;

- Tamper-proof, machine-readable identity documents;

- Biometric data technologies.

It is envisioned a dedicated immigrant tracking system will be in place by October 1, 2002 and that no 'visa-waivers' will be issued to aliens unless their information has been entered on the entry-exit database. Total funding for the proposed scheme is likely to be in excess of US$400 million.

Another main area of focus in terms of border security is the Coast Guard, which will receive a three-fold increase in funding for port, waterway and littoral surveillance. Most of the monies will be used for enhancing defenses of high-risk vessels and coastal facilities (such as nuclear power plants and oil refineries) as well as helping to create an integrated tracking mechanism to monitor all vessels within or transiting US ports and territorial waters. Unfortunately, the Coast Guard fleet is rapidly aging and maintaining it will continue to siphon away resources that could be better spent on actual homeland defense missions.

Finally, moves are being made to upgrade the effectiveness of inspections performed at borders by the Customs Service. Current capabilities allow for roughly only 5 percent of all containers coming to the US to be checked, which greatly increases the odds of terrorists being able to smuggle WMD or other contraband into the country. To offset this, some US$619 million has been added to the 2003 budget to improve the efficiency of the US inspection regime. The funding will be used both to increase the number of customs officers available at main ports of entry and to support the development of new technology that can be used to minimize time-consuming and labor-intensive searches.

6.5.4 Homeland security and technology

One of America's greatest assets in defending the homeland is its extensive technological base. The Bush administration has specifically recognized this advantage and has set aside US$342 million to exploit Information Technology (IT) for general communication and dissemination purposes. Two main priority areas have been identified. First is to increase 'horizontal data sharing' between federal agencies. To this end, the White House has called for the creation of an Information Integration Office within the Department of Commerce to develop and help implement an interagency information architecture for domestic and international counter-terrorism. Second, is to improve 'vertical data sharing' between state and local officials and private stakeholders. In particular, Washington aims to establish a communications system that will allow all concerned entities to access the same network and information base.

A number of options are currently being examined to avail these two objectives. The defense company, Northrop Grumman, for instance, is seeking to build on its 911-style system to link fire and police personnel with local emergency medical facilities, laboratories and public health officials. Several databases are additionally being considered for the Coast Guard that would allow authorities to receive a detailed history of a ship's crew and recent cargoes. Finally, Raytheon is moving to develop a mobile command center that would integrate the various communications equipment used by fire departments, police, the National Guard and hospital personnel. The company is also in the process of finessing a biometrics-based data system that would employ facial recognition technology to identify airport workers.

The Bush administration has been particularly keen to develop IT for safeguarding the US information architecture. The NIPC will remain the country's main bulwark against cyber attacks, acting as the White House's primary office for threat assessment, warning, investigation and response. The Center will receive an additional US$20 million in funding in 2002, which should allow considerable expansion of its IT efforts for critical infrastructure protection. In addition, US$90 million has been allocated to create a Cyberspace Warning Intelligence Network (CWIN) and a Priority Wireless Access (PWA) program. The CWIN will link top government officials with private sector representatives to facilitate coordinated crisis management procedures in the event of a concerted cyber-based attack. The PWA effort is aimed at establishing a secure cellular network that prioritizes the calls of first responders during emergencies. The initiative was borne out of the experience of September 11 when initial search and rescue operations were seriously degraded by the effective 'jamming' of wireless communications airways.

6.5.5 Role of the military
Apart from these four areas, provision is being made for an increased military role in domestic counter-terrorism planning. Although the Posse Comitatus Act of 1878 severely restricts the use of the armed forces for internal contingencies, the US military is perhaps the only institution that possesses the necessary capabilities to handle large-scale terrorist threats in a concerted manner. Such considerations have become particularly salient in light of the destruction caused by the September 11 attacks in New York and Washington, especially in terms of guarding against possible future mass strikes involving chemical, biological, nuclear or radiological weapons.

Indications of the more active role the armed forces are now taking in homeland defense have been moves to create a Northern Command (announced by Secretary of Defense, Donald Rumsfeld and Chairman of the Joint Chiefs of Staff, General Richard Myers, on April 18, 2002) to help DoD better deal with natural disasters, attacks on US soil and other mass domestic contingencies. The new Command will provide for a more coordinated military support infrastructure to assist civil authorities such as the FBI, FEMA and state and local governments and will commence operations (at Peterson Air Force Base, Colorado) on October 1, 2002.

The establishment of Northcom reflects the importance that is currently accorded to the US armed forces in terms of homeland security. Although the primary role of the military will continue to be external defense, its capabilities and training to handle large-scale contingencies make it an indispensable resource for use in counter-terrorism planning and response, particularly in the case of exotic CBRN attacks. What is less clear, however, is how the Command will be coordinated with the White House and what relationship will emerge with the OHS and its Director. Recent events suggest a sub-optimal organizational arrangement may well result. Thus far, defense has tended not to consult with Tom Ridge over recommendations pertaining to homeland security, merely informing him of decisions actually taken (such as the suspension of air patrols over New York city in mid-2002). While this certainly reflects the narrow mandate of the OHS, it also raises the question of how best to use and integrate the military in times of acute national emergency.

6.6 Conclusion
Since September 11, homeland security has emerged as a central theme in the US war on terrorism. The Bush administration has so far provided approximately US$37 billion to support domestic preparedness programs and moves have been instituted to streamline and rationalize the efforts of those agencies and departments that have an active stake in the area of counter terrorism. Nonetheless several problems remain, the OHS is hamstrung by its narrow mandate, the less than tepid support it has received from other federal entities and the ambiguous nature of its overall coordinating powers. Equally, while there has been no shortage of funding to support specific homeland security initiatives, a centralized and effective mechanism for controlling how the money is actually spent has yet to materialize. These issues will need to be dealt with before the US can consider its capabilities adequate for handling large-scale terrorist contingencies that take place on its soil.

CHAPTER 7: SECURITY MEASURES

7.1	Introduction	145
7.2	Understanding the threat	145
7.3	New developments	154
7.4	Information gathering	155
7.5	Threat assessment	155
7.6	Combating the threat	157
7.7	Moving to an alternative existing building	169
7.8	New building design considerations	169
7.9	Operations	177
7.10	Attack reaction	178
7.11	Procuring advice	179

CHAPTER 7: SECURITY MEASURES

7.1 Introduction
Since the events of September 11, 2001 in the United States people everywhere have felt less secure in their places of work. The terrorist threat has, however, been real and persistent for decades and in a wide range of countries. It is a threat which at some level we all have to live with. This does not mean doing nothing about it. There are measures that can be taken to dissuade a terrorist from making a particular building a target, and measures which can limit the impact of such an attack if it takes place. These measures range from the cheap and straightforward to the very expensive and complex, and which are acted on will depend on the level of assessed risk and the resources available. But building managers should be aware of the risk and should undertake some form of security audit to see if there is something they should and could be doing to improve the safety of their staff and premises.

7.2 Understanding the threat
The threat to a building may come for a variety of reasons, from a range of different attackers, with a range of different motives. The actual methods of attack will have to be chosen from among a wide but ultimately limited range, likely to come from among those discussed below.

7.2.1 Large stand-off vehicle bomb
A building protected by a significant stand-off distance between it and any vehicle-borne weapon requires a large bomb to be deployed. Such an attack can represent a serious threat as even a modern building will be heavily damaged by a typical bomb of 1,000 kg equivalent TNT exploding as far away as 40 m. Conventional windows will implode violently, propelling shards of glass at high speed until meeting the resistance of furniture, walls, or occupants. The roof structure is likely to be severely damaged leaving the building open to the elements or attack by other methods. Any lightweight external cladding can be damaged and doors may be destroyed. People caught in the open will sustain injury from the fragmentation of the bomb or surrounding material. As well as impact injuries, ears and lungs may be damaged by blast. People inside will be shocked and disorientated, and perhaps deafened, if only temporarily.

Maintaining an adequate stand-off between the target building and any likely bomb position is important where at all possible because, as the available stand-off distance reduces between the bomb and the target, so the damage will increase disproportionately. This increase is in the order of the inverse of the distance ratio squared. That is, as the stand-off distance halves, for the same bomb the damage caused will equal approximately $(2/1)^2$ or four times the damage at the original distance. At closer ranges the damage becomes even more intense, as the inverse square law progresses to an inverse cube rule and even higher powers. Nevertheless, as the bomb moves closer to its target, the damage, though intense, may be more localized, while at a greater stand-off the blast may encompass the whole building. The car-bomb that partially collapsed the Federal Building in Oklahoma City, in 1995, left 168 dead and damaged 220 buildings in total.

There are two components of blast to be considered in planning to counter a bomb-attack. Firstly there will be the intense positive pressure wave, moving from the seat of the explosion outwards, but this is followed milliseconds later by a lesser negative pressure, or suction, as air is sucked back into the low-pressure zone left at the explosion's center. Thus building-elements such as secure front doors may suffer damage from the initial blast of positive pressure, and yet survive, only to be torn away by the sudden reversal of pressure caused by this secondary suction. This effect can be increased by the phenomenon of 'elastic rebound' in which a steel door may bend elastically under the pressure of the initial blast and then bounce back just as the suction event follows, exacerbating the deformation and leaving the door on the ground outside, unless it was constructed to a very sophisticated design.

Damage may also be caused by high-velocity fragments from the bomb-carrying vehicle or perimeter walls hitting the building. For example an engine block traveling at several hundred miles per hour is difficult to stop, and can do a lot of damage. Given the complex nature of blast, the sides and rear of buildings remote from the explosion may be subjected to lesser but still possibly significant blast effects.

7.2.2 Vehicle bomb close to building
The effect of a large vehicle bomb which explodes close to or, worse, inside, a building, can be catastrophic. Even modern reinforced concrete buildings can be effectively destroyed and heavy casualties may be sustained. In the

case of the American embassy in Beirut, which was destroyed by a suicide car-bomb in 1983, some of the columns failed in tension, meaning that the large, robust multi-storey building had been forced upwards by the blast, causing that failure and leaving debris scattered over a large area. The building occupied by the US Marines at Beirut airport, despite being a reinforced concrete building with walls and floors designed in a robust cellular structure, was completely destroyed in the same year by a suicide truck-bomb being driven into it.

A smaller vehicle bomb detonated in close proximity to a building may not cause total destruction but may, nevertheless, cause severe damage. It may be used to target specific building elements to exacerbate the damage caused, by exploding under a cantilever, for example, or adjacent to a corner column, or perhaps close to a busy reception area.

7.2.3 Proxy vehicle bomb
The deliverers of a vehicle bomb may gain access by brute force, ramming gates or checkpoints; they may achieve the same thing by deception: appearing to deliver building supplies or collecting waste for example. Alternatively, the bombers may use a proxy to deliver the weapon, forcing a member of staff or legitimate visitor to drive a vehicle carrying a bomb into the secure area, perhaps by holding a member of their family hostage, a method used by the Provisional IRA in a series of bombings in Northern Ireland in 1990. This kind of attack is more speculative, since the bombers have less control over the siting of the explosion, which could mean it does not achieve its full destructive potential, as the driver may leave it in the least damaging position available to them. However, even a relatively small device exploding anywhere in the confines of an under-building car-park, for example, could cause a disproportionate amount of damage, the blast effects being increased by the confined space and the added damaging contribution from the fuel in other vehicles in the car-park. Small bombs have the advantage to the bomber that they can be difficult to detect with normal security checks if carefully concealed in a car. They may also be delivered by an unwitting proxy.

7.2.4 Under-site bomb
The underground car-park is one way a bomb may be introduced into the space under a building, and was the method chosen in the case of the first bombing of the World Trade Center in New York in 1993, but there are many

other possible underground access points to be defended against, such as larger sewer pipes, utility access tunnels, ancient storage or access workings, or storm-water drains. Without close control of these passageways it may be possible to accumulate large amounts of explosive close to or under the target building, the detonation of which could cause the building to collapse entirely.

7.2.5 Parcel bomb

Gaining access to the building with small bombs is less of a problem as weapons from a few grams to several kilograms in weight can be posted or delivered to a building, or even to a specific individual within that building. A US physician was seriously injured at a medical center in Dhahran, Saudi Arabia, by a letter-bomb in May 2001. They can also be placed in any convenient recess in the external structure such as window sills, or decorative features such as vases and planters, hidden in reception areas or toilets, or anywhere with public access. A bomb of several kilograms such as could be carried in a briefcase could easily be thrown over a high wall into a fairly precisely chosen area. Many buildings are 'protected' by robust high walls, but in such a case of a lobbed bomb this kind of structure can work to the bomber's advantage, the tight space between walls and building amplifying the damaging effects of the relatively small explosion.

7.2.6 Hand grenade

A specific example of the thrown bomb is the hand-grenade. This may not be capable of causing much direct damage to the building in most cases, the main damaging effect being shrapnel rather than blast. However, with a little practice they can be very accurately thrown, through even a closed window, or an open door, from quite a distance, and cause localized death or severe injury. They also have the advantage of being readily available, cheap, easy to conceal and requiring little training in effective use. They can even be fitted with hooks, so that they can cling to mesh or bars protecting upper-floor windows. As an example of such an attack, a hand-grenade was thrown at the Hurriyat Conference Centre in India, in April 2001, injuring 5 people.

7.2.7 Evacuation attack

A method of attacking staff which would not only cause an immediate problem, but also damage morale in the longer term, would be to attack the escape routes from a building during an evacuation following a bomb alert. Staff gathered together and focused on leaving a building swiftly are very vulnerable to attack, and the bombers may not even have the problem of gaining access to the building in this case, though a device placed in an emergency stairwell rigged to explode during the evacuation would cause severe casualties. The actual purchase, storage and delivery of explosives leaves the attacker vulnerable to detection but a simple smoke-bomb activated during an evacuation could cause a degree of chaos and panic, and while no physical damage may be done, the sense of vulnerability and uncertainty engendered among the staff may be as effectively damaging to morale as a more serious form of attack. It will also bring staff into the open, rendering them vulnerable to more deadly assault.

7.2.8 Rocket-propelled grenade

Bringing the bomb into the building can be achieved by more direct methods. Rocket-Propelled Grenades (RPGs) can punch through most building cladding simply by virtue of their high kinetic energy. The Russian RPG-7 has been manufactured in a number of countries and is relatively easy to come by, is cheap, lightweight, easy to use and effective. With the armor-piercing variety of round, on impact a small shaped charge is detonated releasing a high-velocity molten material allowing it to penetrate several inches of armor-plating. An anti-personnel round is also available. The grenade can be accurately targeted and is effective over a range of up to 500 m. However, unless a fire is caused, only minimal building damage would be sustained and staff casualties limited to the immediate vicinity of the explosion. On the negative side, from the assailant's point of view, the launcher is fairly bulky and requires a space of about 3 m to be used safely. The noise and flames on launch can make the firing location obvious. An RPG-22 anti-armor weapon (range up to 250 m) was used by the Real IRA in an attack on the UK SIS building, in London, in 2000, though no casualties were sustained.

7.2.9 Mortars

Mortar bombs are explosives lobbed on a very high trajectory with a relatively low range. They vary from the light military style of mortar to the kind of heavy improvised device used by the Provisional IRA in an attack on Downing Street, in London, in 1991. If the attack zone is carefully mapped the military-type mortar can be quickly and precisely laid from a location out of sight of the target, even behind another building. The home-made device may also be capable of being set up and fired quite quickly but will typically be less accurate. In the case of the attack on Downing Street, the Prime Minister's residence was damaged but no casualties were sustained. The van launching the weapons through a cut-out in its roof was destroyed in the process.

The light mortar is unlikely to penetrate a building's roof by kinetic energy, so the explosion, while causing severe local damage, will be largely vented into the air, while an accurately fired round from the heavy mortar may penetrate the roof before exploding in the contained office-space below, causing serious damage. If the mortar-bombs land and explode adjacent to the building their effect will be similar to a conventionally- delivered bomb of similar size.

7.2.10 Long-range sniper

The threat to a building and its occupants may also come from firearms. Modern rifles mean that if a line-of-sight exists between the sniper and the target, a trained attacker can shoot a specific target with a high degree of certainty from the security of a position several hundred meters away, which gives a good chance of evading capture following the shooting. For high media-impact, the target needs to be a senior member of staff or high-ranking visitor, although an impact can also be achieved by the random shooting of junior staff. A Palestinian sniper killed 10 people by firing on a checkpoint in the West Bank in March 2002.

The areas most vulnerable to attack are the open ground in front of a building entrance and the offices high in the building with the best views - offices typically occupied by the most senior staff.

Suitable rifles and ammunition are readily available and cheap in many parts of the world, whether military-type or sporting-type weapons, and the military and sport-shooting fraternity provide a large pool of trained marksmen to use them effectively. The latest military-style .50 caliber sniper rifles have been used by terrorist groups such as the IRA and are freely available in the United States. They are very accurate and capable of damaging armored vehicles at distances of up to 1,500 m and, therefore, represent a serious threat to any building.

7.2.11 Close-range gun attack

The longer-range weapon gives greater security to the shooter, but close-range gun attack can be just as effective. Senior staff can be particularly vulnerable on their journey from home to work. If exposed on the way from the house to the car the attacker can simply walk by, shoot the target, drop the weapon and walk away. The same kind of attack may be possible at the work end of the journey, though, typically, security will be tighter there. Even with significant security present such an attack is difficult to defend against if a determined attacker is not concerned about his own escape, as in the case of the assassination attempt on US President Ronald Reagan in 1981 in which his assailant fired six shots from a handgun, hitting four people, including Reagan, despite the close proximity and rapid intervention of the secret services' bodyguards.

The attack may also come during the course of the journey itself, the target coming under attack from someone in another vehicle, or from an attacker on foot waiting at a point where the vehicle has to slow down or stop — circumstances which they may bring about themselves through some form of deception.

Such an attack may also be made inside the building. If an attacker is able to enter a building without suspicion where, for example, there is access for the general public, or where they are able to pose as a bona fide visitor, an effective handgun attack may be made on staff entering the building, other visitors, or receptionists, after which the attacker may simply walk out.

7.2.12 Drive-by attack
If a building can be seen from the road an attacker can shoot at it from a moving or briefly- paused vehicle and swiftly make their escape. This cannot be a precisely targeted attack unless timed to coincide with a VIP visit. Of course casualties may be sustained, even with a handgun, though a more serious threat is offered if automatic weapons are used, whether to staff outside or, in unprotected buildings, inside. An example of such an assault occurred in January 2002 when the US cultural center in Calcutta was sprayed with automatic gunfire by motorcycle-mounted attackers, resulting in the deaths of five policemen and causing 21 other casualties. An attack from a vehicle-mounted heavy machine gun, such as the 'technicals' used in Somalia, could be devastating both in terms of casualties and damage to the building.

7.2.13 Mob attack

Though it may be relatively unfocussed and disorganized, an attack on a building by a mob potentially poses as high a risk to the structure and its occupants as the most precisely planned and sophisticated attack.

Mobs can be organized or develop more spontaneously and the object and intensity of their disapproval can quickly change. With minimal, easily-obtained weapons entrances can be forced, windows broken, vehicles destroyed, interiors stripped, staff attacked, sensitive or valuable equipment or papers spirited away and the buildings burnt down. The US embassy in Skopje, Macedonia, came under such an attack in 1999, leading to serious damage to the building, with many windows being broken, many vehicles destroyed by fire and the staff being forced to take refuge in a panic room. The mob then moved on to attack press and NGO vehicles at a hotel nearby.

Even if kept outside the building, the mob may be able to flow around it, if there are no obstructions, effectively besieging the occupants.

7.2.14 Military-style occupation

Defending a building against a serious military-style attempt to take it over is very difficult. A small group of determined, well-armed, trained personnel will be able to force an entrance to and take full control of almost any building and its staff in a very short space of time unless it is defended by an equally capable and alert security force. The kind of passive defenses appropriate for a civilian building will be easily swept aside by such an assault. In 1997 a group of 19 heavily armed Tupac Amaru militia took over the Japanese embassy in Peru, taking 400 hostages and occupying the building for 127 days.

7.2.15 Infiltration by armed personnel

In addition to an open assault, a building is vulnerable to infiltration by an armed assailant, perhaps entering by covert means, maybe by posing as a legitimate visitor. They may thereby penetrate undetected deep into the building, bearing weapons which might range from handguns to knives to bombs. Clearly such an attacker could kill, injure or take staff hostage. A suicide bomber could cause extensive damage and casualties in such a scenario, even if no further in than the reception zone. Bombs detonating in sensitive parts of the building such as the computer room, or file room, can cause serious operational damage to the organization based there. Of course such information may simply be stolen or copied. While perhaps not typically representing a serious threat to the structure of the building, someone with the necessary expertise or information, having gained such access, could set a bomb in a structurally sensitive location with the hope of destroying the building. Such infiltration may simply have the aim of gaining intelligence for the planning of another form of attack.

7.2.16 Kidnap as leverage
As in the case of the proxy bomb, staff and their families are vulnerable to kidnap, which can be used as leverage to increase the efficacy of a range of attacks, by assisting with the gaining of access or intelligence, or even more direct participation.

7.2.17 Gas attack
Poison gas or disabling powders such as tear gas may be introduced into a building in public areas, or through open windows or, most effectively, in a mechanically vented building, through the air-intake. Even the relatively innocuous example of tear-gas may cause an uncontrolled staff-evacuation, rendering them vulnerable to other forms of attack as in the case above. Anyone with a breathing difficulty could be very seriously affected. It is also very difficult to rid a building of the tear-gas powder as it can get into cabinets, drawers and files. This can be the result of the actions of 'friendly' security forces acting in the building's defense. It may also be the accidental by-product of nearby events that are nothing to do with the building or its occupants.

More deadly are poison gases such as the nerve gas sarin used in the attack on the Tokyo underground in 1995 which killed 12 and hospitalized 493. They are much more difficult to obtain and to deploy effectively. However, they could be introduced into the building's air-intake with devastating effects and, as such, may be relatively tightly targeted, with less of the collateral damage associated with a bomb attack.

7.2.18 Poisoning of water supply
Another form of attack with deadly poisons may be achieved by contaminating the water supply to a building. To do this by introducing the toxin into the main supply is likely to be ineffective due to the volume of water, and has the possibly unwanted side-effect of poisoning the whole area served by that main. But most buildings are supplied via a local connection

to the main and it is common practice to isolate that connection with a stopcock close to the main end. This will generally be sited in an easily accessed public area so that the water supplier can isolate the building for maintenance work or debt control. The lock to the stopcock box, if any, will be very simple and a key easily obtained. By accessing the specific building supply in this way it should be possible to introduce sufficient poison to the target building to achieve the desired result. A plot of this kind was foiled in 2002 when four Moroccans were arrested in Rome in possession of deadly chemicals and maps of the city's water-system marking the US embassy.

7.2.19 Bacterial attack
Deadly bacteria can be introduced into a building through a variety of means. It can be spread throughout a mechanically vented building by contaminating the air supply, perhaps simply by the external air intake. Food and drink supplies, whether to canteens, vending machines or coffee trolleys, can be poisoned at any stage in the supply process. The water supply may be contaminated as above, or the mail system can be used to deliver the bacteria (this can also be used more crudely to deliver, say, broken razor blades). The efficacy of this last method was demonstrated in the spate of anthrax-carrying letters received at a range of premises in the weeks following the September 11 attacks in America, which caused distress and disruption well above and beyond the actual casualties caused, serious as they were.

7.2.20 Infrastructure
Although not directed specifically against the building to be protected, attacks on national infrastructure may nevertheless undermine the building's operational efficiency. Electricity, water and fuel supplies are all vulnerable to interruption, as they can be safely and easily disrupted, being so obvious and too widespread to be properly defended.

7.3 New developments
The events of September 11 brought the deliberate targeted crashing of a hijacked aircraft to the fore as a very effective means of causing enormous damage, loss of life and disruption to civil life. The World Trade Center towers actually seem to have absorbed the initial impact damage quite effectively, only to succumb to the effects of the intense fire fueled by thousands of gallons of aviation spirit. It is likely that techniques of design and construction

will be developed to minimize this risk as the analysis of the incidents progresses, but for now they lie outside the scope of this study. But this example illustrates the fact that over the lifetime of a building new weapons will come into use and techniques of attack will alter. The nature of the threat will change according to new circumstances, and new threatening groups will arise as old ones change their character or fade from the scene. Global, national and political events will create new and unforeseeable problems.

7.4 Information gathering
The planning and effective perpetration of an attack on a building will, to a great extent, depend on good intelligence acquisition. Thus protecting such information as may be protected that would be useful to a potential attacker is an important part of the defensiveprocess. Such information might include the following:

- Local topography and policing;
- Structural, mechanical and electrical details;
- Layout;
- Operation;
- Furniture and fittings;
- Security measures;
- Contingency plans;
- Details of staff and their families;
- Office and staff vehicles;
- Suppliers of services (maintenance, office materials, caterers and so on).

7.5 Threat assessment
Not all threats will be applicable to any particular building. Only a few buildings can be turned into fortresses and rarely would it be appropriate for

them to be. Nevertheless, the possibility of threats arising against a building and its staff must be considered by a responsible management. The process of determining how at risk a building may be, and the relative likelihood of particular forms of attack being made is complex and ultimately imprecise. A series of threat assessments may be necessary to inform the decision making process concerning the nature of the risk to the building in question. Specialist advice may be necessary for this to be effective.

In the current international security situation a wide-range of buildings, perhaps even all buildings, have to be seen to be subject to the terrorist threat. An extended pecking-order of the more at-risk among them might include the following:

- Political/military/diplomatic facilities;
- Nuclear facilities;
- Flag-carrier companies;
- Large multinationals;
- Media/cultural facilities;
- Strategic infrastructure (utilities/bridges/railways/motorways/ports/airports);
- Other expatriate companies;
- Other large companies;
- Medium/small organizations.

In the process of determining the proper response to that threat there will inevitably be a balancing of the probability of any particular form of attack occurring with the costs of taking any action to ameliorate its effects. Possible outcomes of the threat-assessment process will come from among the following options:

Threat assessment 157

1. No action necessary
2. Improve the existing building's security
3. Move to another, already existing building
4. Move to a purpose-built building

Of course within any one of 2, 3 or 4 there will still be a wide range of possible choices which will be informed by the threat assessment (for instance, taking a few low-cost steps to improve the current building's security versus taking a range of substantial and expensive measures). The threat assessment would sensibly be included in any feasibility study conducted into a building project. Because of the sensitivity of the issues and the disproportionately serious consequences of taking the wrong decision, the threat assessments (with their consequent building and operational costs, which will help to inform the choice above) should be made and agreed at the appropriately senior management level. Advice may be sought from a number of quarters, such as local police forces, home embassies if overseas, as well as specialist operators in the field. Representatives of the individual design disciplines involved in preparing the feasibility study should be selected for their experience and awareness of the specifics of designing to improve the security of a building and mitigate the effects of terrorist or insurgency action. Most competent designers will have a sound appreciation of the problems as they affect their particular discipline, but consideration should be given to the appointment of an appropriate building security expert who will have an understanding of the overall picture and manage the process accordingly.

7.6 Combating the threat

An existing building designed to cope with its own weight, the weight of fittings, furniture and occupants, as well as the forces associated with wind and earthquake (where appropriate), depending on local building codes and practices, levels of corruption and so on, may provide an unexpected level of resistance against attack. The weather cladding and standard doors and windows will keep out casual intruders and provide some privacy to the occupants but will not cope with many forms of terrorist assault. In many cases it will not be possible to strengthen buildings to cope with the most serious forms of attack because of their location and the need to keep any construction work within a sensible budget and program. Nevertheless, there are many measures which can be taken to make life more difficult for the potential attacker, perhaps to defeat the efforts of the less organized and committed group or individual and to ameliorate to some degree the effects of any actual attack that may occur.

7.6.1 Large vehicle stand-off bomb

There are two elements to any possible action in this case: keeping the stand-off distance large by making it difficult for the bomber to leave a bomb in a suitable location; and limiting the effects of the bomb should it explode at a range.

Firstly, efforts can be made to secure the perimeter of the site in order to keep the bomb-carrying vehicle away from the buildings. It may be possible where the site and budget allows to build a substantial surrounding wall. Any such wall, new or existing, can be made more secure against bomb attack by fitting entry points with high-as-wall robust gates. Access to the gate can be controlled with chicanes constructed of robust materials - for example, sand-filled oil-drums - forcing attacking vehicles to slow down, thus making it more difficult for them to circumvent security measures. In some circumstances a temporary site closure can be achieved with a heavy vehicle which can be parked across the gate. Earth banks or berms can be constructed on the inner-side to prevent vehicle penetration.

The attempt to keep potential bomb-carrying vehicles away from the site can be assisted by parking controls, so negotiations should be undertaken with the local authorities to ban parking adjacent to the site in high-risk cases, or to build high central reservations in roads opposite the entrances. The Slovakian authorities have recently been very helpful to the US embassy in Bratislava, closing the street to traffic and allowing unsightly concrete barricades in a visually sensitive area to assist with security. This, however, should be seen as an exceptional case and will frequently not be an option for non-governmental buildings.

Mitigation of the effects of the possible explosion in the building itself can be achieved by a variety of measures. Layout is a key element in this that is open to improvement, so the offices should be arranged so that the least important functions, store rooms and so on, should occupy the area facing the likely direction of attack and, conversely, the most important offices should be located as far from the attack and as high up the building as possible.

A competent authority should determine the location of any strong zones in the building to which staff can retreat in the case of an alarm being given. The possibility of improving the security of such a zone should be considered, perhaps by the blocking of windows or putting in new doors.

Windows are a weak point in building's exterior and the flying shards of glass they produce provide their own contribution to the injurious effects of any explosion. Amenity-value means that windows are typically larger than strictly necessary, so it may be possible to reduce their size, and change their position. It may be possible to fit blast-resistant glazing, but it is prohibitively expensive for most situations. Plastic film can be attached to ordinary glass windows to lessen the likelihood of splintering from blast and should be used in conjunction with specially manufactured net curtains designed to billow out and contain large pieces of imploding glass. It has to be said that the range of circumstance in which these measures make a substantial difference to the outcome are limited.

There needs to be a clear policy on evacuation in the case of a bomb threat and this has to be very carefully considered as staff may be safer inside the building than outside.

7.6.2 Smaller vehicle bomb close to building
Much of what was written above concerning the perimeter applies equally in this case, but it should be stressed that at close range, as the distance between the building and the explosion decreases, the damage increases exponentially and so the more vital becomes every millimeter of stand-off that can be achieved. Thus parking against or near the building should be banned if at all possible. Concrete planting boxes or robust posts at the sidewalk's edge will assist with maintaining a minimum standoff.

Again, one way of controlling the damage done by a bomb is to pay attention to the arrangement of functions within the building, with the likely desired targets of an assault to be positioned in the most protected zones of the building, swapping their locations with less high-value targets such as stores and plant or infrequently used offices.

7.6.3 Proxy vehicle bomb
Protection against the delivery of an explosive device by proxy has two elements. Firstly, security procedures at the site should be made as effective

as possible with the resources available and directed equally at staff vehicles as against visitors. Thus, where car-parking areas are maintained, safe car-search areas should be provided at the entrances to the site, along with necessary search equipment such as mirrors, lights and endoscopes and staff trained in their use. The second element is less resource dependent. Staff should be encouraged and trained in the inspection of their own vehicles and should keep their vehicles as secure as possible so that they are less likely to become the unwitting deliverers of a weapon. Chauffeurs should remain with their vehicles whenever they are outside a safe area, reducing the opportunities for a bomb to be attached. The hostage-leveraged proxy-bomb is more difficult to combat but home security is an issue that should be raised with staff. The best way to keep the building secure from this sort of attack is to keep all vehicles at a distance from the building and especially not under it.

7.6.4 Under-site bomb
Placing a bomb under the building is one effective way to increase the damage caused and it also has the advantage to the attacker that it allows the bomb to be placed close to the structure while avoiding conventional security. To combat this approach the space under the building has to be considered as another part of the site that has to be controlled and secure. This will require a survey and any utility suppliers should be consulted to aid with this. Where pipes and tunnels exist, they should be closed off where possible and those that are necessary secured with grills and/or locks, as appropriate. Inspection procedures and supervision should be instituted (avoiding a pattern in any such inspections). CCTV surveillance may be considered.

7.6.5 Parcel bombs
Approaches to dealing with parcel bombs will vary enormously according to perceived risk and available resources. At the more extreme end a post-room remote from other offices can be equipped with devices to investigate conventionally delivered packages, ranging from metal-detectors to X-ray machines to chemical sniffers. Parcels can be opened in a blast-resistant container in a fume cabinet to minimize the effect of any explosion, which will, typically, be fairly limited in its scope, killing or maiming the opener rather than causing large numbers of casualties or seriously damaging the building. If affordable, a security guard can search all bags to limit the chances of a visitor bringing the device in themselves rather than relying on the postal system.

Combating the threat

Clearly this sort of approach is not feasible in most circumstances, and so effective procedures, training and awareness have to substitute for the equipment. Advice should be sought from the police but UK government guidelines note the following as general risk factors when handling deliveries:

- Discolouration, crystals, strange odors or oily stains;
- Powder or powder-like residue;
- Excessive tape or string;
- Unusual size or weight given size;
- Postmark that does not match return address;
- Restrictive endorsements such as 'personal' or 'confidential';
- Excessive postage;
- Handwritten, block-printed or poorly typed addresses;
- Incorrect titles;
- Title but no name;
- No return address;
- Addressed to individual no longer with organization.

One straightforward way of making life difficult for the would-be bomber in any building is to make sure the public areas, including the toilets, are of clean, simple design, and are supervised and kept tidy and free from clutter. The goal being to make obvious anything that should not be there and to minimize the hiding places available for the small hand-delivered explosive device. To this end too, window sills, both inside and out, should be steeply sloped to prevent packages being deposited on them. An aware receptionist can be a highly effective first line of defense.

7.6.6 Thrown bombs and hand grenades

Any windows that could be attacked by this mode should be protected. This might mean locking them shut, or at least limiting the possible opening to only a narrow crack. The glass can be covered with plastic film to make it harder for a thrown device to break through and limit the amount of flying glass in the case of an explosion. Windows can also be shielded with closely-spaced bars or metal screening. Such screens should have only vertical bars on order to counter bombs with attached hooks. Ordinary double-glazing provides some measure of protection, effectively resisting at least a single thrown object.

7.6.7 Evacuation attack

In the case of an emergency the actual process of evacuation can expose staff to greater risk than remaining in the offices thus the decision has to be taken with care. Ideally the evacuation route will be closely controlled with CCTV, locks and frequent inspection to lessen the chances of it being booby-trapped. It should be kept clear of potential hiding-places for individuals or packages for the same reason. In the case of an evacuation being necessary, the gathering area used by the evacuees should be screened from outside sight and where this is not possible the risk to staff that is posed by being concentrated together in an unprotected place should be lessened by simply taking the names of the evacuees and then having them disperse.

7.6.8 Rocket-propelled grenade

An RPG round, having been designed to deal with military armored vehicles, will penetrate most forms of construction. Fire extinguishers should be readily available (which there should be regardless, though at risk premises should consider increasing numbers) to deal with any blaze which may follow such an attack.

VIPs' cars are very vulnerable to RPGs and any vehicle hit is likely to be destroyed. Therefore avoiding being targeted is the only sure protection, so varying routes and times of journeys is one simple step that can be taken. Swift entry to the site, and concealment of car-parking and transfer on the site is another way of making things difficult for the attacker.

A building can be given some measure of protection from the RPG by anti-rocket screening - heavy metal netting suspended in front of the building with separation of about 1m from the walls. The idea behind the 'Kremlin' netting,

Combating the threat

as it is known, is either that the grenade is triggered by the netting, causing it to detonate before it hits the wall, or it renders the firing mechanism inoperative. This is expensive, difficult to fit, unsightly and very unlikely to be acceptable in a civilian building.

7.6.9 Mortar attack
Little can be done to protect against heavy mortar attack without strengthening the roof and attic floor construction. This may not be feasible from an engineering point of view and would be very expensive if it could be done. Again, metal nets can be used but this may not be acceptable or appropriate in most locations. The range of up to several hundred meters makes adequate stand-off unlikely. If the bomb misses the roof, however, and explodes beside the building, the kinds of measures that would be taken against a more conventionally delivered weapon will have a similar effect.

7.6.10 Long-range sniper
This kind of attack will typically be directed against high-value targets; senior personnel of prominent organizations, visiting VIPs and so on. However, random multiple shootings do occur. The obvious rule is that if a sniper cannot see the target then they cannot shoot at it accurately. Thus controlling the risk of sniper attack is in large part about controlling lines of sight into the premises.

Potential targets are most vulnerable as they enter or exit a building, so an internal car-park (preferably not under the building given the possibility of bomb attack above) which allows VIPs to enter without being seen from outside is ideal. Alternatively some sort of covered entrance or 'port cochere' design, in which a VIP car can draw up under cover, will make them less vulnerable as they transfer from vehicle to building. Care should be taken that this does not provide access for a potential bomber. If such a structure is not possible temporary canvas screens that break lines of sight may be an option.

People are still vulnerable inside the building if they can be seen from outside. Narrow windows will help. Shutters, blinds, frosted glass or mirrored/tinted coatings on windows are another way to make life difficult for the shooter outside the building. Bullet-proof glass is an expensive option, is heavy and can be difficult to incorporate in an existing window frame without drawing attention to itself and flagging up an area as important. But it may in some circumstances be suitable for high-risk rooms.

7.6.11 Close-range gun attack
The possibilities open to a close-range assault by a gun-wielding attacker will be limited by basic security measures: separation of visitors and main office space, for example, will make it harder for the assailant to get close to their target. In high-risk situations receptionists should be protected by bullet-proof glass screens and all visitors should be subject to metal detector inspection and/or effective hand searches by security staff in an attempt to keep the gun out of the building in the first place. Garden features such as plant-covered trellises can be an attractive but unobtrusive way of interrupting lines of attack. Having secure, easily activated locks on office doors may help staff to keep safe in the event that a shooter does get into the building, if they are given some warning.

As in the case of the longer-range sniper, allowing visitors to drive into a safe zone before having to exit their vehicle will reduce their vulnerability to this form of assault during transfer to the building.

In some sites the public may have access very close to ground-floor windows, rendering any occupants of the rooms behind vulnerable to a close-range gun-attack. These windows should be either bullet-proof or non-transparent in some way (as above), or the rooms left unoccupied.

7.6.12 Drive-by gun attack
This is a much more random form of attack. If feasible a high-wall will make such an attack less effective. Any security-staff at the entrance will be most vulnerable though equally anyone entering or exiting may become a target too. Thought should be given to providing protection for staff at the door - keeping their inspection point inside rather than out for example. In extreme cases, protected enclosures may be necessary, with sandbags and so on. Staff should have a prearranged escape route to be used after sounding the alarm should they see an attack developing. Once again such an attack may be timed to coincide with a specific visitor's arrival, so protecting transfers from vehicles as above will also protect against drive-by attack.

Ground-floor offices will be particularly at risk, so windows should be privacy-screened as above, though this may afford less protection than in the case above as the shooter may not require a specific target, especially with automatic weapons. Therefore, where possible, ground-floor rooms facing the street should become store-rooms or used for purposes not involving prolonged occupation. Staff should be moved away from outer walls.

It may be useful, where possible, to manage the traffic in front of the building with chicanes, central divides, road humps and so on, with the aim of making things difficult for shooters in attacking vehicles. Even if they had little effect in case of actual attack, such visible measures may help to deter attack by giving an impression of preparedness and control.

7.6.13 Mob attack

Attack by a mob may be directed at a specific building, one which cannot hide its identity perhaps, such as an embassy or particular commercial premises, in which case there is little that can be done to stop an attack happening. But an attack may also occur more spontaneously or opportunistically, in response to some perceived provocation. This may typically result from the building being associated in some way with a particular country. Therefore one way to reduce the chances of becoming the subject of such an attack would be to avoid showing national paraphernalia such as flags. Large or well-known corporations which may generate opposition and anger due to the nature or nationality of their business might consider the prominence and location of any identifying plaques and so on. McDonalds operate everywhere as McDonalds; Walls Ice Cream operate very widely too, but under local business names, which would seem more effective at keeping a low profile, politically-speaking, while maintaining the possibility of commercial promotion.

Steps that may be taken to reduce the impact of a mob attack, should one actually occur, would include security measures like fitting robust external doors and windows, and supplying them with shutters and bars. Secure internal doors will slow down anyone who does get inside, and may keep staff safe. Even ordinary curtains on vulnerable windows will help to reduce the danger from thrown rocks. They look normal but can be closed in the event of such attack.

One of the risks of a mob attack is that it can develop into a siege. Gaps between buildings should be walled off and free-standing buildings can be provided with a wall across the site to delay encirclement. Staff should be provided with an escape route to the rear of the building, or through an adjoining building if possible. The possibility of an evacuation attack (see above) should be taken into account when deciding whether or not to evacuate, though the time available for making such a decision may be very limited.

7.6.14 Military-style occupation
Such an assault cannot be realistically defended against by anything other than a capable military force and so the security of the building is not the issue in this case. Dealing with such an attack is about managing relations with the attackers to protect the well-being of such staff as they have in their control. Therefore it is important that internal communications, staff-training and the decision-making process are adequate for a quick and safe handover of power to the invaders.

7.6.15 Kidnapping
This is an effective way for attackers to gain leverage over staff and is difficult to combat. A staff-member under compulsion may be able to circumvent many of the measures discussed so far. Agreed procedures, such as parking in specified areas or informing security, may fall down in the event of a threat to oneself or one's family. Making life difficult for kidnappers involves action well beyond the building site in question and impinges on the stuff of ordinary life. High-risk individuals will of course take specialist advice and accept a substantial imposition from security measures, but for most staff this is neither affordable nor acceptable. However, special steps that can be taken include varying times and routes of journeys. Parents might consider delivering children to and from school and everyone should have robust locks on doors and windows at home and use them. It all amounts to taking ordinary home security seriously for, beyond that, little else can be done.

7.6.16 Gas attack
The building's own ventilation system can be exploited to maximize the effects of an attack by poison gas. For this reason the air-intakes for a mechanically vented building should be carefully controlled by frequent inspection and/or CCTV. If at all possible the intakes should be relocated to a remote and high position. Remotely controlled dampers should be fitted to the air intakes so that they can be swiftly closed at need. Street disturbances not associated with the building or its occupants may be the

Combating the threat 167

source of contamination by riot-control substances such as tear gas, so such events should be carefully monitored.

Open doors and windows can also be exploited by this form of attack, especially by tear-gas type canisters. Bars and/or double-glazing should be considered for vulnerable windows. Plastic film on windows reduces the chance of penetration by a hurled canister too. Double doors reduce the risk of penetration at entrances.

The general rules on tidiness, clean lines of sight and control of visitors will help to limit an attacker's options, as it will be harder to leave gas-containers in the building without them being noticed.

7.6.17 Poisoning water supply

In this case the attacker exploits a vital service entering the building, the water supply, to introduce potentially deadly poisons into what may be otherwise secure premises. Defending against this type of assault requires it to be made more difficult for the attacker to access the water supply. Thus any stopcocks or access panels on the building's supply that lie outside the site, should be brought inside the site if at all possible. If this cannot be done then it should be requested of the water-supplier that secure locks should be placed on any access points and stopcocks and frequent inspections made.

Bottle-delivered water may also be vulnerable to tampering and contamination, especially to cooled water dispensers. Security procedures should be agreed with the supplying company, with tamper-proof seals used and so on.

7.6.18 Bacterial attack

Both the above methods - air and water supply - may also be used to deliver a bacterial weapon, and hence the approaches outlined above will be equally appropriate. But deadly bacteria may also be delivered in a variety of other ways. Any foodstuffs brought in from outside suppliers may be vulnerable to bacterial contamination, whether for canteens and dining rooms or any trolley service.

Protection against a determined attack of this kind is difficult but making sure suppliers are considering this kind of security is one thing that can be done and making any home staff involved in catering aware is also important.

Locks on refrigerators and food stores and good supervision and security in food preparation areas will hinder the efforts of those wishing to introduce a contaminant. An open kitchen door that allows access to bins or for deliveries, or simply for ventilation, is a weak-point for any infiltrator to gain access for whatever reason.

Following the attacks in the US in 2001, the most notorious way of making such an attack is to send an ordinary letter containing the bacterial agent. It is simple, effective and produces an impact out of all proportion to the actual risk posed. Thus, to avoid disruption, procedures have to be in place to deal with such an attack or suspected attack. Preventing all such letters reaching their target can only be done by opening all letters and parcels in the post-room. Staff there can be protected with the correct gloves and masks, and perhaps more serious clothing and equipment. Advice should be taken. Opening letters in a fume cupboard with external air extraction will reduce contamination risks but there should be awareness of where the air is venting to - out into a busy street would be counter productive in the event of an attack. Bio-filters may be installed but they would be expensive and may require on-site specialist maintenance.

Where staff have to open their own mail, they should be made aware of the problem and know what to do. Letters should be opened carefully with a letter opener to minimize contact with or disturbance of the contents. Envelopes should not be blown into to facilitate opening and contents should not be poured out. Hands should be kept away from the face and washed afterwards when dealing with mail.

Running through a busy office holding a suspected bacteria-contaminated package to get to the bin/bathroom/window should be avoided. It should be put down carefully and left alone. If a suitable container, such as a waste bin, is immediately to hand it could be placed in that and covered with a lightweight lid. This should be followed by the closing of windows, evacuation of the room and turning off air-circulation equipment such as air-conditioning and fans. The possibly contaminated person should keep apart from others and isolation of those from the contaminated room would also be sensible until expert advice has been taken. The rest of the building should be evacuated.

7.7 Moving to an alternative existing building

A move may be required if the building already occupied is unable to be rendered adequately secure, or if it will cost an exorbitant amount to do so. Alternatively, a move may be indicated for other reasons, perhaps the end of a lease or if more space is needed. New-build may not be available or affordable, so a different existing building must be sought. Whatever the reason for the move, security should be a consideration in the choice of the new premises.

If security is the reason for the move, the first thing to be assessed is whether or not the new premises offer an improvement. Key to this will be the availability of a greater stand-off from a potential vehicle bomb. As the device with the greatest lethal and destructive potential and one commonly used by terrorists, increasing the distance between the building and the bomb is the most effective thing to be done in protecting staff and operations. The neighbors and neighborhood and the effects on journeys by staff and visitors should be considered to ensure that the move is not increasing risk in unlooked for ways.

The availability of secure but remote parking would be an important factor informing the choice, as would the possibility of installing some means of transferring VIPs from vehicle to building out of public view.

A strong basic construction should be looked for - reinforced concrete or steel frame and reinforced concrete floors resist most attacks better than masonry wall and timber floors but the lightweight cladding on many such modern buildings may be less resistant to penetration than ordinary masonry.

The new building should have the capacity to arrange usage so that vulnerable parts of the building contain less important functions - plant rather than people, for instance - and allow effective separation of public and private areas.

In general the choice of building will be informed by the principles of the ideal model described below.

7.8 New building design considerations

What follows is a description of an ideal building from a security point of view, and as such it represents a goal that will rarely be achieved in its entirety in practice and would be only appropriate or realistic for a narrow range of circumstances - perhaps police stations in areas of political unrest, national government offices, or the embassy of a prominent (and wealthy) state. Nevertheless, the thinking informing such a response can be applied in a less complete way according to what is possible, appropriate or affordable. At its most basic the approach requires as robust an exterior as is feasible, with secure doors and windows, a separation of public and private areas and control over who and what passes from one to the other, as well as engendering a 'security mindedness' among staff.

7.8.1 The site
The first factor to consider is the site. This should ideally be large enough to allow a 40 m stand-off from any public road or unsecured adjacent lot over which a lot of the blast-effects of even quite a large bomb will be dissipated; an adequately large site will also allow for proper vehicle parking and control. It should not be overlooked in order to reduce the potential for intelligence-gathering or sniper-fire from outside. The site should not be traversed by tunnels or large drains, to prevent infiltration by attackers, or the placement of an under-site bomb. Local planning constraints should not preclude the construction of a high perimeter wall. For the sake of varying entry and granting escape, the site should be accessible by two routes.

7.8.2 The perimeter
Once a site has been chosen, securing the perimeter on the site is perhaps the most essential part of the process. This requires a robust wall, high enough to control sight-lines and robust enough to prevent a vehicle such as a heavy truck crashing through, whether to bring armed men into the compound or to deliver an explosive device. This can be achieved relatively cheaply with a comparatively light wall, preferably made of reinforced concrete. The reinforcement should be placed in each face of the concrete and overlapped to ensure that the concrete hangs together even in failure. Such a wall should then be backed on the inside by a substantial earth bank or berm. For maximum efficacy this berm should be higher than the axle of a truck (at least 1.2 m). Any truck crashing into the wall will meet an immovable vertical mass which it will not be able to climb and with suitable soft landscaping the berm can be turned into an attractive feature. Any decorative elements on the wall should not be capable of being used as climbing aids, nor should they facilitate the concealment of packages or even people, thus the wall line should be kept as clear and simple as possible to allow easy

New building design considerations

visual control from as few points as possible - for example an outward curving wall may require surveillance at either end and might still have a blind-spot at its apex, whereas a perfectly straight wall will need watching only from one point.

If allowed by the authorities the wall should be topped by devices to deter climbers, such as broken glass in mortar, metal spikes and so on. However too much trust should not be placed in such measures as a determined and trained attacker will be able to swiftly overcome them. An alternative or additional deterrent is to grow something spiky against the inner side of the wall. Bougainvillea in the right climate is appropriately difficult to penetrate but will look attractive. If the planting extends about 2 m from the base of the wall this will cause even a determined attacker to pause for consideration before leaping off the wall into the site, and may stop the more casual intruder.

All the walls should be robust enough to resist crowd pressures, as even a fairly amicable mob could become agitated if a wall they were pressing against collapsed and caused injury.

The perimeter wall should be set back from the road at vehicle entrances so that the vehicle can move off the road into the safety of the site without having to slow down too much. This is the point of maximum vulnerability: the location makes it a predictable event and the low speed makes the vehicle an easy target for an attack, whether by firearm, RPG, a lobbed bomb or hand-grenade or even the triggered detonation of a nearby vehicle bomb. Radio links to VIP cars will allow such vehicles to seep in without pausing. All gates should be as high as the perimeter wall, non-transparent, ideally of robust steel construction with hinges and fastenings of commensurate strength. A small flap, protected with heavy mesh and openable from the inside, will allow observation of the outside.

Inside each gate there should be a robust vehicle barrier set far enough back from the gate to allow the gates to shut behind an entering vehicle. The gate and barrier should be interlocked so that only one can be open at a time. This area should have side barriers to prevent the vehicle driving around the barrier: these can be formed of attractive landscaping features.

7.8.3 The layout of the site
The site should be divided into two main zones. The first zone will contain the

main site entrance, all non-VIP car-parking, stores, fuel-storage (carefully designed to prevent unauthorized use) garbage-disposal arrangements, any plant that does not have to be housed in the main building, an entry-control office, as well as a controlled staff entrance. Progress to the inner compound (for VIP vehicles only) must only be made through a vehicle air-lock, approached by a dog-leg, in which such vehicles can be searched. The airlock should have robust gates at either end, interlocked so that only one gate can be open at any one time and high reinforced concrete walls to ensure the safety of the occupants while they are searched. Access to the air-lock for searches should be from the adjacent entry-control office.

The entry-control office should be of robust construction with bullet-proof glass in the reception area. It should have robust document/parcel pass-through facilities. For visitors on foot there should be an airlock with a door at each end interlocked so that only one can be open at a time. The airlock should be controlled by the receptionist who should be able to see into it. The office should be linked to the incident-control room in the main offices so that in an emergency all the gates, doors and any barriers can be locked and only released from the main office.

If many visitors are expected, the routes through the second zone to the main office for them and the staff should be screened from each other as well as from outside the site, to reduce the risk of the interchange of weapons, or attack, or perhaps even verbal assault by annoyed visitors. Such a screen could be constructed from lightweight fencing or of hedging, and need only be about 2 m high to achieve these ends.

The second inner zone should be subdivided with a wall like that at the perimeter, arranged to delay a mob approaching from the main entrance flowing around and encircling the building. Gates in the wall should be controlled from the incident control room and be capable of sustaining the pressure that can be exerted by a mob. Emergency exits from the office should open onto the subdivision remote from the main entrance. With sensitive planting and soft landscaping all these walls can be made into attractive features avoiding any prison-like effect. A second vehicle-entrance to the site, providing an alternative route in and out, should be located in this zone. This allows VIP vehicles to vary their route, obviously according to no discernible pattern, rendering them less liable to attack as they enter or exit the site, as well as allowing evacuation in case the main entrance is blocked,

New building design considerations 173

by a mob for instance. In order that this secondary exit does not become a weak point in the site's security the gate needs to be as robust as the main gate, though it may be appropriate to dispense with the sophistication of a concealed air-lock, as this gate will not be used by the bulk of visitors. But a barrier to prevent tailgating should be incorporated in the layout, limiting the possibility that an attacking vehicle could use the access granted to a legitimate visitor to force its way in behind. No vehicle should be allowed to park against the building.

Ideally CCTV cameras should overlook at least the perimeter walls and entrances. The monitoring screens should be located in the incident control room. In terms of an 'ideal' security solution, clearly there is an option here to attempt to monitor the whole site. This obviously requires more resources both in terms of staff and equipment, but may have the downside of damaging staff-morale with its 'Big Brother' implications. Any landscaping within the site should fulfill its normal decorative function but should be considered carefully, especially as planting matures, so that it does not provide concealment for attackers.

If the site is sloping, the possibility of cutting the building, in part or in whole, into the hillside to enhance protection against all long-distance attacks should be considered. There should be no outside windows, doors or vents to any basements. Access and servicing must be provided from within the building. The building should have clean simple lines to allow easy supervision and to prevent concealment of bombs or attackers. Any projecting building elements, such as cantilevers, eaves, solar screens or verandahs should be of minimal size and lightweight construction to reduce the risk of blast-pressure concentrations. Rebates to windows or any other openings in the walls should be cut at a steep angle to prevent packages being lodged there.

7.8.4 The main building

Layout
The building should comprise three areas: the public part of the reception or waiting room; the plant rooms; and the main offices, isolated as much as possible from the other zones and accessible only after screening at reception. It may be possible to arrange the public and plant-rooms to give some protection to the offices. The structure of the public areas can be kept

separate from that of the offices and designed to vent any explosion to the outside. Security lights should be placed at a distance from the structure, facing outwards so that security guards can patrol between them and the building in the safe dark-zone. The idea is to produce an onion-type defense; if one ring fails there is another inside still to be challenged.

To limit the possibility of being targeted transferring between car and building, the VIP entrance to the office building should have a drive-in covered port cochere entrance, separate and out of sight from the public entrance.

To prevent a build up of mob-pressure, external doors should be approached via a ramp or steps set at right angles to the doors.

The reception area should maintain separation between staff and public, with a bullet-proof ceiling-high screen to the counter. The reception office should have an exit for staff from the reception zone to the main building via a very robust door, ideally placed out of sight from the public area, and capable of being locked swiftly. It should be simple enough that it can be used effectively by panicky people in a hurry. This lock should also be controllable from the incident room inside the main building. The reception area should also contain a post-room with facilities for checking suspect packages. In the light of the US anthrax attacks, all mail may have to be opened here in a secure fume-cupboard type facility.

Access from the reception area to the main building is effectively the building's last line of defense and it should therefore be impossible for anyone other than staff and cleared visitors to cross that boundary. Access should be via locking robust doors controlled by the reception staff, and this entrance should be managed either by turnstiles or by having to pass through a small air-lock with locking doors at both ends, overlooked by reception staff, interlocked so that one door cannot open until the other shuts. This is to prevent an intruder gaining access by tailgating an authorized visitor.

There should be an incident control room close to reception with CCTV monitoring, control over alarms, air-intakes (which should be placed at a high level) and able to lock all external doors.

New building design considerations 175

If there are to be no basements in the building and if protection against an unexpectedly high-level of attack is considered to be a desirable option, then a secure zone can be created cheaply in the middle of the ground-floor area. This zone could form a conference room in normal usage for example. It would be protected from above and below by the structure's reinforced concrete floors and by the reinforced concrete walls of the surrounding corridors and outside walls. Windowless and provided with a very robust door, this would provide a secure staff refuge for a limited period of time. Keeping it stocked with water and providing at least some sort of toilet facilities in case of emergency would be sensible. It would be sensible to site the Incident Control Room here as it should be located where it is best placed to survive an attack.

Staff security can also be enhanced by providing all offices with robust doors with quick and easy locking mechanisms. They should also have silent alarms connected to the incident control room in addition to an internal voice alarm system. Staff need to be able to inform the control room of a threat and be informed by them.

The structure
The ideal form of construction to mitigate the effects of attack may be more expensive than a conventional structure but it is inherently so robust that it may prove attractive nevertheless. This is the in situ (poured in place rather than formed from pre-cast units, so that the joints are as strong as the rest of it) reinforced concrete egg-crate design. In this approach all external walls and roofs are designed to either totally survive the maximum feared bomb-blast, or to fail in terms of deflection and cracking while still protecting the occupants. This means that the building will either remain totally serviceable in structural terms, or else it will become unserviceable but in such a way as the safety of the occupants is not threatened. The bullet-resistance of reinforced concrete floors also means that higher offices gain some protection from ground-level shooters due to the trajectory imposed on them.

It should be noted that this structure does not have to have a concrete blockhouse appearance as conventional cladding can be incorporated to provide weather tightness, a suitably attractive design and to disguise the building's defenses.

Unfortunately, walls usually have to have holes made in them and, for security purposes, the design of the windows is a key problem, since what is most desirable is directly contradictory to what is most safe. Windows can be seen through, shot through and are vulnerable to blast damage but, in most office buildings, good-sized windows are considered an almost essential amenity. Although blast-proof windows or windows combined with blast-resistant louvers are available, they are prohibitively expensive for general use. Thus, while they may be specified in this ideal situation, in most cases some alternative approach must be found. Cheaper and less resistant glazing is available but, in the case of a failure, the danger to occupants from high-velocity glass particles is very real.

One method of limiting the risk posed by the weak point caused by a window is to fit narrow vertical windows. With such a design it is easier to move desks and seats out of line of the window, making it more difficult to see in and lessening the area vulnerable to flying glass in the event of an explosion, while still maintaining a degree of amenity value. In more vulnerable locations, such as ground-floor back of sidewalk situations, high-level narrow horizontal windows, while less pleasing, retain the office's access to natural light. In extreme situations it may be necessary to sacrifice the amenity value and eliminate the windows all together. External doors should open into a lobby substantially greater in cross section than the door itself, to form an airlock and to spread the blast should the outer door fail. Both inner and outer doors should berobust and the locks controlled from the incident room.

For effective long-term operation some degree of flexibility must be designed into a building but all internal walls which could be considered permanent, such as those to stairwells, corridors, toilets and some offices, should be built of in situ reinforced concrete and tied into the external walls and reinforced concrete floors. Typically, main reinforcing bars are laid in one face of concrete floors and beams, providing strengthening against the vertical loading induced by gravity and wind; but adding another layer of reinforcing bars at the other face is relatively cheap and helps to counteract the tensile stresses caused by blast imposing upward pressure on a floor. Additional reinforcing to the linkage of column and beam will help to reduce the risk of collapse.

Since it is possible to target even quite a high roof with a mortar bomb it is important to maintain the strong outer shell at this location too, so the roof should also be constructed of in situ reinforced concrete. To increase its resistance to mortar attack the roof should be made up of a double layer; the first acting as a burster-plate, detonating the bomb, the second containing the blast and any debris from the first layer. In cases where it is necessary to contain plant inside the main building, the plant room can act as this double layer. Access for maintenance, however, should be possible from the outside without going through the building.

This method of constructing a building so that it comprises a series of robust, reinforced concrete boxes has the additional benefit that if an attack should occur that exceeds the planned - for level of threat and an explosion does take place somewhere inside the building, the structure may be able to contain the problem, leaving the bulk of the building unaffected.

7.9 Operations

The most secure building design will be severely compromised by ineffective operation; and conversely a building designed with little or no thought for security may be made much more secure if operated in an effectively security-minded fashion.

The finest lock on a door is useless if it is not locked. Therefore, step one is to keep possible entries to the building locked when not in use and actually to use all security measures that are available, such as alarms and so on.

The access and movement of visitors must be controlled, so that they cannot make an attack on staff directly, leave a dangerous device or gather intelligence. Thus buildings that do not need public access should grant entry only to visitors vouched for by staff. This may mean waiting outside or in a secure reception area. Visitors should be logged in and out and carry a badge showing their status. Where possible, clear zoning should be established, with rules about who is allowed where that are adhered to.

To limit the risk posed by staff members, a vetting procedure should be carried out where feasible. At the very least references should be sought and checked out for all staff, however casual.

People from suppliers and maintenance companies provide another possible method of ingress for the attacker or intelligence-gatherer, therefore the number of companies dealt with should be limited, references sought and relationships developed. A request to deal with the same individuals each visit makes the process easier and changes can then be checked.

The attacker or intruder will be less effective if they do not know the layout of the building, therefore architectural plans should be controlled as far as is possible and staff should be made aware of the risk-factor in disseminating knowledge about the building.

Staff records should be kept secure; the more an attacker knows about staff the easier it is to arrange deception, kidnapping and so on. All data should be kept secure and backed-up remotely and securely to allow the speedy resumption of operations in case of loss of data for any reason.

The building should be kept tidy and well-maintained. Back-up supplies of water and provision of a generator, where appropriate, will reduce the impact of a loss of services.

Emergency plans should be developed and staff should be trained in what to do in the event of an emergency. They should know where to go, how to evacuate, how to deal with fire, suspect parcels and so on. Practice should be regular to keep the training effective.

Such plans should be made in conjunction with local emergency services such as the police and the fire brigade. Liaison should also be made and maintained with the local embassy in the case of overseas locations.

7.10 Attack reaction

An Incident Control Officer (ICO) should be appointed, with two designated deputies to cover absences. There should also be three designated search wardens for each floor - more in the case of particularly large offices.

The ICO will assess the situation initially and then inform staff of the appropriate response; start searches in the case of a bomb-warning or lock doors in case of an intruder, for example. To this end an effective public address system is important.

In the case of an alarm being given, all staff should search their own offices and floor wardens should also search their part of the escape route. When the ICO is satisfied that the escape route is clear, floor wardens commence the evacuation and check that their floor is clear. They also make sure those with special needs receive assistance.

Floor wardens list their colleagues at the collection point and coordinate with the ICO. If the area is not secure they disperse the staff.

The policy on a military style takeover must be quite clear. Resistance is likely to be futile and dangerous so there must be some prepared method of surrendering control, ordering staff to unlock doors and so on to ensure as peaceful a hand over as possible.

7.11 Procuring advice

Police forces in many countries will offer advice on crime prevention, including terrorist crime in many cases. However, at the level of professional architecture and engineering, designing in building security beyond the demands of ordinary crime has been given limited attention up to now apart from some very obvious high-risk targets. But there has been a vast increase in awareness of the problem and a demand for information and advice following the events of September 11, 2001.

Conventional advice still holds true however: having and reviewing contingency plans for what to do with people, data and products in case of an emergency; training staff to carry out security procedures; and controlling access to the building can be effective ways of limiting the likelihood or effectiveness of a terrorist attack. Effective staff-training and the upkeep of that training, is key, and a trained and aware receptionist is a significant resource in security terms that even the smallest of offices can deploy.

Nevertheless, faced with the extended possibility of a range of terrorist attacks, all organizations should now consider designing their facilities to aid security, in the case of new-build or adapting existing premises. There are some private companies involved in the latter business, often with ex-army or ex-police staff, which can offer advice from an operations point of view.

However, to arrive at an effective new building solution, the client should appoint a professional building security adviser to their in-house team at the earliest possible moment. Such a figure can advise on any feasibility studies to be carried out and on the preparation of the initial design briefs and selection of consultants. They should keep at least a watching brief on the project during design development and construction to ensure the integrity of the security philosophy.

CHAPTER 8: BEST PRACTICES FOR RESPONSE TO TERRORIST ATTACKS

8.1	Pre-event planning	183
8.2	Components common to all terrorist responses	184
8.3	Components specific to different types of terrorist attack	190
8.4	Summary of basic steps in response	206

CHAPTER 8: BEST PRACTICES FOR RESPONSE TO TERRORIST ATTACKS

Terrorism is both a state and a federal crime. However, all incidents are manifested locally, and initial reaction to them will be provided by local crisis and consequence organizations. When these incidents are large, they will involve multiple organizations. Therefore, both in the planning and response phases, local crisis and consequence personnel must interact with external entities with, in some cases, broader authority over the incident, and in other cases, with near equal power but radically different mission, operational procedures, perceptions, and cultures. They must operate with political crisis managers and co-response organization from a unified command structure. Maniscalco, PM, and Christen, HT, *Understanding terrorism and managing the consequences*, Upper Saddle River, NJ: Prentice Hall, 2002, p12.

This chapter outlines practical steps that responders may undertake before, during, and after a terrorist attack and focuses on necessary actions when an event has occurred. It discusses generic response capabilities that can be applied regardless of the type of incident as well as special responses needed in the event of a large-scale or exotic attack.

8.1 Pre-event planning

Pre-event planning is essential to any terrorist response structure. Three aspects are especially important: the creation of single incident management and command systems; the appropriate identification of specialized response capabilities; and the institution of protocols for sharing intelligence information.

8.1.1 Creation of Single Incident Management and Command Systems

When a large number of responding organizations must function together under conditions of extreme stress, it is critical for a familiar working relationship to be established before an incident occurs. The best way to achieve this is to conduct planning and training within a single Incident Management System/Incident Command System (IMS/ICS) that has clearly defined and agreed roles and responsibilities. In the absence of such a framework, the consequence manager may find it difficult to administer an incident effectively, particularly when a large unified command structure is required. Past terrorist attacks have demonstrated that events can pose challenges in terms of scale, duration and range of hazards. It is therefore critical that all response entities are fully familiar with one another's protocols and Standard Operating Procedures (SOPs).

8.1.2 The identification of specialized response capabilities
Terrorist attacks can cover the entire scale from suicide bombings and anthrax hoaxes, to large-scale bombings and chemical attacks. The varied and unpredictable nature of these events makes it unlikely that any one locality, regardless of its size and resources, will be completely prepared for all eventualities. During planning, therefore, relevant officials need to identify where special capabilities exist - locally, regionally or nationwide - for dealing with particular threat scenarios, including:

- Tactical operational teams capable of responding to terrorists armed with sophisticated weapons;

- Hazardous materials (HAZMAT) teams capable of containing large-scale or localized chemical or biological contamination;

- Emergency management teams capable of triaging, treating andtransporting large numbers of patients with unusual injuries;

- Search and rescue teams capable of responding to structural collapses.

8.1.3 Information/intelligence sharing
A final consideration in preparing for possible terrorist incidents is to ensure that local emergency managers are able to receive threat information from federal or national intelligence agencies. Whenever possible, mechanisms should be in place to expedite the clearing of these individuals, allowing them to receive classified data that can then be `scrubbed' and appropriately disseminated to responders on the ground.

8.2 Components common to all terrorist responses
Regardless of scale, duration and type of contingency being addressed, several features are common to all types of terrorist response actions.

8.2.1 The incident management system
Establishing a single incident management system is a key aspect of preplanning for any response to a terrorist incident; it is also a vital element in

any action that is subsequently initiated. An IMS is usually created to coordinate response actions by standardizing terminology, resource allocations, support functions and chains of command. The system typically begins with an incident manager and consists of secondary supporting liaison, safety and public information officers who oversee and direct four main functional areas:

- Operations, which include such things as mass casualty emergency management response, fire/rescue activities, public health operations, tactical law enforcement and HAZMAT actions;

- Logistics, which are generally concerned with supporting and servicing response teams on the ground;

- Planning, which normally entails the development of an Incident Action Plan (IAP) and the gathering and dissemination of data to avail decision-making;

- Administration, which is mostly concerned with finance, time keeping and worker's compensation units.

8.2.2 Integrated leadership at the scene

Because terrorist incidents typically necessitate a large contingency of police, fire/rescue and emergency management personnel - each with their own chain of command - mechanisms need to be in place to establish a system of integrated leadership at the scene of the attack. In certain localized cases, it may be sufficient to have the ranking law enforcement officer acting as sole incident manager, with emergency personnel and fire/rescue representatives operating at the branch level. More complex, large-scale contingencies, however, often require the establishment of a unified joint management team based out of a single command vehicle or Emergency Operations Center (EOC). Responsibility for the establishment of these integrated leadership posts generally falls to the planning section of the IMS.

8.2.3 Co-ordination with the military

In many instances, the IMS may co-ordinate with the military to facilitate response actions. In these cases, the armed forces would normally be incorporated under an on-site unified management and command structure with access to issues, communications and plans. At the operational level, the military can work as a separate branch in its own right or as part of existing search, rescue, medical and emergency management teams. With respect to logistics and communications, however, the army's role is generally executed separately, although supplies equipment and facilities can be made available for both civilian and military responders.

In the United States, cooperation between the IMS and the military has been greatly availed by the fact that both act according to largely similar command and control systems. This has minimized the danger of conflicting actions resulting from unknown or unfamiliar terminology, particularly at the sectional level. The US military delineates the IMS command functions in the following manner:

> S-1: administration
> S-2: intelligence
> S-3: plans and operations
> S-4: supplies and logistics.

8.2.4 Resource requirements

Regardless of the overall response framework, only equipment and supplies that are immediately available can be delivered to the scene right after an event. Terrorism response therefore requires a `push logistics' system to transport additional material such as:

- Personal Protective Equipment (PPE): protective suits and respiratory equipment for all response personnel, bulletproof vests for law enforcement;

- Decontamination equipment: Tyvek suits for patients, red bags (used to contain potentially infectious material), cleaning equipment, privacy shelters, run-off control materials, and decontamination showers;

- Medications: drugs such as atropine, antidotes, and vaccines;

- Morgue materials: body bags, collection bags, and tags;

- Medical supplies: oxygen, ventilators, intravenous (IV) tubes, airway adjuncts, basic life support (BLS) trauma supplies, and disposable litters;

- Crime scene supplies: evidence bags, film, tags, forms, perimeter control;

- Detection equipment: gas and liquid sampling equipment, chemical, biological and radiological detection kits;

- Communications equipment: radios, cell and satellite telephones;

- Vehicles: ground and air evacuation, trucks to carry supplies, refrigerated trucks for medicines and potentially infectious bodies.

These supplies should be prepackaged and stored for rapid deployment. Plastic nesting boxes are especially useful in this regard, as they are easy to load, lightweight, and highly transportable. If material has a limited shelf-life, it is vital that it is checked and, if necessary, replaced at standard intervals to ensure that it is ready when needed. While localities may not be able to purchase and store all of the necessary supplies and equipment to protect an entire population, the logistics branch should ensure that there are at least enough medications and PPE on hand for first responders and mutual aid personnel. If these individuals are not adequately protected, the remaining population will be at far greater risk.

8.2.5 Initial actions
Initial reports of a terrorist event are unlikely to be accurate; therefore first responders must mentally prepare themselves for a variety of scenarios. At the beginning there are many unknowns and the attack may in fact be in motion as medical, search and rescue units arrive. The scene may be a 'hot zone' contaminated with chemical, biological or radiological material. Individuals may still be firing weapons (on both sides) and partially exploded devices, secondary devices or booby traps, fires, collapsed structures may also be extant. When a responder arrives, therefore, they should attempt to take in and evaluate the entire scene before attempting to focus on his/her specific area of expertise.

If a secondary device is found or suspected, everyone within a 1,000 ft radius should be immediately evacuated. If the scene is still 'active', first responders should retreat to a safe distance or, at the very least, seek shelter behind solid objects until the situation settles down. If the event is non-violent or in a post-incident phase, a Forward Boy Line (FBL) should be erected to define the boundaries of the contaminated area and initial triage efforts should be instituted. Once immediate medical issues have been attended to, the focus should be on establishing an IMS to manage and integrate on-going response actions.

Safety is of paramount concern in the early stages of a terrorist incident and should be based on the '2 in 2 out' protocol established under the US Occupational Health and Safety Administration (OHSA). This requires that two responders enter an emergency zone together, remain in contact with each other and exit at the same time while two additional personnel provide constant external backup and support. Alternatively, responders could usefully practice the LACES principle, which is based on the following five precepts:

- Lookout: a person is assigned responsibility for surveying the scene from a distance and warning responders of any imminent danger;

- Awareness: all responders remain cognizant of their situational surrounds and stand ready to react to unexpected developments;

- Communications: an effective communications channel is established between all responders that includes both direct voice and hand signals as well as portable radios;

- Escape: an evacuation route is mapped out before entry to any unstable area;

- Safety zones: a secure area is established to provide distance, shielding and upwind protection from the incident site.

All terrorism incidents, regardless of size, are crime scenes. Therefore, in addition to other considerations, initial actions must take account of establishing a valid chain of custody to secure potential evidence that can be used in court. These include such things as firearms, tools, written communications, bullets, shell casings, cigarette butts, clothes, bomb fragments, chemical containers, blood, hair, tissue, fingerprints, tire traces and footprints, among others. First responders should log observations as soon as possible and communicate the location of weapons, devices and suspects to the incident manager or law enforcement branch immediately. Just as importantly, they should exercise care to not taint evidence on the ground by observing the following guidelines and procedures:

- Do not touch evidence if possible;

- If evidence must be moved for tactical reasons, note, log and, where practical, photograph the original location;

- Avoid evidence contamination by establishing a single path through the scene for responders;

- Minimize the number of personnel working on site;

- Check shoes for imbedded evidence.

8.2.6 Scene control
Scene control is necessary both to prevent civilians and the media from congregating at an incident site and to allow for established entry points where response personnel and units can log in for tracking purposes. The erection of a secure perimeter around a terrorist attack area should be instituted as quickly as possible and, to the extent that it is feasible, minimized in geographic scope so as not to unduly drain the resources of law enforcement.

One component of scene control that often presents unique problems pertains to media regulation. Because freedom of the press is an intrinsic value common to most liberal democracies, newspaper and television crews have to be given access to terrorist incident scenes. However, in allowing such latitude there is always the danger that irresponsible or inaccurate reporting will work to hamper the effectiveness of rescue operations, heighten public anxiety or otherwise feed terrorists' sense of self-achievement. Managing media activities at the scene of a major disaster can, thus, emerge as a somewhat vexing issue. Several possible solutions can be advanced to address this dilemma:

- The formation of a media pool that can be escorted on a supervised tour of cleared areas by the IMS safety officer and law enforcement;

- The establishment of media protocols based on voluntary reporting guidelines;

- The institution of a Joint Information Center (JIC) to disseminate accurate, consistent, timely and easy to understand information for the general well-being of the community. In the United States, JICs form a pivotal point of information following a major disaster and act to collate data from the White House Press Office, the Public Affairs Officers (PAOs) from involved agencies at the Federal Emergency Management Administration (FEMA) headquarters and the Disaster Field Office (DFO).

8.3 Components specific to different types of terrorist attack

8.3.1 Conventional attacks
In the case of routine incidents or small mass casualty events, an incident manager would follow the protocols outlined above without a written plan (although they may utilize an incident checklist as an aid). In response to a conventional explosive that affected more than one or two people, triage, treatment and transport would normally be sector operations under the lead of an emergency management branch director. If more than a few people were injured, several units typically would be committed to patient treatment and evacuation (ground and/or air ambulances). In these instances, the transport sector would coordinate with medical control to determine which medical facilities are appropriate and ready to receive patients. Simultaneously, the fire rescue and law enforcement branches would work to suppress fires, rescue trapped individuals, secure the site and process crime scene evidence. Few terrorist events are small enough to allow one person to coordinate all response actions single handedly. Therefore, early in the process, a safety officer should also be identified to provide additional guidance and direction.

8.3.2 Large-scale incidents

In an average response, essential (if not all) resources generally are available. In major complex and protracted events, however, the logistical needs expand exponentially. Radio and other communications networks fail or require expansion and vehicles must have sufficient fuel on hand. Medical supplies are quickly depleted and lights are needed at night. In addition, hazardous materials, health and public works branches are almost always required on site. There is also the added demand for crew rehabilitation, food and water, sleeping facilities, sanitation measures and mental health counseling.

Because of the complexity, duration and sheer amount of resources and personnel needed to respond to a major incident, a written IAP is generally required. These plans are important in that they allow others to understand the complexity of a particular situation and contribute in areas where they can make the biggest impact. When a response lasts more than 12 hours, an IAP is normally written, briefed and distributed to operational shifts in the guise of functionally specific checklists. In the US, these documents take the following form:

ICS 200, IAP Cover: documents the actions developed by the Command, specifies the control objectives, tactics to meet the objectives, resources, organization, communications plan, medical plan and other appropriate information for use in field operations.

ICS 201, Incident Briefing: provides the Command with basic information regarding the incident situation and the resources allocated to the incident and serves as a permanent record of the initial response. The ICS 201 form is prepared by field command for presentation to the IMT along with a more detailed oral briefing.

ICS 202, Incident Objectives: describes the basic incident strategy and control objectives for use during each operational period, includes information on safety and weather. The ICS 202 form is completed by the Planning Section and approved by Command in conjunction with the Objectives Meeting.

ICS 203/207, Organizational Assignment List/Organization Chart: provides information on the response organization and personnel staffing including branch directors and division/group supervisors. The ICS 203/207 forms are prepared and maintained by the Resource Unit under the direction of the Planning Section Chief and updated when the number of personnel assigned to the incident increases or decreases or a change in assignment occurs.

ICS 204, Field Assignment List: informs Operations Section personnel of incident assignments and transmits this data to field command and appropriate members of the IMT. The ICS 204 form is prepared under direction of the Planning Section Chief using guidance from ICS Form 202, ICS Form 215 and Operations Section Chief.

ICS 205, Incident Radio Communications Plan: provides information on the assignments for all communications equipment for each operational period. Information from the Incident Communications Plan on frequency assignments can be placed on the appropriate Field Assignment form (ICS Form 204). The ICS 205 form is prepared by the Communications Unit Leader.

ICS 206, Medical Plan: provides information on incident medical aid stations, transportation services, hospitals and medical emergency procedures. The ICS 206 form is prepared by the Medical Unit Leader and reviewed by the Safety Officer.

ICS 209, Incident Status Summary: summarizes incident information for IMT members and external parties and provides data to the Information Officer for preparation of media releases. The ICS 209 is prepared by the Situation Unit and updated at intervals set by the Command or Planning Section Chief. The form is distributed to the Command, Planning Section Unit Leaders, the Joint Information Center (or PIO, if no JIC is established) and external parties. It is also posted in the Incident Situation Display located at the EOC.

ICS Form 211 Check-In/Out List: delineates personnel and equipment arriving at or departing from various incident locations, including staging areas, security posts, base camps, heli-bases, and the FCP and ICP. Managers at these locations record the information and give it to the Resource Unit as soon as possible.

ICS Form 213, General Message: records incoming messages that cannot be orally transmitted to the intended recipients; transmits EOC and other incident personnel messages via radio or telephone to the addressee; sends any message or notification to incident personnel, which require hard-copy delivery. The ICS 213 form can be initiated by Incident dispatchers or any other relevant personnel. One copy should be sent and one copy retained by the person who initiates the message.

ICS Form 214, Unit Log: records details of unit activity including specialized team activity (for example, Strike Team). ICS 214 is initiated and maintained by Command, field command, and Unit Leaders. Completed logs are forwarded to supervisors who provide copies to the Documentation Unit.

ICS Form 215 Operational Planning Worksheet: communicates the resource requirements for the next operational period and is used by the Planning Section to complete Field Assignment Lists (ICS 204s) and by the Logistics Section for ordering resources for the incident. The document may also be employed as a source document for resource information on other ICS Forms such as ICS 209. The ICS 215 form is initiated by the appropriate members of the General Staff. It is recommended that the format be drawn on the chalkboard or whiteboard and, when decisions are reached, the information is recorded on the form.

ICS Form 219S, T-Cards (Colored Cards) - Resource Unit: records status and location of resources, transportation, and support vehicles and personnel, providing a visual display (cards are displayed in resource status racks where they can be easily retrieved). Information comes from several sources including but not limited to:

- ICS Briefing (ICS Form 201);
- Check-In/Out List (ICS Form 211);
- Resource/Materials Request/Order (ICS Form 222);
- Organization-supplied Information Cards (maintained by the Resource Unit until demobilization).

ICS Form 220, Air Operations Summary: provides information on air operations including the number, type, location and specific assignments of helicopters and fixed-wing aircraft. The ICS 220 form is completed by the

Transportation Unit of the Logistics Section or the Air Operations Branch Director.

ICS Form 222, Resource Materials Request Order: reports personnel or equipment needs of responders. A requester fills out the form and passes it through appropriate channels for delivery to the Logistics Section's Supply Unit. The Supply Unit logs in the request, either orders the item, fills it out of existing supplies/contracts, or forwards it on to Contracts for action. Documentation is maintained per company/agency procedures for ordering and tracking requests.

Incident Map: a map of hard or soft copy, or aerial photo depicting the site.

Safety Plan: safety objectives and hazard warnings prepared by the safety officer. It becomes significantly more complicated in a biological, chemical, radiological or nuclear event.

For incidents that last more than 24 hours, the planning section chief would normally give a formal briefing of the IAP every 12 hours in the planning briefing cycle. This timeframe may shorten to eight hours to reflect shift changes or extend to 24 hours when significant night operations are not required. Typically all section and division level commanders and relevant unit leaders will attend the briefing and receive a copy of the IAP (which, in the case of a large-scale event, may be more than 10 pages in length).

8.3.3 Exotic

Incidents where Chemical, Biological Radiological or Nuclear (CBRN) agents are involved will likely begin as emergency medical and fire/rescue operations then evolve into body recovery/identification and disposal contingencies that take place in cooperation with criminal investigative organizations. This can pose both logistical and mental health challenges for first responders, particularly those who lack concerted training and experience in unconventional fatality management.

Initial dispatch information is unlikely to present a clear picture in the event of an exotic attack. In fact, an incident may first be reported simply as an individual suffering from unusual respiratory difficulties or skin lesions and it may take many days to correctly identify the agent and respond accordingly.

As such, first responders must look for indicators and keep in mind the following:

- Suspect a chemical agent when multiple non-trauma patients present with similar symptoms;

- Check for patients who may be scattered throughout a crowd or facility;

- Seek convergent responders that are exhibiting symptoms;

- Attempt to prevent direct exposure or transfer of agents from victims to responders;

- Notice unusual odors;

- Do not pass a FBL where multiple casualties have fallen from non-trauma injuries - it is likely to indicate a zone of contamination;

- Monitor radio traffic from other units indicating multiple victims;

- Establish a hot zone quickly.

Set up decontamination areas and remove mobile patients quickly to these sites. Normally, decontamination is handled on-site. The goal here is to contain an incident and prevent cross contamination or having to decontaminate multiple sites. This is generally handled through the setting up of a 'hot zone' (an area that immediately surrounds the incident site). Within the hot zone are victims and persons in protective equipment only. Access to the hot zone is controlled through entry control points and anyone who is not wearing Personal Protective Equipment should be allowed to enter. Victims in the hot zone are given only what treatment is necessary to move them to the 'warm zone'. The warm zone is where basic triage and decontamination occur. The warm zone immediately surrounds the hot zone and access is controlled through entry control points. Patients who have been decontaminated are then moved to the cold zone for more comprehensive treatment or for transport to medical facilities. The reason for this process is to keep the contamination isolated at the scene;

- Call for special teams to quickly control hot zone entry;
- Arrange for decontamination areas for mass casualty patients.

At the patient treatment level, responses to incidents involving chemical or radiological materials will not be substantially different from procedures that are brought to bear in the case of HAZMAT spills or accidents. However, the scene will be quite different, both due to the fear and uncertainty that the public and possibly responders are likely to experience and because the incident site will, itself, be a crime scene.

As in an accidental release, responders should practice the 2 in 2 out protocol. They should attempt to determine the scope of the hot zone, approximate the number of patients, and delineate a mechanism of injury. Moves should be made to erect an effective system of perimeter control as soon as possible to prevent the further spread of infectious agents and to ensure victims do not leave the scene with criminal evidence that may be needed for criminal prosecution. Infrastructure that is likely to be contaminated should also be tagged so it can be appropriately cleaned at a later date.

Experience with large-scale industrial accidents indicates that controlling victims in these types of situations can be problematic. Typically patients leave before they are adequately evaluated, triaged, treated and decontaminated. Those who remain often become impatient if equipment and supplies for treatment are limited; if they feel relatively well; or if they have to wait extensively before receiving attention. Finally, individuals tend to be unwilling to strip naked for decontamination purposes, especially when such procedures have to be performed in an environment that is not private.

Response personnel must do as much as they can under the circumstances. Communication of timely and valid information to the victims will help them do what is needed to protect themselves and ensure the safety of others. However, in almost every case, it is certain that some individuals will 'escape' from the hot zone, either knowingly or unwittingly. It is therefore vital that responders immediately communicate the nature, scale and dimensions of the contingency with which they are faced so that local emergency medical facilities can develop a plan for decontaminating and quarantining those that may independently present themselves at a later time. In the case of the Aum

Shinrikyo subway attacks in Tokyo, victims walked from the scene to local hospitals. Situations like these indicate that hospitals should be prepared to conduct decontamination. In these instances, decontamination prior to admission must be a priority and all hospitals anticipating the delayed arrival of potential victims should move to initiate strict entry control procedures. Responders should also constantly monitor the boundaries of the hot zone and be on alert for sudden changes in wind direction and/or speed, both of which can radically alter the size and location of a HAZMAT site.

Whenever possible, patients not directly exposed to exotic agents should be attended to on-site to reduce the pressure on medical facilities dealing with primary victims. Records of these individuals should be kept for after-action reports and made available to law enforcement authorities to avail future investigations. Treatment should take place in a secure and effective decontamination site. Ideally these areas should be located upwind from the contamination source; on a downhill slope or flat ground with provisions for water run-off and, if possible, near a health care facility. Typically decontamination would be divided into gross, secondary and definitive:

- In gross decontamination, victims should be evacuated from the high-risk area, stripped and rinsed from head to toe with water;

- In secondary decontamination, victims should be given a rapid wash with a 0.5 per cent sodium hypochlorite solution (a 10 to 1 dilution of household bleach), preceded and followed by a full-body rinse. In the case of mustard gas, do not decontaminate with bleach as it will increase the damage caused by the agent by increasing its rate of absorption;

- In definitive decontamination, victims should be given a full head o toe sodium hypochlorite wash until they are clean (with certainbiological agents this may need to continue for at least 10 minutes) followed by a thorough water rinse.

For those exposed to radiation, rapid removal of clothing and the institution of a full body chemical-water wash/rinse is generally the most effective form of treatment. Healthcare workers and responders providing this type of decontamination should wear surgical attire or disposal garments made of Tyvek to reduce potential exposure. Material must be carefully disposed of after use and any industrial vacuum cleaners brought in for site-cleaning purposes should be fitted with HEPA filters to prevent the release of radioactive particles into the air.

As in a large-scale event, a medical branch typically will be assigned to the operations section of an IMS. A chemical attack will be managed by an extension of the hazardous materials approach, with emphasis on detection, PPE and patient decontamination. The fire/rescue branch will normally assist in these operations and provide the management structure for HAZMAT contingencies, including PPE provision, victim evacuation and risk determination. Safety personnel will also be involved, addressing such issues as law enforcement weapons control, potential fire zones, perimeter security, chemical contamination area entry, PPE suit selection and decontamination procedures.

The onset of an unannounced biological attack will be gradual and difficult to recognize. Mass casualties at a single scene are unlikely because viral and bacterial effects take days or weeks to manifest. The exception to this general rule is biological toxins which have a rapid onset time and may be confused with nerve agents as their symptoms are similar. Patients may be spread across medical facilities throughout a region, state, the nation, or the globe. However, once an attack is recognized, health and medical response entities are likely to be overwhelmed by the ill and the frightened. The main functions of on-site emergency personnel would be to: limit the environmental expansion of the incident; protect the unaffected population through evacuation or dissemination of information; and establish shelters and decontamination sites for those unable to leave the scene or return home. In performing their role, first responders must take adequate measures to protect themselves by following basic decontamination procedures as outlined above and at all times wear PPE.

8.3.4 Medical response to an exotic attack

Medical facility response
A large-scale unconventional chem-bio attack will require hospitals to alter their normal SOPs and respond to the demands of an event that may include a large number of casualties, individuals suffering from unknown agents, unusually serious injuries or psychosomatic symptoms. Medical receiving facilities need to be alerted by on-site emergency personnel near the

beginning of an event to give them time to prepare for immediate and possibly delayed patient influxes. Hospitals should have several backup networks to ensure receipt of information including auxiliary power and backup communications systems. Since regional or national transportation may be impacted by a terrorist event, a medical facility should also have a plan for backup laboratory facilities and procedures when they are unable to use their usual diagnostic services.

Security is a critical element in any medical facility response. Because protective personnel often rotate and may not be permanently stationed at hospitals, it is useful to have security checklists and protocols in a pocket guide format for each guard. These guides should be concise and contain only critical information. The medical facility leadership should brief security officers as information arrives to prepare them for the influx of patients, media, relatives, friends and onlookers. Armed officers may be also be necessary to monitor and regulate entry to the emergency room and related treatment areas.

Contaminated patients en route to the hospital require a special security plan. Based on past experience, in mass casualty events, more than half the patients arrive in private vehicles. As noted above, security should be positioned to direct these individuals. Moreover, all vehicles must necessarily be assumed to be contaminated and should be diverted to a special staging area where they can be decontaminated at a later time and secured to prevent further spreading. The public will generally be resistant to leaving their vehicles and a system for transporting unaffected, decontaminated individuals should therefore be put in place as soon as possible. Records should also be kept of vehicles left at the site.

Specific response steps that a hospital may undertake include:

- Activation of the hospital's disaster plan;
- Recall of critical personnel;
- Institution of security lock-down;
- Accreditation of volunteers;

- Modification of standing orders and procedures for patient care as necessary;
- Establishment of mechanisms to discharge able patients as quickly as possible;
- When appropriate, termination of the hospital disaster plan.

Basic medical response to specific exotic agents

Primary therapeutic care of victims involved in an exotic attack will take place off-site. Nonetheless, response personnel should still have a basic understanding of the toxins, viruses, bacteria and chemicals that are likely to be used in terrorist attacks and appropriate treatment procedures that need to be instituted for these agents. Relevant medical management procedures are discussed below.

Nerve agents

Nerve agents such as Tabun, Sarin, Soman, GF and VX are capable of killing within seconds to minutes at appropriate concentrations. They exist at room temperature as liquids with volatility varying from that of water to light motor oil. Nerve agents inhibit or block the activity of the enzyme acetyl cholinesterase, which breaks down the neurotransmitter acetylcholine that helps to transfer messages from one nerve to another. The accumulation of the neurotransmitter continues to stimulate the organ, resulting in hyper stimulation throughout the body. Signs of nerve agent exposure include pupil contraction, tearing, salivation, runny nose, sweating, abdominal cramping, vomiting, diarrhea, muscle twitching and paralysis. At high concentrations this will result in a loss of consciousness, seizures, breathing cessation and death. Antidotes are available that work well if administered in time.

Patient care begins with decontamination, administration of antidotes and ventilation if needed. Large amounts of water containing hypochlorite, or any material, including dirt, can be used to remove nerve agents from the skin of patients. If clothing is wet with the agent, it must be removed in the hot zone before the patient reaches the decontamination unit. When treating a severely impacted unconscious patient, attend to the airway, breathing and circulation first unless airway resistance makes this impossible.

Nerve agent antidotes include Atropine, Pralidoxime Chloride, Diazepam and

Morphine. Atropine works to dry the gland and stop smooth muscle contraction but does not impact skeletal muscles. Atropine should be given in 2 to 6 mg doses and be administered every 5 to 10 minutes until secretions have diminished noticeably and breathing has improved or airway resistance has decreased (if the patient is being ventilated). Atropine can be administered intramuscularly (IM), intravenously (IV), or endotracheally (ET). Atropine should not be administered by IV until ventilation has begun.

Pralidoxime removes the nerve agent from the enzyme allowing it to function, but it does not reverse clinical effects in the gland and smooth muscle. It is not effective against soman but, if an initial identification of agent has not been made, administering it will do little harm. Initially 1 g of Pralidoxamine is given through an IV drip over 20 minutes and administered hourly for a total of three doses. Valium or morphine can also be used as anticonvulsants. The Mark I device used by the US military employs two spring-powered injectors, one with atropine (2 mg) and one with Pralidoxamine (600 mg) to effectively administer the antidotes.

Cyanide

Cyanide, available in both gaseous and solid forms, can also kill within minutes. It interferes with the oxygen metabolizing capacity of the body. Symptoms of low-level exposure may be difficult to recognize but include a brief period of rapid and deep breathing, feelings of anxiety, agitation, dizziness, weakness, nausea with or without vomiting, trembling and redness of the skin. At higher concentrations, victims lose consciousness (loss of consciousness may be sudden), experience seizures and suffer cardiac arrhythmias. Cyanide can be measured in the blood for confirmation. Death can take place as suddenly as eight minutes after exposure.

Care includes removing the patient from the area, decontamination and treatment with a two-phase antidote regime incorporating nitrite and sodium thiosulfate. Finally medical personnel should administer oxygen and correct acidosis. Specific treatment includes the following considerations for conscious, breathing casualty: No antidotes. If the victim is unconscious, and not breathing: Amyl nitrite perle via bag ventilator (first aid, only until IV drugs can be given); sodium nitrite, 300 mg IV; sodium thiosulfate, 12.5 g IV. Half these doses might be administered later if there is no response to the first dose.

Nitrite is administered first, which removes cyanide from the cells by changing normal hemoglobin to methemoglobin (which attracts the poison). It is available as amyl nitrite, which comes both in a 'perle' format (that must be broken and placed in a breathing bag for the patient to inhale) and as sodium nitrite (which is packaged in an ampoule containing 300 mg in 10 ml for IV administration). Sodium thiosulfate is given next, generally by IV. The antidote comes in an ampoule containing 12.5 g in 50 ml.

Vesicants

Lewisite and sulfur mustard are the major agents that are used as chemical weapons to cause blisters. Mustard smells like garlic, onions or mustard. It is not an effective weapon in cold weather but will produce a vapor in warmer conditions. Exposure to sulfur mustard vapors can cause irreversible damage to tissues within minutes; however, immediate clinical signs are not apparent. The latent period after exposure ranges from two to 24 hours, averaging four to eight hours after initial contact. Early symptoms include irritated and burning eyes, severe conjunctivitis, swelling of the lids and corneal edema. The skin of a patient will be red and appear similar to a sunburn. Small blisters may develop around the edges of the irritation, which gradually meld to form large blisters in the form of second degree burns. Inhalation of mustard damages the inner layer of the airways and results in burning of the sinus, nasal bleeding, sore throat, laryngitis and shortness of breath. Severe damage provides an excellent environment for subsequent infection (usually approximately four days after exposure), damage to the bone marrow and the lining of the gastrointestinal tract.

Patients require immediate decontamination, within a minute if possible, however they should not be decontaminated with hypochlorite solutions as this will increase the agent's absorption into the skin. Skin damage can be reduced if treated within 30 minutes. Patients arriving for care hours after the incident should be given soothing lotions for the skin; frequent irrigation and application of antibiotics for blistered areas; and limited fluid replacement. Eyes should be washed and ophthalmic ointment or drops applied as soon as possible, followed later by topical antibiotic, a mydriatic (that prevents adhesion of lens to iris), and Vaseline (at the edges of the lids). Ophthalmologists may also apply topical steroids within the first 24 hours. Steam inhalation and cough suppressant can be used to treat airway involvement. Voice changes may indicate the need for an immediate insertion of an endotracheal tube.

Lewisite smells like geraniums and is more volatile than mustard. Its topical damage is similar to mustard but it does not degrade marrow, the gastrointestinal tract or lymphatic tissue. Unlike mustard, it damages systemic capillaries allowing leaking of intravascular volume which may result in hypovolemic shock in severe cases. The topical irritation due to Lewisite is immediate, causing pain within seconds of contact.

Treatment is similar to that of mustard. However, there is an antidote for the systemic effects of the agent called British-Anti-Lewisite (BAL). This is a drug used for heavy metal poisoning, which can be administered only in the hospital.

Pulmonary agents

Pulmonary agents, including phosgene and chlorine, cause fluid to accumulate in the lungs with little damage to other tissues. At high concentrations phosgene causes immediate but transient irritation in the eyes, nose and upper airways. Normally patients feel short of breath two to 24 hours after exposure. If this occurs more than six to eight hours after initial contact, then effects are usually not severe enough to cause death. Although victims may be asymptomatic, they should not be released for at least six hours as deadly symptoms can start suddenly. Management of patients experiencing severe symptoms is twofold. First they should be kept at absolute rest, even if they appear healthy; second, they should be given oxygen, especially in cases where the victim is experiencing shortness of breath.

Anthrax

Bacillus anthracis can generally incubate for one to six days, however the incubation period is dose dependent and can last as long as 69 days. Initial symptoms such as fever, malaise, fatigue and cough resemble the flu. Death occurs within 24 to 36 hours of the onset of severe symptoms. Anthrax is not contagious and can be treated with high doses of antibiotics such as ciprofloxacin or doxycycline. Six pre-vaccination shots with annual boosters will prevent the disease. Vaccination after exposure may prevent infection or reduce severity of symptoms. Medical personnel should practice secretion and lesion precautions. Sporicidal agents should be used for decontamination of exposed surfaces.

Cholera
The effects from cholera may appear one to five days after exposure with sudden onset of vomiting, abdominal distention, and pain with little or no fever, followed rapidly by diarrhea. Fluid losses may exceed five to 10 liters per day. Water and electrolytes should be administered with antibiotics such as tetracycline and ampicillin that shorten the duration of diarrhea. A licensed killed vaccine is available, but is only effective for six months. Careful hand washing should be carried out by attending medical personnel.

Plague
Pneumonic plague incubates for two to three days. Symptoms include high fever, chills, hemoptysis and toxemia. Patients die from respiratory failure and circulatory collapse. Bubonic plague incubates for two to 10 days and results in a high fever, swollen lymph nodes and may spread to the central nervous system, lungs and throughout the body. Plague can be diagnosed through culture or Gram stain of lymph node aspirates. Early administration of antibiotics is effective in conjunction with supportive therapy when necessary. A vaccine is available, but it must be administered six times in the first 18 months followed by biannual boosters. Medical personnel should practice secretion and lesion precautions and patients with pneumonic plague must be isolated. Heat, disinfectants and ultraviolet light destroy the bacteria.

Tularemia
Tularemia can present in two forms. The first is characterized by ulcers, high fever, chills and malaise; the second by fever, headache, substernal discomfort, prostration, weight loss and a nonproductive cough. Patients can be diagnosed through X-rays or cultures. A two-week course of tetracycline, administered early, is effective. An investigational new attenuated live vaccine is available. Medical personnel should practice secretion and lesion precautions. Heat and disinfectants destroy the bacteria.

Q Fever
Q fever exposure generally results in non critical fever, cough and chest pain ten days after exposure. Diagnosis may be confirmed serologically. Tetracycline or doxycyline administered orally for five to seven days may limit the illness. A vaccine is available, but severe local reactions may occur in those already immune. Secondary contamination is not a risk and decontamination is accomplished with soap and water or a weak hypochlorite solution.

Smallpox

Smallpox incubates between nine days and two weeks, beginning with malaise, fever, vomiting, headache and backache. Two to three days later characteristic lesions appear that become pustular vesicles. They are more abundant on the face and extremities and develop simultaneously. There is no effective treatment, although researchers are examining new antiviral medications. Immediate vaccination should be undertaken for all exposed personnel who should then be isolated for at least 16 to 17 days. Individuals must be treated as soon as possible following exposure and patients are treated as infectious until all scabs separate.

Venezuelan Equine Encephalitis (VEE)

VEE victims experience sudden onset with malaise, spiking fevers, severe headache, nausea, vomiting and sore throat. Patients require only supportive therapy and a vaccine is available, which should be given as an IND. Blood and body fluid precautions should be used by medical personnel treating VEE. The virus can be destroyed by heat and disinfectants. Viral Hemorrhagic Fevers (VHFs)

VHFs are febrile illnesses that can be further complicated by bleeding, shock and edema. Typical symptoms include watery diarrhea and dehydration. Treatment involves disinfection with hypochlorite, although ribavirin and convalescent plasma can also be effective in the case of Argentine hemorrhagic fever. Isolation and barrier nursing procedures are required.

Botulinum toxins

Exposure to botulinum can result in respiratory failure within 24 to 36 hours after initial contact. There are no clinical methods of diagnosis, but botulinum should be suspected if multiple victims present with descending bulbar, muscular and respiratory weakness. Intubations and ventilator assistance is vital to treat respiratory failure and tracheostomies may be necessary. Administration of a botulinum antitoxin (IUND) may prevent or decrease progression and shorten recovery times (Pentavalent toxoid is available as an IND for those at high risk). Soap and water and hypochlorite are effective as immediate remedial therapies. The toxin is not dermally active.

Staphylococcal Enterotoxin B (SEB)

Three to 12 hours after aerosol exposure to SEB, victims may experience fever, chills, headache, myalgia and nonproductive cough that can last up to four weeks. Patients may also experience nausea, vomiting and diarrhea after ingestion. High levels of exposure can result in death. Patients that present with febrile respiratory syndrome but no chest X-ray abnormalities are strongly indicative of SEB exposure. Supportive care is required, including, if necessary, artificial ventilation and fluid management is important. Responders should wear protective masks and use hypochlorite and soap and water as effective disinfectants. Exposed food must be destroyed.

Ricin
Exposure to ricin will result in weakness, fever, cough and hypothermia about 36 hours after aerosol exposure followed in the next half day by hypotension and cardiovascular collapse. Diagnoses is difficult but a large cluster of patients experiencing these symptoms would indicate exposure to ricin as a biological agent. Supportive care is required and no antidote is available. Protective masks are the best prevention measure for first responders. Water and hypochlorite or soap should be used to decontaminate surfaces. Ricin is not volatile.

Trichothecene Mycotoxins (TM)
Exposure to TM causes skin irritation, pain and redness, nose, throat and chest pain, itching, sneezing and cough. Ingestions of high concentrations of the toxin can result in death and is normally indicated by the appearance of yellow droplets ('yellow rain') on clothes. No specific antidote is available but superactive charcoal is effective against ingested mycotoxin. Garments should be removed and decontaminated with soap and water. Eyes should be irrigated with large amounts of saline. Responders should wear PPE at all times.

8.4 Summary of basic steps in response
The basic steps in a response are listed below. Many overlap.

- Event reported;
- Arrival of professional first responders;
- Scene surveillance;
- Operational functions assigned to responders;
- Determine who is in charge;
- Establish command post (Command vests allow sector officers to be readily identifiable);
- Triage, treat and transport primary patients;
- Create Incident Action Plan (IAP);

Summary of basic steps in response 207

- Institute perimeter security and traffic control;
- Prevent victims from leaving the scene;
- Establish a media pool and arrange media tour when possible;
- Log in new units as they arrive;
- Alert hospitals and clinics about potential arrival of victims who have left the scene;
- If an incident involves a structural collapse, call in urban search and rescue team(s);
- Provide triage, basic medical care, and movement of patients to treatment areas;
- Decontaminate patients;
- Retrieve hostages (if necessary);
- Bomb disposal;
- Reduce scene area as quickly as possible;
- Decontaminate buildings, equipment, vehicles, (civilian and military responders);
- Setup sites to decontaminate civilian responders (military);
- Initiate long-term investigations, conducted by law enforcement personnel at the local state and federal levels (which may last forseveral years).

APPENDIX: THE INTERNATIONAL RESPONSE TO TERROISM: LEGAL CONVENTIONS, INSTITUTIONAL BODIES AND REGIONAL INITIATIVES

Legal measures adopted through the United Nations (UN)

The global community, acting through the UN, has enacted several conventions to combat international terrorism. Rather than trying to define terrorism per se, which has proven largely fruitless given the subjective and prerogative undertones surrounding the term - these agreements aim: first to outlaw practices that are implicitly deemed to be terrorist in nature; and second regulate activities that contribute to such violence.

To date, the most important conventions have included:

- The Tokyo (1963) Hague (1970) and Montreal Conventions (1973), which are variously aied at counter in aviation hijacking and sabotage;

- The Convention on Protected Persons (1973), which aims to counter attacks carried out against diplomats;

- The Hostages Convention (1979), which aims to counter kidnappings and abduction of civilians and non-combatants;

- The International Maritime Organization (IMO) Convention (1988), which aims to counter attacks against shipping and fixed platforms at sea;

- The Convention on Marking Plastic Explosives for the Purpose of Identification (1991), which aims to prevent and prohibit the manufacture and international transfer of unmarked plastic explosives - particularly as it pertains to terrorist attacks and acts of aircraft sabotage.

The conventions are designed to suppress international terrorism by establishing a regulatory framework for cooperation among participating states. To accomplish this goal, the accords require that signatories:

- Cooperate to prevent, within their sovereign jurisdictions, the various types of offences covered by the conventions;

- Exchange all relevant information at their disposal, if such offences have been committed within their territories;

- Coordinate administrative and judicial measures to ensure any who have violated the conventions are brought to justice. In essence, this means offenders must either be extradited to the country where the alleged transgression first took place or, failing that, are submitted to trial before the apprehending state's own authorities (the principle of 'extradite or try');

- Fully adhere to the rules and decision-making procedures that underscore each of the respective conventions.

Although these UN initiatives do represent a symbolic commitment on the part of the global community to act against international terrorism, the conventions that make up this regulatory framework suffer from a number of serious deficiencies. In particular the accords:

- Are not really international in scope; even with respect to those agreements that have been in force for many years, the number of signatories is disappointingly low;

- Suffer from a major loophole in that they do not apply to offences that are carried out for political purposes (which all terrorist attacks inevitably are). This stipulation reflects the general sensitivity that exists in the international community to the dangers inherent in political persecution;

- Have not been implemented vigorously, even among those states that are parties to the agreements. In many cases, signatories have been prepared to ignore their commitments under the conventions if it suits their national interest to do so. In this manner, the accords have been more permissive than obligatory in nature.

Improving the general effectiveness of the UN legal framework will require concerted moves to address each of these shortcomings. First and most fundamentally, there needs to be a major push to induce those members of the global community that have not already signed and ratified the conventions to do so. The goal should be to have as close to universal application as possible.

Second, a Standing Committee on International Terrorism should be established to ensure that the conventions are effectively implemented and that parties to the agreements actually abide by their commitments. One way to achieve this would be to require that signatories make available annual reports outlining the specific steps they have taken to enforce the agreements enacted in their name. A precedent for this type of vetting procedure already exists in the guise of mechanisms that are used to assess adherence to such agreements as the International Convention on Human Rights (ICHR) and Convention against Illicit Traffic in Narcotic Drugs and Psychotropic Substances.

Finally, moves need to be instituted to fill the political loophole that is currently serving to mitigate the effectiveness of major UN enforcement agreements. To this end, it has been suggested that protocols should be attached to the Tokyo, Hague, Montreal, Protected Persons, Hostages and IMO Conventions affirming that political defense can never be used in relation to the offences covered by each of the agreements. It is pertinent to note in this context that the deliberate targeting of civilians has long been regarded a war crime under the international law of armed conflict, irrespective of the political motivations driving such attacks.

Institutional measures: international police cooperation (INTERPOL)

Interpol represents perhaps the most ambitious attempt that has been initiated to foster global police cooperation. The body has an international membership that, as of 2002, consists of 179 countries spread over five continents (see Table One). The aims of Interpol, as set out in Article 2 of its constitution, outline a commitment to:

- Ensure and promote the widest possible cooperation between the criminal police authorities of member states;

- Establish and develop all institutions likely to contribute effectively to the suppression and prevention of ordinary crimes (author emphasis on ordinary crimes).

Article 3 of Interpol's constitution specifically bars its members from intervention in, or investigation of military, political, racial or religious matters. This stipulation, when taken in conjunction with Article 2's emphasis on ordinary crimes, meant that for many years terrorism was regarded as beyond the legitimate ambit if the organization.

Attitudes began to change, however, with the upsurge in international terrorist activity from the late 1960s onwards. An important turning point came in 1984 when the Interpol General Assembly passed a resolution on "Violent Crime Commonly Known as Terrorism." The purpose of this modification was to give practical guidance in the interpretation of Article 3. Specifically it was determined that the article should not debar member states from sharing and acting on terrorism information so long as such data was not used solely for political purposes. Interpol delegates were thus encouraged to share counter-terrorist intelligence as freely as their national laws allowed.

The 1984 resolution led to the formation of a dedicated International Terrorist Unit in January 1986, which, for the first time, formally recognized the existence of a specific anti-terrorist function for Interpol. The Unit adopted a set of guidelines in May 1986 that have since set the ground rules for sharing terrorist-related information among Interpol members.

Despite these developments, much criticism has been directed at Interpol over its general effectiveness in anti-terrorism work. Two main issues have been consistently highlighted: First, although Interpol has been recognized with a formal anti-terrorist function since 1986, the bulk of its member states continue to adhere to the principle that they should not become involved in political, religious or racial matters - that is the very areas that stimulate acts of terrorism in the first place. Indicative of this reticence, investigation of terrorism currently represents no more than two to three percent of Interpol's entire workload.

Second, Interpol, itself, does not represent a secure forum in which to exchange terrorist-related information. Western states have repeatedly expressed grave reservations about the ability of certain delegates to handle sensitive data in an appropriate manner - claiming that these states either lack sufficient experience or inclination to afford proper protection to classified material. More to the point, because Interpol's membership includes regimes that are known to have been major sponsors of international terrorism, notably Syria, Libya and Iran, it is generally not considered to offer a secure environment in which to share information pertaining to extremist or militant activities.

Regional measures

The weaknesses inherent in the UN and Interpol regulatory framework have prompted several states to undertake more geographically limited measures of their own. These initiatives have either been adopted on a regional basis or through institutional forums composed of politically or economically like-minded states.

Measures implemented by West European states

- The Terrorism, Radicalism, Extremism and Violence International (TREVI) system of consultation - a joint ministerial, intelligence and police information exchange forum set up in 1976. During the 1980s and early 1990s, TREVI acted as the main vehicle for coordinating counter-terrorism action in Western Europe;

- The European Convention on the Suppression of Terrorism (ECST), a Council of Europe initiative, which aims to ensure that the use of political defense can never be used in relation to offences commonly recognized as terroristic in nature;

- The Police Working Group on Terrorism (PWGOT) - a practical police and intelligence network established in 1979 to facilitate the coordination of operational measures against international terrorism;

- Europol - a centralized police and intelligence body originally set up by the member states of the European Union in 1992 (as part of the EU's so-called Third Pillar on Judicial and Home Affairs Cooperation) to facilitate the fight against major organized crime. In 1997, however, the EU's Treaty of Amsterdam officially recognized terrorism as a legitimate area of concern falling within the overall parameters of Europol's mandate.

Measures enacted in Central and Southeast Asia

- The Association of Southeast Asian Nations (ASEAN) Chiefs of National Police (ASEANAPOL) – an intelligence and police forum set up in the 1980s to discuss issues pertaining to transnational crime throughout Southeast Asia. Although initially most of the dialogue in the group focused on the activities of drug traffickers, it has increasingly begun to take on a more discrete anti-terrorism focus;

- The Commonwealth of Independent States (CIS) Counter-Terrorism Center – set up and primarily funded by Moscow in December 2000 to maintain a database of information on international terrorism;

- The Shanghai Cooperation Organization – established in 1996 to fight terrorism emanating from Afghanistan and generally promote regional stability throughout Central Asia. The Group currently consists of China, Russia, Kyrgyzstan, Tajikistan, Kazakhstan and Uzbekistan.

Measures implemented by major industrialized states - the G7 Group

The G-7 is composed of US, UK, Canada, France, Italy, Japan and Germany. Since 1997, Russia has also been included in G7 Summit meetings and is currently involved in all but financial and certain economic discussions.

The G7 Anti-Terrorism Agreement (1986), which obliges signatories to:

- Deny entry into their respective territories of suspected terrorists;

- Forge closer cooperation between security and police forces;
- Place strict restrictions on diplomatic missions suspected of being involved in terrorism; and
- Provide for closer operational cooperation against terrorism.

The G7 Anti-Terrorism Declaration (1996), which aims to improve the practical fight against international terrorism by committing signatories to:

- Improve transport safety (especially in relation to aircraft);
- Fight arms trafficking, including nuclear, chemical and biological weapons;
- Increase police and intelligence cooperation;
- Improve national counter-terrorism capabilities;
- Cooperate to prevent the abuse and exploitation of charities and front companies by subversive groups.

Suggested international measures

A number of measures have been suggested to enhance the overall effectiveness of the international community's response to terrorism:

- The establishment of a global court with the power to try and convict those who have committed international terrorist crimes;
- Most suggestions in this regard envisage a tribunal with jurisdiction over a lengthy list of international crimes and with an elaborate subsidiary court structure including a procurator, public defender, commission of inquiry, prosecutor, and a board of clemency and parole;
- The major advantage of an international criminal court is that it would obviate the need for extradition. The principal problem, however, is that states would almost certainly be unwilling to concede legal sovereignty to an international body, particularly in relation to their own citizens.

The establishment of a global convention on extradition

This suggested initiative envisions expanding the concept of universal jurisdiction to cover forms of international crime that cannot be considered political in nature and linking it to the principle of extradite or try. A convention of this sort would help to fill the political defense loophole that currently exists in the UN regulatory framework but would still have to overcome the legal and political differences that exist in state approaches to international crime.

The establishment of an international anti-terrorism rapid response team

The creation of a semi-permanent rapid reaction force to deal with terrorist incidents that have clear international ramifications (such as aircraft hijackings, attacks using weapons of mass destruction) has also been suggested. An international unit of this sort would arguably have a deterrent value against groups that operate on a transnational basis and could be deployed to deal with terrorist incidents in countries that are not experienced in countering this mode of violence.

There are, however, a number of fundamental problems with the proposal:

- Practical problems - many states would reject any idea of an international rapid response team operating in their jurisdiction;

- Conceptual problems - principally identifying the specific circumstances under which a force of this sort would be deployed (which bears in on the general problem of defining terrorism);

- Financial difficulties - most notably identifying how to pay for the creation and maintenance of such a force;

- Perceptual problems - does the threat of terrorism actually warrant the creation of an international rapid response team?